Street & Smith's
Guide to Pro Basketball 1997–98

Also by the Editors of Street & Smith's
Published by Ballantine Books:

**Street & Smith's
Guide to Baseball**

**Street & Smith's
Guide to Pro Football**

Street & Smith's Guide to Pro Basketball 1997–98

By the Editors of
Street & Smith's

★ ★ ★

Consulting Editor
Scott Gray

BALLANTINE BOOKS • NEW YORK

Copyright © 1997 by Advance Publications, Inc.

All rights reserved under International and Pan-American Copyright Conventions.
Published in the United States by
Ballantine Books, a division of Random House, Inc., New York, and simultaneously in Canada by Random House of Canada Limited, Toronto.

http://www.randomhouse.com

ISBN 0-345-40851-9

Manufactured in the United States of America

Cover Photo of Michael Jordan
© Tim O'Dell/Active Images

Player photos appear courtesy of the individual teams and/or NBA Photos except where noted.

First Edition: October 1997

10 9 8 7 6 5 4 3 2 1

Table of Contents

Joe Smith

Acknowledgments

We appreciate the assistance afforded us by the league offices and the departments of media relations of the 29 NBA teams.

Ballantine Books provides an All-Star roster of dedicated professionals. Cathy Repetti is the prototypical point guard, able to make perfect decisions under pressure. Mark Rifkin moves well without the ball, then swoops in for the alley oop. Nick Sywak buries treys at will, and Philip Cornell dominates the boards. No team in the publishing industry can match the all-around talents of Carlos Beltrán, George Davidson, Betsy Flagler, Caron Harris, and Steve Palmer.

Indispensable as always, Gioia Di Biase designed the cover and the internal layout.

Instant offense was provided by Paul Bratt, Leota and Richard Gray, Heather Poort, Dave Roberts, Paul Stone, and Gene Taback.

Toni Kukoc

Introduction

This is going to be interesting. The overlords of the NBA have wisely decided to make some changes to the rules. Here's a rundown of the new edicts:

Defenders can no longer forearm check. It might result in more cheap fouls but should also create more freedom for creativity off the dribble.

The calling-timeout-while-flying-out-of-bounds play is history, and not a moment too soon. What used to be a heads-up play was becoming a nuisance.

Thanks to the new "no charge" zone, players on their way to the hoop won't have to worry about defenders camping near the basket to take a flop.

The three-point circle goes back to 23 feet, nine inches, except in the corners, where it will remain as is. It may cut down on the wanna-be-all-things-to-all-people gunners jacking it up at a 33-percent clip. Then again, don't count on it.

As you are no doubt aware, Chicago followed 72 with 69 and defended its NBA crown. The Bulls are expected to be intact for one more run, but it won't be a cakewalk. The Knicks and Heat keep getting tougher in the East, while Utah, Houston, San Antonio, Seattle, and the Lakers are each vying for the honor of dethroning Air in his farewell campaign.

For anyone who doesn't know the position-numbers code, this book will be more enjoyable if you understand the following designations: point guard (one), shooting guard (two), small forward (three), power forward (four) and center (five).

Have a great season!

Kevin Garnett

National Basketball Association

1996–97 FINAL STANDINGS

Eastern Conference

Atlantic Division	Won	Lost	Pct.
Miami	61	21	.744
New York	57	25	.695
Orlando	45	37	.549
Washington	44	38	.537
New Jersey	26	56	.317
Philadelphia	22	60	.268
Boston	15	67	.183

Central Division	Won	Lost	Pct.
Chicago	69	13	.841
Atlanta	56	26	.683
Charlotte	54	28	.659
Detroit	54	28	.659
Cleveland	42	40	.512
Indiana	39	43	.476
Milwaukee	33	49	.402
Toronto	30	52	.366

Conference First Round: Chicago 3, Washington 0; Atlanta 3, Detroit 2; Miami 3, Orlando 2; New York 3, Charlotte 0

Conference Semifinals: Chicago 4, Atlanta 1; Miami 4, New York 3

Conference Finals: Chicago 4, Miami 1

1996–97 Final Standings (Continued)

Western Conference

Midwest Division	Won	Lost	Pct.
Utah	64	18	.780
Houston	57	25	.695
Minnesota	40	42	.488
Dallas	24	58	.293
Denver	21	61	.256
San Antonio	20	62	.244
Vancouver	14	68	.171

Pacific Division	Won	Lost	Pct.
Seattle	57	25	.695
L.A. Lakers	56	26	.683
Portland	49	33	.598
Phoenix	40	42	.488
L.A. Clippers	36	46	.439
Sacramento	34	48	.415
Golden State	30	52	.366

Conference First Round: Utah 3, L.A. Clippers 0; L.A. Lakers 3, Portland 1; Seattle 3, Phoenix 2; Houston 3, Minnesota 0

Conference Semifinals: Utah 4, L.A. Lakers 1; Houston 4, Seattle 3

Conference Finals: Utah 4, Houston 2

NBA Finals: Chicago 4, Utah 2

1996–97 NBA STATISTICAL LEADERS

Points Per Game

	G	PTS	PPG
Michael Jordan	82	2431	29.6
Karl Malone	82	2249	27.4
Glen Rice	79	2115	26.8
Mitch Richmond	81	2095	25.9
Latrell Sprewell	80	1938	24.2
Allen Iverson	76	1787	23.5
Hakeem Olajuwon	78	1810	23.2
Patrick Ewing	78	1751	22.4
Kendall Gill	82	1789	21.8
Gary Payton	82	1785	21.8

Rebounds Per Game

	G	REB	RPG
Dennis Rodman	55	883	16.1
Dikembe Mutombo	80	929	11.6
Anthony Mason	73	829	11.4
Ervin Johnson	82	913	11.1
Patrick Ewing	78	834	10.7
Chris Webber	72	743	10.3
Vin Baker	78	804	10.3
Loy Vaught	82	817	10.0
Shawn Kemp	81	807	10.0
Tyrone Hill	74	736	9.9
Karl Malone	82	809	9.9

Assists Per Game

	G	AST	APG
Mark Jackson	82	935	11.4
John Stockton	82	860	10.5
Kevin Johnson	70	653	9.3
Jason Kidd	55	496	9.0
Rod Strickland	82	727	8.9
Damon Stoudamire	81	709	8.8
Tim Hardaway	81	695	8.6
Nick Van Exel	79	672	8.5
Robert Pack	54	452	8.4
Stephon Marbury	67	522	7.8

Field Goal Percentage

	FG	FGA	FG%
Gheorge Muresan	327	541	.604
Tyrone Hill	357	595	.600
Rasheed Wallace	380	681	.558
Shaquille O'Neal	552	991	.557
Chris Mullin	438	792	.553
Karl Malone	864	1571	.550
John Stockton	416	759	.548
Dale Davis	370	688	.538
Danny Manning	426	795	.536
Gary Trent	361	674	.536

Three-Point Field Goal Percentage

	3FG	3FGA	3FG%
Glen Rice	207	440	.470
Steve Kerr	110	237	.464
Kevin Johnson	89	202	.441
Joe Dumars	166	384	.432
Mitch Richmond	204	477	.428
Reggie Miller	229	536	.427
Dell Curry	126	296	.426
Terry Mills	175	415	.422
Mario Elie	120	286	.420
Voshon Lenard	183	442	.414

Free Throw Percentage

	FT	FTA	FT%
Mark Price	155	171	.906
Terrell Brandon	268	297	.902
Jeff Hornacek	293	326	.899
Ricky Pierce	139	155	.897
Mario Elie	207	231	.896
Reggie Miller	418	475	.880
Malik Sealy	254	290	.876
Hersey Hawkins	258	295	.875
Darrick Martin	218	250	.872
Glen Rice	464	535	.867

Steals Per Game

	G	STL	SPG
Mookie Blaylock	78	212	2.72
Doug Christie	81	201	2.48
Gary Payton	82	197	2.40
Eddie Jones	80	189	2.36
Rick Fox	76	167	2.20
David Wesley	74	162	2.19
Allen Iverson	76	157	2.07
John Stockton	82	166	2.02
Greg Anthony	65	129	1.98
Kenny Anderson	82	162	1.98

Blocks Per Game

	G	BLK	BPG
Shawn Bradley	73	248	3.40
Dikembe Mutombo	80	264	3.30
Shaquille O'Neal	51	147	2.88
Alonzo Mourning	66	189	2.86
Ervin Johnson	82	227	2.77
Patrick Ewing	78	189	2.42
Vlade Divac	81	180	2.22
Hakeem Olajuwon	78	173	2.22
Kevin Garnett	77	163	2.12
Marcus Camby	63	130	2.06

1996–97 SINGLE-GAME HIGHS

Minutes: 58, Charles Barkley, Houston versus L.A. Lakers, November 12 (2 OT)

Points: 51, Michael Jordan, Chicago versus New York, January 21

Field Goals: 24, Hakeem Olajuwon, Houston versus Denver, January 30

Three-Point Field Goals: 9, Steve Smith, Atlanta versus Seattle, March 14

Free Throws: 22, Latrell Sprewell, Golden State at L.A. Clippers, March 10

Rebounds: 33, Charles Barkley, Houston at Phoenix, November 2

Offensive Rebounds: 15, Jayson Williams, New Jersey versus Minnesota, January 9

Defensive Rebounds: 25, Charles Barkley, Houston at Phoenix, November 2

Assists: 23, Nick Van Exel, L.A. Lakers at Vancouver, January 25

Blocked Shots: 12, Vlade Divac, Charlotte versus New Jersey, February 12

Steals: 10, Clyde Drexler, Houston at Sacramento, November 1

Eddie Jones

PROJECTED 1997–98 FINAL STANDINGS

Eastern Conference

Atlantic Division	Won	Lost	.Pct.
New York	59	23	.720
Miami	56	26	.683
Washington	47	35	.573
Orlando	44	38	.537
Philadelphia	34	48	.415
New Jersey	30	52	.366
Boston	21	61	.256

Central Division	Won	Lost	.Pct.
Chicago	65	17	.793
Atlanta	52	30	.634
Charlotte	51	31	.622
Detroit	45	37	.549
Milwaukee	39	43	.476
Indiana	38	44	.463
Cleveland	32	50	.390
Toronto	30	52	.366

Western Conference

Midwest Division	Won	Lost	.Pct.
Utah	58	24	.707
San Antonio	56	26	.683
Houston	53	29	.646
Minnesota	41	41	.500
Dallas	18	64	.220
Denver	16	66	.195
Vancouver	15	67	.183

Pacific Division	Won	Lost	.Pct.
L.A. Lakers	60	22	.732
Seattle	54	28	.659
Portland	48	34	.585
Phoenix	39	43	.476
Sacramento	33	49	.402
L.A. Clippers	31	51	.378
Golden State	24	58	.293

NBA Finals: Chicago 4, L.A. Lakers 1

Dikembe Mutombo

Atlanta
HAWKS

Franchise History: Entering the league as the Tri-Cities Blackhawks in 1949–50, the franchise later made moves to Milwaukee and St. Louis before landing in Atlanta. Bob Pettit—playing with a broken left wrist—brought St. Louis a championship in 1957–58. The team went to Atlanta in 1968–69, where it wallowed in mediocrity until the arrival of Dominique Wilkins in the early '80s. The Hawks have resurged somewhat under head coach Lenny Wilkens in recent seasons.

1996–97 Review: The signing of free agent pivot Dikembe Mutombo supplied the element that had been missing in Atlanta. With the finger-wagging enforcer in the middle, Christian Laettner was able to play his natural position at power forward, where he put together an All-Star season. With guards Mookie Blaylock and Steve Smith lighting up the perimeter, the Hawks soared to a 56-win campaign. They slipped by Detroit in the first round of the playoffs, then were trampled by Chicago in the conference semis.

1997–98 Preview: Lenny Wilkens has proven to be a master at making the most of limited talent, but he is currently blessed with four players who each rate among the NBA's top ten at their respective positions. Unfortunately, every member of the quartet has at least one prominent flaw that could keep the team from advancing beyond last year's accomplishments. It is difficult to envision Smith or Laettner playing better than they did in 1996–97, but that may be what it will take for the Hawks to move up.

Hawks Veteran Roster

No	Player	Pos	Ht	Wt	Exp
17	Jon Barry	G	6-4	205	5
10	Mookie Blaylock	G	6-1	185	8
33	Tyrone Corbin	F	6-6	225	12
35	Darrin Hancock	G/F	6-7	212	3
44	Alan Henderson	F	6-9	235	2
42	Henry James	F	6-8	220	6
32	Christian Laettner	F/C	6-11	245	5
15	Priest Lauderdale	C	7-4	343	1
55	Dikembe Mutombo	C	7-2	250	6
28	Ivano Newbill	C	6-9	245	2
3	Ken Norman	F	6-8	228	10
5	Eldridge Recasner	G	6-3	190	3
8	Steve Smith	G	6-8	215	6

Head Coach: Lenny Wilkens

Hawks 1997 Draft Picks

Rookie	College	Position
Ed Gray (1-22)	California	Guard
Alain Digbeu (2-50)	France	Guard
Chris Crawford (2-51)	Marquette	Forward

At about 6-3, Ed Gray is not the ideal height for a shooting guard, and he may struggle to get shots off versus many NBA twos. He does play with above-average quickness and court sense, and there is no doubting his ability to score at the collegiate level. He compiled six 30-point games last season. Alain Digbeu is a 6-5 shooting guard who was known in Europe as "the king of dunks." Chris Crawford registered nine 20-point games as a senior, and he shot .373 (85 for 228) from three-point distance in his collegiate career.

Hawks Scouting Report

Guard: Point guard Mookie Blaylock posted a career high in scoring and topped the NBA in steals last season. An unrepentant gunner, he paced the Hawks in field goal attempts but shot a tepid .432 while ranking just 21st in the league in assists. He is the soul of the Hawks, and his mix of strengths and weaknesses defines the team as a whole. Steve Smith broke the 20-ppg barrier for the first time as a pro, and he dished out more than four assists per game for the first time since 1993–94. One of the NBA's tallest twos, he handles the ball like a point guard. He was hampered by knee problems early in his career, and he remains prone to injuries. Capable of scoring from the high post or the perimeter, only his susceptibility to cold streaks keeps him from being a perennial All-Star. **Grade: A–**

Forward: Power forward Christian Laettner enjoyed the most productive season since his rookie year, starting all 82 games and making his All-Star debut. He is tough and smart in the paint, with a sweet touch from midrange and good passing skills. It hasn't necessarily shown up in his statistics, but Alan Henderson looks like a potential starter at small forward. The 16th pick overall in the 1996 draft, he sat out more than half of his second season with a viral illness but came back to flash terrific energy and a quality balance of skills. **Grade: B**

Center: A rare combination of height, extension, agility, and timing makes Dikembe Mutombo the top shot blocker in the NBA. His overall defense is probably overrated—he makes half the number of steals as Olajuwon, and he will occasionally loaf in transition—but no center protects the middle better than Mutombo. Massive (7-4, 343) pivot project Priest Lauderdale is short on experience but very long on length. **Grade: B+**

Hawks 1996–97 Player Statistics

	G	MIN	FG	FGA	FG%	FT	FTA	FT%	3FG	3FGA
Smith	72	2818	491	1145	.429	333	393	.847	130	388
Laettner	82	3140	548	1128	.486	359	440	.816	31	88
Blaylock	78	3056	501	1159	.432	131	174	.753	221	604
Mutombo	80	2973	380	721	.527	306	434	.705	0	0
Corbin	70	2305	253	600	.422	86	108	.796	74	208
James	53	945	125	306	.408	30	36	.833	76	181
Henderson	30	501	77	162	.475	45	75	.600	0	0
Burton	24	380	39	116	.336	57	68	.838	13	46
Recasner	71	1207	148	350	.423	51	58	.879	58	140
Barry	58	965	100	246	.407	37	46	.804	48	124
Norman	17	220	27	94	.287	4	12	.333	6	38
Lauderdale	35	180	49	89	.551	13	23	.565	0	1
Boyce	22	154	21	63	.333	11	22	.500	2	16
Hancock	24	133	16	35	.457	10	14	.714	0	0
Newbill	72	850	40	91	.440	20	52	.385	0	0
Alston	2	11	0	5	.000	0	2	.000	0	0
Miller	1	14	0	5	.000	0	0	---	0	0

	ORB	REB	AST	STL	TO	BLK	PF	PTS	PPG
Smith	90	238	305	62	176	23	173	1445	20.1
Laettner	212	720	223	102	218	64	277	1486	18.1
Blaylock	114	413	463	212	185	20	141	1354	17.4
Mutombo	268	929	110	49	186	264	249	1066	13.3
Corbin	76	294	124	90	85	7	176	666	9.5
James	27	81	21	11	29	1	98	356	6.7
Henderson	47	116	23	21	29	6	73	199	6.6
Burton	11	41	11	8	26	3	55	148	6.2
Recasner	35	115	94	38	65	4	97	405	5.7
Barry	26	99	115	55	59	3	56	285	4.9
Norman	8	39	12	7	18	3	17	64	3.8
Lauderdale	16	43	12	1	37	9	39	111	3.2
Boyce	7	15	13	10	16	4	17	55	2.5
Hancock	4	18	12	9	11	1	15	42	1.8
Newbill	76	204	24	28	42	15	115	100	1.4
Alston	3	4	0	0	0	0	0	0	0.0
Miller	2	7	0	0	0	0	2	0	0.0

Hawks 1996–97 Team Statistics

Final Record: 56–26

Home Record: 36–5

Road Record: 20–21

Division Record: 17–11

Conference Record: 34–20

Overtime Record: 5–0

Points Per Game: 94.8

Opponents Points Per Game: 89.4

Field Goal Percentage: .446

Opponents Field Goal Percentage: .435

Turnovers Per Game: 15.0

Opponents Turnovers Per Game: 15.5

Offensive Rebounding Percentage: .315

Defensive Rebounding Percentage: .692

Total Rebounding Percentage: .503

Scored Fewer Than 100 Points: 52

Opponents Scored Fewer Than 100 Points: 66

Hawks Clipboard

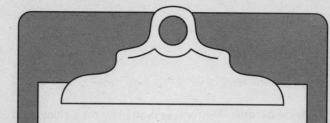

Why the Hawks win: The Hawks play fierce defense, spearheaded by Blaylock outside and Mutombo inside, yet they commit fewer fouls (19.4 per game) than any other NBA team. Atlanta has a fairly balanced offensive attack. Only the Bulls and Jazz won more games at home than the Hawks last season.

Why the Hawks lose: Inconsistency from the perimeter can expose Atlanta's lack of a dominant low-post scorer. Of the ten 50-win teams, only the Hawks failed to log a .500 record on the road.

1996–97 MVP: Dikembe Mutombo

Projected MVP: Christian Laettner

Fast Fact: The Hawks finished next to last in the league in assists last season, dishing out 19 per game.

Jon Barry G

Age: 28
Seasons: 5
Height: 6-4
Weight: 205
College: Georgia Tech

Barry was drafted by the Celtics, sent to Milwaukee, shipped to Golden State, then signed by Atlanta. He is a good passer who can connect from long range, but he has rarely seen quality minutes as a pro.

	G	MPG	FG%	3FG%	FT%	APG	RPG	PPG	BLK	STL
1996–97	58	16.6	.407	.387	.804	2.0	1.3	4.9	3	55
Career	297	13.7	.418	.363	.775	1.8	1.3	4.7	38	255

Mookie Blaylock G

Age: 30
Seasons: 8
Height: 6-1
Weight: 185
College: Oklahoma

Blaylock is a terror when his stroke is steady, but the Hawks might be better off if he would launch fewer three-point attempts and create more open looks for his teammates.

	G	MPG	FG%	3FG%	FT%	APG	RPG	PPG	BLK	STL
1996–97	78	39.2	.432	.366	.753	5.9	5.3	17.4	20	212
Career	594	35.6	.418	.348	.743	7.0	4.2	14.6	224	1460

Tyrone Corbin   F

Age: 35
Seasons: 12
Height: 6-6
Weight: 225
College: DePaul

Corbin has always gotten by on effort rather than athleticism, and he has toiled for no fewer than eight NBA teams. He is still one of the top defensive small forwards in the business.

	G	MPG	FG%	3FG%	FT%	APG	RPG	PPG	BLK	STL
1996–97	70	32.9	.422	.356	.796	1.8	4.2	9.5	7	90
Career	870	26.3	.466	.285	.796	1.9	5.0	9.6	252	1054

Darrin Hancock   G/F

Age: 26
Seasons: 3
Height: 6-7
Weight: 212
College: Kansas

Hanging on for his NBA life, Hancock played nine games for the Bucks, went to Atlanta for two games, San Antonio for one, then back to the Hawks to close the season.

	G	MPG	FG%	3FG%	FT%	APG	RPG	PPG	BLK	STL
1996–97	24	5.5	.457	.000	.714	0.5	0.8	1.8	1	9
Career	133	10.5	.530	.333	.579	0.7	1.3	3.5	10	56

Alan Henderson   F

Age: 25
Seasons: 2
Height: 6-9
Weight: 235
College: Indiana

Henderson, who has a live body and good instincts, sweats the details and fights for defensive position. His season was stunted by viral pancreatitis, but he should figure prominently in Atlanta's future.

	G	MPG	FG%	3FG%	FT%	APG	RPG	PPG	BLK	STL
1996–97	30	16.7	.475	.000	.600	0.8	3.9	6.6	6	21
Career	109	17.6	.451	.000	.596	0.7	4.3	6.4	49	65

Christian Laettner   F/C

Age: 28
Seasons: 5
Height: 6-11
Weight: 245
College: Duke

Laettner, who is more effective facing the basket than posting up, presents a tough matchup for most fours because he stretches the floor with his jumper, then gets to the charity stripe and converts.

	G	MPG	FG%	3FG%	FT%	APG	RPG	PPG	BLK	STL
1996–97	82	38.3	.486	.352	.816	2.7	8.8	18.1	64	102
Career	388	35.2	.477	.272	.815	3.1	8.2	17.2	391	466

Dikembe Mutombo   C

Age: 31
Seasons: 6
Height: 7-2
Weight: 250
College: Georgetown

A prolific rebounder and shot blocker, Mutombo was the NBA's Defensive Player of the Year last season. His offensive repertoire isn't very refined, but he is not a below-average scorer.

	G	MPG	FG%	3FG%	FT%	APG	RPG	PPG	BLK	STL
1996–97	80	37.2	.527	.000	.705	1.4	11.6	13.3	264	49
Career	471	36.9	.524	.000	.659	1.6	12.2	13.0	1750	272

Ivano Newbill   C

Age: 27
Seasons: 2
Height: 6-9
Weight: 245
College: Georgia Tech

Newbill, who played 34 games for the Pistons in 1994–95 and has also seen action in Turkey and the CBA, made the Atlanta roster out of training camp. In two starts for the Hawks, he pulled down 25 rebounds.

	G	MPG	FG%	3FG%	FT%	APG	RPG	PPG	BLK	STL
1996–97	72	11.8	.440	.000	.385	0.3	2.8	1.4	15	28
Career	106	11.1	.412	.000	.378	0.4	2.7	1.3	26	40

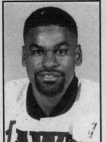

Eldridge Recasner G

Age: 30
Seasons: 6-3
Height: 190
Weight: 3
College: Washington

A well-traveled tweener with a decent shooting touch, Recasner has played in Germany and Turkey overseas, Louisville in the Global League, Yakima in the CBA, and Denver and Houston in the NBA.

	G	MPG	FG%	3FG%	FT%	APG	RPG	PPG	BLK	STL
1996–97	71	17.0	.423	.414	.879	1.3	1.6	5.7	4	38
Career	137	18.2	.417	.419	.875	1.9	1.9	6.2	9	64

Steve Smith G

Age: 28
Seasons: 6
Height: 6-8
Weight: 215
College: Michigan State

Although his lateral quickness isn't exceptional and his perimeter stroke tends to come and go, few off-guards can stop Smith from scoring within 18 feet of the hoop.

	G	MPG	FG%	3FG%	FT%	APG	RPG	PPG	BLK	STL
1996–97	72	39.1	.429	.335	.847	4.2	3.3	20.1	23	62
Career	419	34.7	.440	.338	.826	4.2	3.8	16.8	142	385

Dana Barros

Boston
CELTICS

Franchise History: Boston was an inaugural member of
the league in 1946–47. Ten years later—led by point guard
Bob Cousy and center Bill Russell—the Celtics won their
first of 16 championships. Boston went on to win every
NBA title from 1958–59 through 1965–66, plus two in the
late '60s. The Celtics earned a couple more titles in the
mid-'70s, with Dave Cowens and John Havlicek starring
in the frontcourt. Larry Bird was the driving force behind
three Celtics championships in the '80s.

1996–97 Review: After hovering near the 35-win level for
the past three years, the NBA's most tradition-rich team
finally crashed, eking out just 15 wins last season. The
Celtics went 1–23 in their division, 4–37 on the road. They
allowed a league-worst 107.9 points per game. The team
suffered a rash of injuries, most notably to Dino Radja,
Dana Barros, Pervis Ellison, Greg Minor, and Dee Brown
(none of whom made more than 25 appearances). Antoine
Walker paced Boston in scoring and rebounding.

1997–98 Preview: The Celtics apparently needed to hit
rock bottom before making changes, but now that Rick
Pitino has been hired as head coach, the situation should
begin to improve. Of course, the progress may not show
up in the wins column for a while. The Celtics will again
be hurting for size in the frontcourt, and rookie guards
Chauncey Billups and Ron Mercer figure to undergo the
usual first-year growing pains. The bottom line for Boston's
faithful—don't expect an overnight rebuilding process.

Celtics Veteran Roster

No	Player	Pos	Ht	Wt	Exp
11	Dana Barros	G	5-11	163	8
7	Dee Brown	G	6-2	185	7
29	Pervis Ellison	F/C	6-10	242	8
44	Rick Fox	G/F	6-7	250	6
—	Travis Knight	C	7-0	235	1
9	Greg Minor	G/F	6-6	230	3
8	Antoine Walker	F	6-9	245	1
55	Eric Williams	F	6-8	220	2

Head Coach: Rick Pitino

Celtics 1997 Draft Picks

Rookie	College	Position
Chauncey Billups (1-3)	Colorado	Guard
Ron Mercer (1-6)	Kentucky	Forward
Ben Pepper (2-56)	Australia	Center

Chauncey Billups is a scoring point guard who has good size for the position (6-3, 200). He is quick and athletic, able to beat opponents off the dribble and finish with either hand. His shooting range extends to the NBA three-point arc, and few point guards bring better rebounding to the table. While he was at Colorado, most opponents focused their defenses on stopping him, so he knows how to light it up with a hand in his face. Off-guard Ron Mercer also has above-average height (6-7) for his spot, but he could wind up at the three if his ballhandling and perimeter shooting don't develop. Very quick and explosive, he crashes the boards and works hard on defense. He played two seasons under Pitino at Kentucky, winning a national title in 1996, then finishing second last season.

Celtics Scouting Report

Guard: Dana Barros missed most of last season with a bad ankle, depriving the Celtics of a valuable off-the-bench sparkplug. His smallish size is a liability defensively, and he doesn't have the instincts of a pure point guard, but his perimeter stroke is money. Greg Minor also sat out the bulk of the campaign after foot surgery. A swingman who can play solid defense, connect from midrange, and run the floor, he made 47 starts for Boston two years ago. Dee Brown, whose career has gone straight into the tank, can still be a quality player if he gets into shape and finds some consistency. He was out for 62 games last season with an injured toe. Of course, rookies Billups and Mercer will be given every chance to take the majority of quality minutes at the one and two, respectively. **Grade: C+**

Forward: Antoine Walker joined a list of just seven Boston rookies who have scored 1,000 points. The other six are Dino Radja, who was a veteran of the European pro ranks, and five Hall of Famers. Selected sixth overall in the 1996 draft, Walker finished first among NBA rookies in rebounding, third in minutes, scoring, and steals, and fourth in assists. Eric Williams upped his scoring output to 15.0 ppg in his second season. He's an aggressive, blue-collar worker who has paced the team in free throw attempts in each of the past two years. Rick Fox put together a superb campaign defensively, setting a franchise record for steals with 167. He has a super work ethic and is an above-average passer and rebounder for his position. **Grade: C**

Center: Pervis Ellison could have been one of the great finesse pivots of his day, but rickety knees have made him one of the all-time busts. When healthy he swats shots and can be dominant on the glass. The signing of Travis Knight gives the Celtics a more mobile pivot option. **Grade: C–**

Celtics 1996–97 Player Statistics

	G	MIN	FG	FGA	FG%	FT	FTA	FT%	3FG	3FGA
Walker	82	2970	576	1354	.425	231	366	.631	52	159
Wesley	74	2991	456	974	.468	225	288	.781	103	286
Fox	76	2650	433	950	.456	207	263	.787	101	278
Williams	72	2435	374	820	.456	328	436	.752	2	8
Day	81	2277	398	999	.398	256	331	.773	126	348
Radja	25	874	149	339	.440	51	71	.718	0	1
Barros	24	708	110	253	.435	37	43	.860	43	105
Minor	23	547	94	196	.480	31	36	.861	1	8
Conlon	74	1614	214	454	.471	114	171	.842	2	10
Brown	21	522	61	166	.367	18	22	.818	20	65
Brickowski	17	255	32	73	.438	10	14	.714	7	20
Hawkins	29	326	29	68	.426	12	15	.800	10	31
Ellison	6	125	6	16	.375	3	5	.600	0	0
Driggers	15	132	13	43	.302	10	14	.714	0	9
Szabo	70	662	54	121	.446	45	61	.738	0	1
Hamer	35	268	30	57	.526	16	29	.552	0	2
Lister	53	516	32	77	.416	23	31	.742	0	0

	ORB	REB	AST	STL	TO	BLK	PF	PTS	PPG
Walker	288	741	262	105	230	53	271	1435	17.5
Wesley	67	264	537	162	211	13	221	1240	16.8
Fox	114	394	286	167	178	40	279	1174	15.4
Williams	126	329	129	72	139	13	213	1078	15.0
Day	109	330	117	108	127	48	208	1178	14.5
Radja	44	211	48	23	70	48	76	349	14.0
Barros	5	48	81	26	39	6	34	300	12.5
Minor	30	80	34	15	22	2	45	220	9.6
Conlon	128	323	104	46	109	18	154	574	7.8
Brown	8	48	67	31	24	7	45	160	7.6
Brickowski	6	34	15	5	19	4	42	81	4.8
Hawkins	9	31	64	16	28	1	40	80	2.8
Ellison	9	26	4	5	7	9	21	15	2.5
Driggers	12	22	6	3	6	2	10	36	2.4
Szabo	56	165	17	16	41	32	119	153	2.2
Hamer	17	60	7	2	13	4	39	76	2.2
Lister	66	168	13	8	30	14	95	87	1.6

Celtics 1996–97 Team Statistics

Final Record: 15–67

Home Record: 11–30

Road Record: 4–37

Division Record: 1–23

Conference Record: 8–46

Overtime Record: 2–5

Points Per Game: 100.6

Opponents Points Per Game: 107.9

Field Goal Percentage: .440

Opponents Field Goal Percentage: .503

Turnovers Per Game: 16.4

Opponents Turnovers Per Game: 17.6

Offensive Rebounding Percentage: .294

Defensive Rebounding Percentage: .685

Total Rebounding Percentage: .490

Scored Fewer Than 100 Points: 36

Opponents Scored Fewer Than 100 Points: 16

Celtics Clipboard

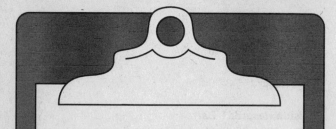

Why the Celtics win: The Celtics have some players who can light it up from the perimeter, plus a few others who will body up on defense. In the rare instances when both come together, they can do some damage.

Why the Celtics lose: Too small and/or too soft at virtually every spot, Boston is always at a defensive disadvantage. The Celtics are equal parts mediocrity and youth, the two primary guarantors of a sub-.500 NBA season.

1996–97 MVP: Antoine Walker

Projected MVP: Chauncey Billups

Fast Fact: Boston allowed opponents to shoot .503 from the field last season; no other NBA team posted worse than a .472 mark.

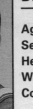

Dana Barros G

Age: 30
Seasons: 8
Height: 5-11
Weight: 163
College: Boston College

Barros was an All-Star for the 76ers back in 1994–95, but he has been a disappointment since arriving in Boston. He was hampered by an ankle injury last season.

	G	MPG	FG%	3FG%	FT%	APG	RPG	PPG	BLK	STL
1996–97	24	29.5	.435	.410	.860	3.4	2.0	12.5	6	26
Career	558	24.8	.465	.415	.860	3.6	2.0	11.6	27	530

Dee Brown G

Age: 29
Seasons: 7
Height: 6-2
Weight: 185
College: Jacksonville

Brown's glory days as a slam dunk champion are all but forgotten, and what remains is the uncertainty of whether he can shoot well enough to stay in the league. Staying healthy would be a good first step.

	G	MPG	FG%	3FG%	FT%	APG	RPG	PPG	BLK	STL
1996–97	21	24.9	.367	.308	.818	3.2	2.3	7.6	7	31
Career	435	29.5	.449	.333	.833	4.2	2.9	12.0	167	631

Marty Conlon   F/C

Age: 30
Seasons: 6
Height: 6-10
Weight: 231
College: Providence

Conlon has an awkward-looking shot and perhaps the least fluidity of any player in the league, but he works hard and knocks down the 16-foot jumper with consistency.

	G	MPG	FG%	3FG%	FT%	APG	RPG	PPG	BLK	STL
1996–97	74	21.6	.471	.200	.842	1.4	4.2	7.8	18	46
Career	350	17.2	.502	.200	.734	1.0	3.6	6.7	67	138

Todd Day   G

Age: 28
Seasons: 5
Height: 6-7
Weight: 184
College: Arkansas

Day is an absolutely fearless shooter; a scary thought considering his career percentage. He has the raw tools but is almost comically erratic in every phase of the game.

	G	MPG	FG%	3FG%	FT%	APG	RPG	PPG	BLK	STL
1996–97	81	28.0	.398	.359	.773	1.4	4.0	14.5	48	108
Career	388	27.9	.408	.339	.744	1.6	3.8	13.8	262	471

Rick Fox G/F

Age: 28
Seasons: 6
Height: 6-7
Weight: 250
College: North Carolina

Fox is stronger than most twos and threes, which gives him an edge defensively despite his lack of great quickness. He has put together two straight solid seasons on both ends of the floor.

	G	MPG	FG%	3FG%	FT%	APG	RPG	PPG	BLK	STL
1996–97	76	34.7	.456	.364	.787	3.8	5.1	15.4	40	167
Career	443	24.7	.464	.356	.772	2.8	3.9	10.7	203	551

Greg Minor G/F

Age: 26
Seasons: 3
Height: 6-6
Weight: 230
College: Louisville

Minor is a borderline starter at either small forward or shooting guard, but he was slowed by injuries last season. He doesn't take many bad shots and is a competent defender.

	G	MPG	FG%	3FG%	FT%	APG	RPG	PPG	BLK	STL
1996–97	23	23.8	.480	.125	.861	1.5	3.5	9.6	2	15
Career	164	19.8	.500	.213	.799	1.5	2.9	8.2	29	83

Dino Radja   F

Age: 30
Seasons: 4
Height: 6-11
Weight: 263
College: None

One of the most well-rounded power forwards in the league—or formerly in the league—Radja was traded to Philly in the offseason, failed a physical, and will probably be back in Europe this season.

	G	MPG	FG%	3FG%	FT%	APG	RPG	PPG	BLK	STL
1996–97	25	35.0	.440	.000	.718	1.9	8.4	14.0	48	23
Career	224	32.6	.497	.000	.735	1.6	8.4	16.7	282	201

Antoine Walker   F

Age: 21
Seasons: 1
Height: 6-9
Weight: 245
College: Kentucky

Walker registered two triple-doubles last year (putting him a mere 67 behind Larry Bird on Boston's all-time list). His perimeter shooting is suspect to say the least, but otherwise he looks like a future star.

	G	MPG	FG%	3FG%	FT%	APG	RPG	PPG	BLK	STL
1996–97	82	36.2	.425	.327	.631	3.2	9.0	17.5	53	105
Career	82	36.2	.425	.327	.631	3.2	9.0	17.5	53	105

David Wesley G

Age: 27
Seasons: 4
Height: 6-0
Weight: 196
College: Baylor

Now at the point in Charlotte, Wesley doesn't get much attention from the national media, but he is productive. Taken as a whole, his numbers stack up with some of the NBA's upper-echelon point guards.

	G	MPG	FG%	3FG%	FT%	APG	RPG	PPG	BLK	STL
1996–97	74	40.4	.468	.360	.781	7.3	3.6	16.8	13	162
Career	267	26.3	.449	.388	.770	4.9	2.6	10.5	37	382

Eric Williams F

Age: 25
Seasons: 2
Height: 6-8
Weight: 220
College: Providence

Williams, who turned in 19 20-point performances last year, isn't especially explosive or quick, but he is strong and aggressive. He takes it to the rack and either finishes or gets to the foul line.

	G	MPG	FG%	3FG%	FT%	APG	RPG	PPG	BLK	STL
1996–97	72	33.8	.456	.250	.752	1.8	4.6	15.0	13	72
Career	136	28.7	.450	.278	.719	1.5	4.0	13.0	24	128

Anthony Mason

Charlotte
HORNETS

Franchise History: Starting in 1988–89, the Hornets had the distinction of finishing last in three different divisions in their first three seasons of existence. Charlotte escaped the cellar in the franchise's second year in the Central, 1991–92, then gradually moved up toward a 50-victory campaign in 1994–95, thanks to the All-Star play of Larry Johnson and Zo Mourning. The trading of Mourning due to contract concerns caused the Hornets to fall back to .500 in 1995–96.

1996–97 Review: The Hornets rebuilt quickly in the wake of Zo's exit. The player they got for Mourning, swingman Glen Rice, finished third in the league in scoring. Dealing first-round pick Kobe Bryant to L.A. for Vlade Divac gave Charlotte flexibility at center. And swapping Johnson for Anthony Mason at forward improved the team in every phase of the game. In his first season as head coach, Dave Cowens fashioned the best record in team annals, but the Hornets were eliminated by New York in the first round.

1997–98 Preview: Charlotte fired the first salvo of the 1997 free agency period, landing point guard David Wesley, who scored almost 17 ppg for Boston last year. Few teams can cool off Charlotte's perimeter shooting and interior mobility during the regular season, but playoff basketball demands a higher brand of intensity. The same Knicks who went 1–3 against the Hornets in the 82-game grind handled them easily in the postseason. Charlotte still lacks the requisite defensive presence to win when it counts.

Hornets Veteran Roster

No	Player	Pos	Ht	Wt	Exp
30	Dell Curry	G/F	6-5	205	11
00	Tony Delk	G	6-2	189	1
12	Vlade Divac	C	7-1	260	8
52	Matt Geiger	C	7-1	245	5
14	Anthony Mason	F	6-8	250	8
21	Ricky Pierce	G	6-4	215	15
41	Glen Rice	F/G	6-8	220	8
31	Malik Rose	F	6-7	250	1
34	Tony Smith	G	6-4	205	7
—	David Wesley	G	6-0	196	4

Head Coach: Dave Cowens

Hornets 1997 Draft Picks

Rookie	College	Position
None		

First-Round Picks Since 1988

1996	Kobe Bryant	None	Guard
	Tony Delk	Kentucky	Guard
1995	George Zidek	UCLA	Center
1994	No Pick		
1993	Greg Graham	Indiana	Guard
	Scott Burrell	Connecticut	Forward
1992	Alonzo Mourning	Georgetown	Center
1991	Larry Johnson	UNLV	Forward
1990	Kendall Gill	Illinois	Guard
1989	J.R. Reid	North Carolina	Center
1988	Rex Chapman	Kentucky	Guard

Hornets Scouting Report

Guard: David Wesley's ratio of recognition to production isn't very high, but this could be the season in which his name becomes known. Playing point for the struggling Celtics last year, he finished sixth in the league in minutes, fifth in steals per game, tied for 12th in assists (ahead of Anderson, Payton, Brandon, Blaylock, etc.), and among the top 40 in scoring. He can connect from long range but is more of a penetrator than a three-point bomber. At the two, Dell Curry takes the majority of the minutes but rarely starts. A deadeye with a perfect release, his accuracy from long distance is uncanny. Clutch veteran Ricky Pierce joined the Hornets late last season and averaged more than 30 mpg and 15 ppg in his final 16 starts. Charlotte received a spark from rookie Tony Delk, who sat out 21 games due to coach's decisions but shot a whopping .464 in 112 tries from beyond the arc. **Grade: B–**

Forward: Glen Rice emerged as a full-fledged superstar last year, scorching the nets on a nightly basis. In the final 50 games, he averaged nearly 30 points per contest on .492 shooting. His range is phenomenal, but he can also get to the rack and finish with flair. Anthony Mason is a unique talent at the four, capable of matching up defensively at any position, running the offense as a point-forward, and scoring at will in the paint. He was the only player in the NBA to rank among the top 25 in both rebounding and assists last season. **Grade: A+**

Center: Vlade Divac has fine passing skills and a nice feel for the game. He is also one of the better rebounders and shot blockers in the league. Matt Geiger is a solid backup when healthy, but he missed 33 games last season because of back problems. Although foul prone, he is surprisingly agile on the offensive end. **Grade: B+**

Hornets 1996–97 Player Statistics

	G	MIN	FG	FGA	FG%	FT	FTA	FT%	3FG	3FGA
Rice	79	3362	722	1513	.477	464	535	.867	207	440
Mason	73	3149	433	825	.525	319	428	.745	1	3
Curry	68	2078	384	836	.459	114	142	.803	126	296
Divac	81	2840	418	847	.494	177	259	.683	11	47
Pierce	60	1250	239	497	.481	139	155	.897	42	95
Geiger	49	1044	171	350	.489	89	127	.701	6	20
Bogues	65	1880	204	443	.460	54	64	.844	60	144
Delk	61	867	119	256	.465	42	51	.824	52	112
Smith	69	1291	138	337	.409	38	59	.644	32	99
Royal	62	858	62	146	.425	94	117	.803	0	2
Addison	41	355	49	122	.402	22	28	.786	8	20
Rose	54	525	61	128	.477	38	62	.613	0	2
Chambers	12	83	7	31	.226	3	4	.750	2	3

	ORB	REB	AST	STL	TO	BLK	PF	PTS	PPG
Rice	67	318	160	72	177	26	190	2115	26.8
Mason	186	829	414	76	165	33	202	1186	16.2
Curry	40	211	118	60	93	14	147	1008	14.8
Divac	241	725	301	103	193	180	277	1024	12.6
Pierce	36	121	80	28	68	9	97	659	11.0
Geiger	100	258	38	20	67	27	153	437	8.9
Bogues	25	141	469	82	108	2	114	522	8.0
Delk	31	99	99	36	68	6	71	332	5.4
Smith	38	94	150	48	73	19	110	346	5.0
Royal	52	154	25	23	47	11	100	218	3.5
Addison	19	45	34	8	17	3	52	128	3.1
Rose	70	164	32	28	41	17	114	160	3.0
Chambers	3	14	4	1	9	0	14	19	1.6

Hornets 1996–97 Team Statistics

Final Record: 54–28

Home Record: 30–11

Road Record: 24–17

Division Record: 14–14

Conference Record: 34–20

Overtime Record: 5–0

Points Per Game: 98.9

Opponents Points Per Game: 97.0

Field Goal Percentage: .471

Opponents Field Goal Percentage: .460

Turnovers Per Game: 14.7

Opponents Turnovers Per Game: 13.9

Offensive Rebounding Percentage: .287

Defensive Rebounding Percentage: .681

Total Rebounding Percentage: .484

Scored Fewer Than 100 Points: 46

Opponents Scored Fewer Than 100 Points: 49

Hornets Clipboard

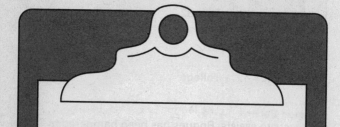

Why the Hornets win: If the Hornets have a healthy point guard who can get the ball to perimeter marksmen Rice, Curry, and Delk, they can be tough to stop. At the free throw line and beyond the arc, there isn't a better shooting team in the league.

Why the Hornets lose: The defense has improved, but it remains middle of the road compared to the rest of the NBA. The Hornets have been outrebounded on average for nine consecutive seasons.

1996–97 MVP: Anthony Mason

Projected MVP: Anthony Mason

Fast Fact: The Hornets played 21 sets of back-to-backs (i.e., games on consecutive nights) last year, going 14–7 on the front end and 11–10 on the back end.

Muggsy Bogues G

Age: 32
Seasons: 10
Height: 5-3
Weight: 141
College: Wake Forest

The league's all-time leader in ratio of turnovers to assists, Bogues has been hampered by knee problems in recent seasons and may have to retire. His smallish size is an obvious shortcoming on defense.

	G	MPG	FG%	3FG%	FT%	APG	RPG	PPG	BLK	STL
1996–97	65	28.9	.460	.417	.844	7.2	2.2	8.0	2	82
Career	709	30.2	.460	.276	.815	8.4	2.8	8.3	31	1192

Dell Curry G

Age: 33
Seasons: 11
Height: 6-5
Weight: 205
College: Virginia Tech

Curry isn't a great ball handler, passer, or defender, but he has been arguably the top perimeter shooter in the league this decade. He has shot at least .400 from three-point range in each of the past six years.

	G	MPG	FG%	3FG%	FT%	APG	RPG	PPG	BLK	STL
1996–97	68	30.7	.459	.430	.803	1.7	3.1	14.8	14	60
Career	794	23.6	.461	.399	.848	2.0	2.7	13.2	208	835

Tony Delk   G

Age: 23
Seasons: 1
Height: 6-2
Weight: 189
College: Kentucky

Delk doesn't have the height of a two or the passing skills of a one, but he is a clutch shooter who is deadly from downtown. He'll make an excellent catalyst off the bench if he can't crack the starting five.

	G	MPG	FG%	3FG%	FT%	APG	RPG	PPG	BLK	STL
1996–97	61	14.2	.465	.464	.824	1.6	1.6	5.4	6	36
Career	61	14.2	.465	.464	.824	1.6	1.6	5.4	6	36

Vlade Divac   C

Age: 29
Seasons: 8
Height: 7-1
Weight: 260
College: Serbia

Divac topped all NBA pivots in assists per game last season, and he was seventh in the league in blocked shots. His all-around numbers put him among the upper half at his position.

	G	MPG	FG%	3FG%	FT%	APG	RPG	PPG	BLK	STL
1996–97	81	35.1	.494	.234	.683	3.7	9.0	12.6	180	103
Career	601	30.3	.508	.230	.705	2.8	8.7	12.5	1009	748

Matt Geiger C

Age: 28
Seasons: 5
Height: 7-1
Weight: 245
College: Georgia Tech

An odd case, Geiger can look almost nimble on offense, yet his ratio of blocks to fouls (about one to five) is the stuff of a defensive statue. He works hard and looks scary.

	G	MPG	FG%	3FG%	FT%	APG	RPG	PPG	BLK	STL
1996–97	49	21.3	.489	.300	.701	0.8	5.3	8.9	27	20
Career	320	21.4	.534	.298	.711	0.6	5.4	8.3	188	158

Anthony Mason F

Age: 31
Seasons: 8
Height: 6-8
Weight: 250
College: Tennessee State

Mason had a remarkable year, rating third in the NBA in rebounding and third among forwards in assists. He paced the league in minutes per game and logged the first four triple-doubles of his career.

	G	MPG	FG%	3FG%	FT%	APG	RPG	PPG	BLK	STL
1996–97	73	43.1	.525	.333	.745	5.7	11.4	16.2	33	76
Career	492	32.1	.525	.200	.696	2.9	8.0	10.4	138	337

Ricky Pierce   G

Age: 38
Seasons: 15
Height: 6-4
Weight: 215
College: Rice

Twice the NBA's Sixth Man of the Year and still one of the craftiest off-the-bench scorers in the game, Pierce has played for five franchises in the past four seasons.

	G	MPG	FG%	3FG%	FT%	APG	RPG	PPG	BLK	STL
1996–97	60	20.8	.481	.442	.897	1.3	2.0	11.0	9	28
Career	930	25.0	.495	.322	.876	1.9	2.4	15.4	147	759

Glen Rice   G/F

Age: 30
Seasons: 8
Height: 6-8
Weight: 220
College: Michigan

Rice has refined his always-explosive abilities and taken his game to an All-Star level. He rang up an electrifying streak of 28 straight 20-point games and topped the NBA in three-point accuracy.

	G	MPG	FG%	3FG%	FT%	APG	RPG	PPG	BLK	STL
1996–97	79	42.6	.477	.470	.867	2.0	4.0	26.8	26	72
Career	636	37.0	.463	.406	.842	2.3	4.8	20.5	204	734

Donald Royal F

Age: 31
Seasons: 7
Height: 6-8
Weight: 218
College: Notre Dame

Royal came to Charlotte in a deal with Golden State for Scott Burrell. He has superb first-step quickness and no fear when taking the ball to the rack, but his offensive skills are otherwise nothing special.

	G	MPG	FG%	3FG%	FT%	APG	RPG	PPG	BLK	STL
1996–97	62	13.8	.425	.000	.803	0.4	0.4	3.5	11	23
Career	473	17.2	.477	.000	.767	1.0	2.9	6.5	98	240

Tony Smith G

Age: 29
Seasons: 7
Height: 6-4
Weight: 205
College: Marquette

Smith, who scored nearly 24 ppg as a senior at Marquette, has been used strictly for defensive purposes as a pro. His range, accuracy, ballhandling, and passing are all subpar.

	G	MPG	FG%	3FG%	FT%	APG	RPG	PPG	BLK	STL
1996–97	69	18.7	.409	.323	.644	2.2	1.4	5.0	19	48
Career	444	16.1	.432	.312	.691	1.9	1.6	5.6	77	307

Jason Caffey

Chicago
BULLS

Franchise History: The Bulls entered the NBA in 1966–67, going through the usual growing pains before finding success in the mid-'70s, when they reached the conference finals twice. After a decade's worth of mediocrity, Chicago drafted Michael Jordan third overall in 1984. The franchise won its first of three straight championships in 1990–91, lost the crown for two seasons while Jordan played minor league baseball, then bounced back to win a league-record 72 games and another ring in 1995–96.

1996–97 Review: The Bulls continued their dominance, and only a 7–4 April kept them a game short of 70 wins. Jordan and Scottie Pippen were an unstoppable tandem, as always, but several key role players—Dennis Rodman and Toni Kukoc among them—were hampered by injuries. The Bulls didn't always play their best in the playoffs, but they met little resistance from Washington (3–0), Atlanta (4-1), and Miami (4–1) en route to the Finals, where Utah put up a fight before succumbing in six.

1997–98 Preview: With a ring for each finger and a chance for one more, the Bulls are back for another run at the title. Nobody knows better than Jordan what it takes to be a champion, and he will be driven by the desire to go out on top in what is expected to be his swan song. Perhaps because the Bulls have set such a high standard the past two seasons, there are murmurs of impending downfall anytime they fail to go up 3–0 in a playoff series. Of course, the unbelievers tend to fall silent at season's end.

Bulls Veteran Roster

No	Player	Pos	Ht	Wt	Exp
1	Randy Brown	G	6-2	191	6
30	Jud Buechler	F/G	6-6	228	7
35	Jason Caffey	F	6-8	256	2
9	Ron Harper	G	6-6	216	11
23	Michael Jordan	G	6-6	216	12
25	Steve Kerr	G	6-3	181	9
7	Toni Kukoc	F/G	6-11	232	4
13	Luc Longley	C	7-2	292	6
33	Scottie Pippen	F/G	6-7	228	10
91	Dennis Rodman	F	6-6	220	11
34	Bill Wennington	C	7-0	260	10

Head Coach: Phil Jackson

Bulls 1997 Draft Picks

Rookie	College	Position
Keith Booth (1-28)	Maryland	Forward
Roberto Duenas (2-58)	Spain	Center

Keith Booth was the final draft choice of the first round (there was no official 29th selection, due to the forfeiture of Washington's pick). Tough and unselfish, he was used in a complementary role for three years before stepping up as Maryland's scoring leader last season. He has the right size (6-6, 226) for a shooting guard but is more of a scorer than a shooter. He'll probably swing between the two and the three if he stays in the league for a while. He is a super rebounder for his size, having nabbed slightly under eight caroms per game as a senior. Roberto Duenas, the final player drafted, is a 7-2 center who will probably continue to play in Europe.

Bulls Scouting Report

Guard: It all begins, oddly enough, with Ron Harper at the point. Once a perennial 20-ppg scorer, he has adapted to being a defensive stopper who takes his points as they come. Long arms, an off-guard's size, and great footwork allow him to shut down the drives of opposition ones. At the other guard spot, Chicago has a player who simply is the sport of basketball—Steve Kerr. Just kidding. The man the masses know as M.J., Air, or just plain Mike continues to set the all-time standard for his position. The NBA's top scorer last season for the ninth time in his career, he has developed a deadly jump shot to go with his uncheckable dribble-drive arsenal. His skills are utterly complete, his execution is unselfish and efficient, and his passion for winning is nonpareil. As for Kerr, he is always in the right spot and is money from long distance. **Grade: A+**

Forward: Despite swirling trade winds and questions (sometimes spoken, sometimes not) about his intangibles, Scottie Pippen is the best all-around player in the league, not including the one who has a cologne named after him. His position is small forward, but he distributes the ball like a one, scores like a two, rebounds like a four, and works the low post like a five. Dennis Rodman, the greatest rebounder ever, at least among non-centers, lost 27 games to injuries and suspensions during the regular season, then did nothing special in the playoffs. Jason Caffey did a solid job in the Worm's absence. Toni Kukoc was also hurt for much of the year, but he is akin to a 6-11 point guard, in terms of ballhandling and range, when healthy. **Grade: A+**

Center: Australian seven-footer Luc Longley eats space and chips in nine points per night. Bill Wennington gives the Bulls six fouls and can pull opposition pivots away from the basket with his midrange set shot. **Grade: C+**

Bulls 1996–97 Player Statistics

	G	MIN	FG	FGA	FG%	FT	FTA	FT%	3FG	3FGA
Jordan	82	3106	920	1892	.486	480	576	.833	111	297
Pippen	82	3095	648	1366	.474	204	291	.701	156	424
Kukoc	57	1610	285	605	.471	134	174	.770	50	151
Longley	59	1472	221	485	.456	95	120	.792	0	2
Kerr	82	1861	249	467	.533	54	67	.806	110	237
Caffey	75	1405	205	385	.532	139	211	.659	0	1
Williams	9	138	26	63	.413	11	15	.733	0	0
Harper	76	1740	177	406	.436	58	82	.707	68	188
Rodman	55	1947	128	286	.448	50	88	.568	5	19
Brown	72	1057	140	333	.420	57	84	.679	4	22
Wennington	61	783	118	237	.498	44	53	.830	0	2
Parish	43	406	70	143	.490	21	31	.677	0	0
Simpkins	48	395	31	93	.333	28	40	.700	1	4
Buechler	76	703	58	158	.367	5	14	.357	18	54
Steigenga	2	12	1	4	.250	1	2	.500	0	2

	ORB	REB	AST	STL	TO	BLK	PF	PTS	PPG
Jordan	113	482	352	140	166	44	156	2431	29.6
Pippen	160	531	467	154	214	45	213	1656	20.2
Kukoc	94	261	256	60	91	29	97	754	13.2
Longley	121	332	141	23	111	66	191	537	9.1
Kerr	29	130	175	67	43	3	98	662	8.1
Caffey	135	301	89	25	97	9	149	549	7.3
Williams	14	33	12	3	11	5	20	63	7.0
Harper	46	193	191	86	50	38	138	480	6.3
Rodman	320	883	170	32	111	19	172	311	5.7
Brown	34	111	133	81	58	17	116	341	4.7
Wennington	46	129	41	10	31	11	132	280	4.6
Parish	42	89	22	6	28	19	40	161	3.7
Simpkins	36	92	31	5	35	5	44	91	1.9
Buechler	70	164	32	28	41	17	114	160	3.0
Steigenga	0	3	2	1	2	1	1	3	1.5

Bulls 1996–97 Team Statistics

Final Record: 69–13

Home Record: 39–2

Road Record: 30–11

Division Record: 24–4

Conference Record: 44–10

Overtime Record: 2–0

Points Per Game: 103.1

Opponents Points Per Game: 92.3

Field Goal Percentage: .473

Opponents Field Goal Percentage: .436

Turnovers Per Game: 13.5

Opponents Turnovers Per Game: 15.8

Offensive Rebounding Percentage: .359

Defensive Rebounding Percentage: .693

Total Rebounding Percentage: .526

Scored Fewer Than 100 Points: 30

Opponents Scored Fewer Than 100 Points: 57

Bulls Clipboard

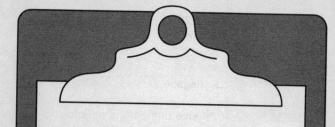

Why the Bulls win: Because they have solid to superb defenders at all five spots, the Bulls rarely need to double-team or rotate. Jordan and Pippen create a steady stream of points, while complementary players such as Kerr and Kukoc can put the final nail in an opponent's coffin.

Why the Bulls lose: On rare occasions, Jordan and Pippen go cold on the same night. If nobody picks up the slack, and the opponent can make some jump shots while controlling the boards, Chicago can be beaten.

1996–97 MVP: Michael Jordan

Projected MVP: Michael Jordan

Fast Fact: Phil Jackson owns the highest playoff winning percentage among head coaches in league history (.736, 92–33).

Randy Brown   **G**

Age: 29
Seasons: 6
Height: 6-2
Weight: 191
College: New Mexico State

A fierce one-on-one defender, Brown is committed to shutting down his matchups, but his rate of personal fouls per minutes played (one to nine) is on the high side for a defensive specialist.

	G	MPG	FG%	3FG%	FT%	APG	RPG	PPG	BLK	STL
1996–97	72	14.7	.420	.182	.679	1.8	1.5	4.7	17	81
Career	399	15.3	.439	.219	.673	1.8	1.7	4.7	108	443

Jason Caffey   **F**

Age: 24
Seasons: 2
Height: 6-8
Weight: 256
College: Alabama

Caffey saw more action in his second season, owing to Rodman's bad behavior and knees. He posted just under nine points and eight rebounds in his 19 starts at the four.

	G	MPG	FG%	3FG%	FT%	APG	RPG	PPG	BLK	STL
1996–97	75	18.7	.532	.000	.659	1.2	4.0	7.3	9	25
Career	132	14.8	.505	.000	.642	0.9	3.1	5.5	16	37

Ron Harper   G

Age: 33
Seasons: 11
Height: 6-6
Weight: 216
College: Miami (Ohio)

An invaluable part of Chicago's title success, Harper scores 13 points per game fewer then he used to, but his defense and ballhandling make up for the lack of scoring.

	G	MPG	FG%	3FG%	FT%	APG	RPG	PPG	BLK	STL
1996–97	76	22.9	.436	.362	.707	2.5	2.5	6.3	38	86
Career	765	32.2	.451	.292	.720	4.2	4.4	15.5	579	1424

Michael Jordan   G

Age: 34
Seasons: 12
Height: 6-6
Weight: 216
College: North Carolina

A five-time Finals MVP, Jordan is the ultimate clutch competitor. A superstar scorer who also relishes playing defense, he currently ranks third on the league's all-time steals list.

	G	MPG	FG%	3FG%	FT%	APG	RPG	PPG	BLK	STL
1996–97	82	37.9	.486	.374	.833	4.3	5.9	29.6	44	140
Career	848	38.6	.509	.340	.843	5.6	6.3	31.7	783	2165

Steve Kerr G

Age: 32
Seasons: 9
Height: 6-3
Weight: 181
College: Arizona

Kerr, who buried the shot that closed out Utah in the Finals, finished second in the NBA in three-point accuracy last season. His assist-to-turnover ratio was an outstanding four to one.

	G	MPG	FG%	3FG%	FT%	APG	RPG	PPG	BLK	STL
1996–97	82	22.7	.533	.464	.806	2.1	1.6	8.1	3	67
Career	589	19.9	.495	.477	.847	2.2	1.3	6.8	33	367

Toni Kukoc F/G

Age: 29
Seasons: 4
Height: 6-11
Weight: 232
College: Croatia

Kukoc lacks the bulk to bang with the big boys down low, but he is a fearless shooter who was the team's third-leading scorer last season despite making only 15 starts.

	G	MPG	FG%	3FG%	FT%	APG	RPG	PPG	BLK	STL
1996–97	57	28.2	.471	.331	.770	4.5	4.6	13.2	29	60
Career	294	27.6	.477	.338	.758	4.0	4.5	13.3	106	307

Luc Longley C

Age: 28
Seasons: 6
Height: 7-2
Weight: 292
College: New Mexico

Longley's lack of aggressiveness can be frustrating, but he does a competent job of clogging the middle. He has surprising range for his size and is a reliable shooter from 16 feet.

	G	MPG	FG%	3FG%	FT%	APG	RPG	PPG	BLK	STL
1996–97	59	24.9	.456	.000	.792	2.4	5.6	9.1	66	23
Career	373	20.5	.464	.000	.754	1.5	4.9	6.9	415	196

Scottie Pippen F/G

Age: 32
Seasons: 10
Height: 6-7
Weight: 228
College: Central Arkansas

Pippen ranked first among the Bulls in assists and steals last season, second in rebounding and scoring. He lacks Jordan's intangibles but is otherwise his equal at this stage of their respective careers.

	G	MPG	FG%	3FG%	FT%	APG	RPG	PPG	BLK	STL
1996–97	82	37.7	.474	.368	.701	5.7	6.5	20.2	45	154
Career	789	35.7	.485	.329	.688	5.3	6.9	17.9	721	1692

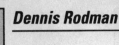

Dennis Rodman   F

Age: 36
Seasons: 11
Height: 6-6
Weight: 220
College: Southeastern Oklahoma State

Rodman's season included the usual boring assortment of look-at-me antics, plus a minor knee injury. He paced the league in rebounding for the sixth year in a row but was inconsistent in the playoffs.

	G	MPG	FG%	3FG%	FT%	APG	RPG	PPG	BLK	STL
1996–97	55	35.4	.448	.263	.568	3.1	16.1	5.7	19	32
Career	796	31.3	.530	.237	.588	1.7	13.0	7.8	500	552

Bill Wennington   C

Age: 34
Seasons: 10
Height: 7-0
Weight: 260
College: St. John's

Wennington has had three straight seasons of .490-plus field goal accuracy, but his ratio of personal fouls to blocked shots last year was a comical 12 to one.

	G	MPG	FG%	3FG%	FT%	APG	RPG	PPG	BLK	STL
1996–97	61	12.8	.498	.000	.830	0.7	2.1	4.6	11	10
Career	627	14.0	.469	.114	.784	0.6	3.1	4.7	229	207

Terrell Brandon

Cleveland
CAVALIERS

Franchise History: One of the least successful franchises of the past 25 years, the Cavaliers have won a meager four playoff series since joining the NBA in 1970–71. The Cavs did win a division title in 1975–76, led by forwards Jim Brewer and Campy Russell, but they lost to Boston in the conference finals. In the latter half of the '80s, the Cavs had a couple of 50-win seasons and made several playoff appearances (including a trip to the conference finals in 1991–92), but they never found a way to get past the Bulls.

1996–97 Review: Head coach Mike Fratello's slow-down system almost worked another miracle, as the Cavaliers finished above .500 and missed the postseason by just one game, despite an absence of offensive talent. Point guard Terrell Brandon paced the Cavs in scoring, but he couldn't keep the team from going 11–16 in the final two months. In the regular season finale, Cleveland battled Washington for the eighth playoff spot but lost 85–81. The Cavs set a league record for fewest points allowed per game (85.6).

1997–98 Preview: The Cavaliers wound up with two picks in the lottery, but neither figures to make much impact at the outset. Coach Fratello is seemingly able to squeeze a winning record from any group of players who follow his formula of gritty defense and molasses offense, but he'll have another severe talent drought this season. With the franchise's sad-sack history of injuries, mediocrity, and missed opportunities, don't expect the Cavs to receive the good fortune they'll need to win 40 games.

Cavaliers Veteran Roster

No	Player	Pos	Ht	Wt	Exp
1	Terrell Brandon	G	5-11	180	6
35	Danny Ferry	F	6-10	235	7
32	Tyrone Hill	F	6-9	245	7
11	Zydrunas Ilgauskas	C	7-3	238	1
33	Donny Marshall	F	6-7	230	2
52	Vitaly Potapenko	C	6-10	280	1
3	Bob Sura	G	6-5	200	2

Head Coach: Mike Fratello

Cavaliers 1997 Draft Picks

Rookie	College	Position
Derek Anderson (1-13)	Kentucky	Guard
Brevin Knight (1-16)	Stanford	Guard
Cedric Henderson (2-45)	Memphis	Forward

Derek Anderson was projected as a top-five pick before a knee injury—the second of his collegiate career—aborted his senior season. He tore his left ACL as a sophomore at Ohio State, then blew out the right one 19 games into last year. He was averaging 17.7 points per game before the injury. Scouts love his all-around skills. He elevates high and quick and can score off picks or create off the dribble. He'll make the extra pass, chip in on the boards, and play hard defense. Brevin Knight follows in the footsteps of smallish point guards such as Damon Stoudamire and Cleveland's own Terrell Brandon. He topped the nation in assists last season and converted 41 percent of his three-point attempts. His playmaking ability is obviously first rate, and he has the freaky quickness that can cause havoc for opposition point guards on both ends of the floor.

Cavaliers Scouting Report

Guard: Primarily a backup in his first four years with the Cavaliers, Terrell Brandon has been an All-Star the past two seasons. A small but quick point guard who creates shots for teammates who can't get their own, he blows by defenders who must play him tight to stop his jumper. The team's overall lack of firepower tends to limit his assist totals (he ranked just 19th in the league), and he sometimes tries to do too much by himself. Second-year shooting guard Bob Sura saw action in all 82 games, including 23 as a starter. He was on fire toward season's end, contributing roughly 16 points, five assists, and five boards per contest. Aggressive and athletic, he likes to take the rock to the rack but is deeply inconsistent from the perimeter. Cleveland's two lottery picks, Knight and Anderson, will contend for minutes at the one and two, respectively. **Grade: B**

Forward: Bouncing back from injuries sustained in a car wreck, Tyrone Hill regained the form that made him an All-Star in 1994–95. He manages to score in double figures through sheer will, and his work on defense and under the glass is top notch. He was one of only two qualifiers to shoot .600 last season, and he ranked tenth in the league in rebounding. Danny Ferry became a starter for the final 29 games and hit 42 percent of his three-point tries, but he is a poor defender and rebounder who rarely creates for others. Backup small forward Donny Marshall had some success from beyond the arc in his second season, but his shooting in general was inconsistent. **Grade: C–**

Center: The Cavaliers could feature a distinctly Eastern European flavor in the paint, with Vitaly Potapenko and Zydrunas Ilgauskas slated to be at center. The former is a potential double-digit scorer, while the latter missed his entire rookie season with a foot injury. **Grade: D**

Cavaliers 1996–97 Player Statistics

	G	MIN	FG	FGA	FG%	FT	FTA	FT%	3FG	3FGA
Brandon	78	2868	575	1313	.438	268	297	.902	101	271
Mills	80	3167	405	894	.453	176	209	.842	86	220
Hill	74	2582	357	595	.600	241	381	.633	0	1
Phills	69	2375	328	766	.428	125	174	.718	85	216
Ferry	82	2633	341	794	.429	74	87	.851	114	284
Sura	82	2269	253	587	.431	196	319	.614	53	164
Potapenko	80	1238	186	423	.440	92	125	.736	1	2
West	70	959	100	180	.556	27	56	.482	0	0
Marshall	56	548	52	160	.325	38	54	.704	33	87
Lang	64	843	68	162	.420	35	48	.729	0	6
Geary	39	246	22	58	.379	5	11	.455	8	21
Scott	16	50	8	16	.500	4	11	.364	0	0
Thomas	19	77	9	24	.375	1	1	1.000	2	12

	ORB	REB	AST	STL	TO	BLK	PF	PTS	PPG
Brandon	48	301	490	138	178	30	177	1519	19.5
Mills	118	497	198	86	120	41	222	1072	13.4
Hill	259	736	92	63	147	30	268	955	12.9
Phills	63	245	233	113	135	21	174	866	12.6
Ferry	82	337	151	56	94	32	245	870	10.6
Sura	76	308	390	90	181	33	218	755	9.2
Potapenko	105	217	40	26	109	34	216	465	5.8
West	69	186	19	11	52	55	142	227	3.2
Marshall	22	70	24	24	32	3	60	175	3.1
Lang	52	127	33	33	50	30	111	171	2.7
Geary	4	15	36	13	15	2	36	57	1.5
Scott	8	16	0	0	0	3	6	20	1.3
Thomas	3	13	8	2	6	1	7	21	1.1

Cavaliers 1996–97 Team Statistics

Final Record: 42–40

Home Record: 25–16

Road Record: 17–24

Division Record: 13–15

Conference Record: 26–28

Overtime Record: 2–4

Points Per Game: 87.5

Opponents Points Per Game: 85.6

Field Goal Percentage: .453

Opponents Field Goal Percentage: .441

Turnovers Per Game: 14.5

Opponents Turnovers Per Game: 16.2

Offensive Rebounding Percentage: .294

Defensive Rebounding Percentage: .719

Total Rebounding Percentage: .506

Scored Fewer Than 100 Points: 66

Opponents Scored Fewer Than 100 Points: 72

Cavaliers Clipboard

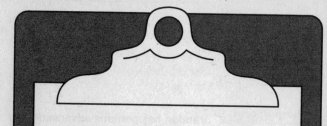

Why the Cavaliers win: The Cavaliers must dictate tempo, protect the ball, and connect from the perimeter. Brandon usually needs to dominate for the Cavs to win.

Why the Cavaliers lose: Injuries and bad luck appear to always be factors, and the Cavs often seem to be outgunned on the court. The shortage of post-up scorers puts extra pressure on the team's outside shooters, while the overall lack of point production leaves the defense in almost constant "must stop" situations.

1996–97 MVP: Terrell Brandon

Projected MVP: Terrell Brandon

Fast Fact: The Cavaliers were 14–2 last season in games in which they scored at least 100 points.

Terrell Brandon G

Age: 27
Seasons: 6
Height: 5-11
Weight: 180
College: Oregon

Brandon has perhaps advanced from being a well-kept secret to being slightly overrated, but he is definitely the best player the Cavaliers have. He led the team in scoring, steals, and assists last season.

	G	MPG	FG%	3FG%	FT%	APG	RPG	PPG	BLK	STL
1996–97	78	36.8	.438	.373	.902	6.3	3.9	19.5	30	138
Career	457	26.6	.446	.360	.868	4.9	2.7	12.7	142	621

Danny Ferry F

Age: 31
Seasons: 7
Height: 6-10
Weight: 235
College: Duke

One of the biggest draft busts in NBA history (second overall in 1989), Ferry is a borderline starter at this stage of his career. He shoots the three and makes his free throws but does little else.

	G	MPG	FG%	3FG%	FT%	APG	RPG	PPG	BLK	STL
1996–97	82	32.1	.429	.401	.851	1.8	4.1	10.6	32	56
Career	541	21.5	.444	.386	.835	1.6	3.2	8.4	201	262

Tyrone Hill   F

Age: 29
Seasons: 7
Height: 6-9
Weight: 245
College: Xavier

Hill gets the job done with a strong, wiry body and hard work. He almost never misses a shot from ten feet in, and he crashes the offensive boards like a man possessed.

	G	MPG	FG%	3FG%	FT%	APG	RPG	PPG	BLK	STL
1996–97	74	34.9	.600	.000	.633	1.2	9.9	12.9	30	63
Career	475	26.3	.529	.000	.649	0.8	8.4	9.6	239	349

Antonio Lang   F

Age: 25
Seasons: 3
Height: 6-8
Weight: 230
College: Duke

Thrown in as part of the deal that sent Hot Rod Williams to Phoenix for Dan Majerle, Lang reached a career high in games played last year but was generally a nonfactor in his two seasons with the Cavs.

	G	MPG	FG%	3FG%	FT%	APG	RPG	PPG	BLK	STL
1996–97	64	13.2	.420	.000	.729	0.5	2.0	2.7	30	33
Career	117	10.8	.454	.000	.727	0.4	1.6	2.6	44	47

Donny Marshall F

Age: 25
Seasons: 2
Height: 6-7
Weight: 230
College: Connecticut

Marshall lacks exceptional size or quickness for his position, and his field goal percentages for the past two seasons are abysmal, but he does have three-point range.

	G	MPG	FG%	3FG%	FT%	APG	RPG	PPG	BLK	STL
1996–97	56	9.7	.325	.393	.704	0.4	1.3	3.1	3	24
Career	89	8.3	.338	.351	.674	0.3	1.1	2.8	4	32

Chris Mills F

Age: 27
Seasons: 4
Height: 6-6
Weight: 216
College: Arizona

Mills is an aggressive defender who overachieves on the boards, despite his tweenerish size. He doesn't handle the ball particularly well but can finish his drives or pull up from long distance.

	G	MPG	FG%	3FG%	FT%	APG	RPG	PPG	BLK	STL
1996–97	80	39.6	.453	.391	.842	2.5	6.2	13.4	41	86
Career	319	34.7	.442	.375	.819	2.1	5.4	12.6	178	272

Bobby Phills   G/F

Age: 28
Seasons: 6
Height: 6-5
Weight: 220
College: Southern

One of the better wing defenders in the NBA, Phills has been limited by nagging injuries in recent years. He makes the most of his skills but is not a prolific scorer for a shooting guard.

	G	MPG	FG%	3FG%	FT%	APG	RPG	PPG	BLK	STL
1996–97	69	34.4	.428	.394	.718	3.4	3.6	12.6	21	113
Career	334	27.4	.443	.399	.747	2.5	3.0	10.5	88	410

Vitaly Potapenko   C

Age: 22
Seasons: 1
Height: 6-10
Weight: 280
College: Wright State

A wide body and a decent shooting touch make Potapenko an intriguing project. His work ethic is excellent, and he registered a couple of 20-point games in his rookie campaign.

	G	MPG	FG%	3FG%	FT%	APG	RPG	PPG	BLK	STL
1996–97	80	15.5	.440	.500	.736	0.5	2.7	5.8	34	26
Career	80	15.5	.440	.500	.736	0.5	2.7	5.8	34	26

Bob Sura G

Age: 24
Seasons: 2
Height: 6-5
Weight: 200
College: Florida State

Sura gets off the floor and finishes with style, and he is a fine passer with good court sense. He responded well to being a starter late last season, but an iffy jump shot may hinder his playing time.

	G	MPG	FG%	3FG%	FT%	APG	RPG	PPG	BLK	STL
1996–97	82	27.7	.431	.323	.614	4.8	3.8	9.2	33	90
Career	161	21.2	.423	.331	.641	3.9	2.8	7.9	54	146

Mark West C

Age: 37
Seasons: 14
Height: 6-10
Weight: 246
College: Old Dominion

West has been around forever and is one of the best at blocking shots, banging inside, and turning caroms into layups. His career is winding down but he may have a few fouls left to give.

	G	MPG	FG%	3FG%	FT%	APG	RPG	PPG	BLK	STL
1996–97	70	13.7	.556	.000	.482	0.3	2.7	3.2	55	11
Career	1004	19.4	.584	.000	.573	0.4	5.2	6.1	1372	318

Robert Pack

Dallas
MAVERICKS

Franchise History: Dallas came into the league in 1980–81 and quickly put together an outstanding team, featuring 1981 draft picks Mark Aguirre, Jay Vincent, and Rolando Blackman, and 1983 rookies Dale Ellis and Derek Harper. The Mavericks won 55 games in 1986–87 and came within one win of the NBA Finals the following season. Dallas has fallen apart in the past five years, having put all hope in three young guns—Jason Kidd, Jamal Mashburn, and Jim Jackson—all of whom were traded last season.

1996–97 Review: Kidd was the first of the trio to go, sent to Phoenix in a multiplayer swap that netted swingman Michael Finley. Dallas was 16–28 when Don Nelson was hired as general manager. He promptly traded Mashburn to Miami, then sent Jackson to New Jersey in a nine-player deal that brought Shawn Bradley and Robert Pack. The Mavericks used an NBA-record 27 players, were the third-lowest-scoring team in the league, and wound up with a worse (24–58) record than they had the year before.

1997–98 Preview: The hiring of Nelson as GM, and the aforementioned housecleaning, did nothing to alter the impression that this is one confused franchise. It is not likely that head coach Jim Cleamons will still be on the Dallas bench after midseason, and unless Nellie can locate someone on whom to unload his personally assembled collective of mediocrity (Robert Pack? Shawn Bradley?), Mavericks fans are going to see enough blah basketball to last a lifetime.

Mavericks Veteran Roster

No	Player	Pos	Ht	Wt	Exp
44	Shawn Bradley	C	7-6	248	4
4	Michael Finley	G/F	6-7	215	2
45	A.C. Green	F	6-9	225	12
12	Derek Harper	G	6-4	206	14
13	Martin Muursepp	F	6-9	235	1
31	Ed O'Bannon	F	6-8	220	2
14	Robert Pack	G	6-2	190	6
6	Khalid Reeves	G	6-3	201	3
20	Erick Strickland	G	6-3	210	1
40	Kurt Thomas	F	6-9	230	2
52	Samaki Walker	F	6-9	258	1

Head Coach: Jim Cleamons

Mavericks 1997 Draft Picks

Rookie	College	Position
Kelvin Cato (1-15)	Iowa State	Center
Bubba Wells (2-35)	Austin Peay	Forward

The Mavericks lost their lottery pick in the Eric Montross trade—Boston used it to take Ron Mercer at number six. Dallas got the 15th pick from Minnesota, selected Cato, then delivered him to Portland for Australian seven-footer Chris Anstey. A former junior tennis star, he has excellent footwork for his size. He did not play organized ball until age 17 but has developed enormously in five years, and his work in exhibition games versus college teams was very impressive. Bubba Wells would have paced the nation in scoring as a senior last season but didn't play enough games to qualify. He has steel rods in both ankles because of stress fractures.

Mavericks Scouting Report

Guard: Robert Pack makes a lot of things happen at the point, but not all of them are good for his team. He is quick and strong, able to drive and finish in traffic, but his assist-to-turnover ratio (2.08:1 last season, 1.92:1 career) is on the poor side, and his shooting is wildly erratic. He is also injury prone, having not played more than 55 games in any of the past three seasons. Explosive leaper Michael Finley will be at the off-guard spot. He hasn't missed a game in his two years as a pro and has averaged exactly 15 ppg in both. He defends with vigor, chips in on the glass, and has proven to be a more consistent shooter than expected. One-two tweener Khalid Reeves has been a minor component in three major trades, but he has yet to find a permanent position. This should be veteran point guard Derek Harper's last season in uniform. **Grade: C**

Forward: Ed O'Bannon was college basketball's Player of the Year in 1994–95, but he has been an utter bust as a pro. He can't shoot, is too slow and soft for his position, etc. Rookie scoring machine Bubba Wells will compete for time at the three, as will Martin Muursepp, a European youngster whose rights were owned by three different teams last year. Samaki Walker missed 34 games of his rookie campaign with injuries, but he flashed a spark of NBA ability when healthy. Kurt Thomas suffered a broken ankle, spoiling his second NBA season and delaying his Dallas debut. A.C. Green, who hasn't missed a game in ten years, still scraps for caroms and tip-ins. **Grade: F**

Center: Shawn Bradley leads the league in blocked shots, scores in double figures, snags eight boards per game, and improves a little more each year. Expectations aside, he is a mid-quality NBA pivot. Australian rookie Chris Anstey figures to be Bradley's backup. **Grade: C+**

Mavericks 1996–97 Player Statistics

	G	MIN	FG	FGA	FG%	FT	FTA	FT%	3FG	3FGA
Finley	83	2790	475	1071	.444	198	245	.808	101	280
Pack	54	1782	272	693	.392	196	243	.807	31	112
Bradley	73	2288	406	905	.449	149	228	.654	0	8
Dinilovic	56	1789	248	570	.435	121	151	.801	85	236
Strickland	28	759	102	256	.398	65	80	.813	28	92
Harper	75	2210	299	674	.444	95	128	.742	60	176
Reeves	63	1432	184	470	.391	65	87	.747	83	227
Green	83	2492	234	484	.483	128	197	.650	1	20
Thomas	18	374	39	105	.371	35	46	.761	0	1
Walker	43	602	83	187	.444	48	74	.649	0	1
Muursepp	42	348	54	131	.412	44	70	.629	4	24
O'Bannon	64	809	93	279	.333	31	35	.886	18	70
Watson	23	340	31	72	.431	12	16	.750	4	12
Sasser	8	69	9	23	.391	0	0	.000	1	3
King	11	103	11	22	.500	2	7	.286	0	0
Dreiling	40	389	34	74	.459	11	27	.407	1	1

	ORB	REB	AST	STL	TO	BLK	PF	PTS	PPG
Finley	88	372	224	68	164	24	138	1249	15.0
Pack	28	146	452	94	217	6	139	771	14.3
Bradley	221	611	52	40	134	248	237	961	13.2
Danilovic	29	136	102	54	116	9	160	702	12.5
Strickland	21	90	68	27	66	5	75	297	10.6
Harper	30	137	321	92	132	12	144	753	10.0
Reeves	34	119	226	34	108	9	159	516	8.2
Green	222	656	69	70	74	16	145	597	7.2
Thomas	31	107	9	12	25	9	67	113	6.3
Walker	47	147	17	15	39	22	71	214	5.0
Muursepp	35	67	20	12	18	11	58	156	3.7
O'Bannon	50	148	39	29	20	12	97	235	3.7
Watson	18	47	33	22	24	4	34	78	3.4
Sasser	1	8	2	3	2	0	11	19	2.4
King	11	27	1	2	6	1	14	24	2.2
Dreiling	19	76	11	8	9	7	65	80	2.0

Note: Not all players are shown.

Mavericks 1996–97 Team Statistics

Final Record: 24–58

Home Record: 14–27

Road Record: 10–31

Division Record: 9–15

Conference Record: 16–36

Overtime Record: 1-3

Points Per Game: 90.6

Opponents Points Per Game: 97.0

Field Goal Percentage: .436

Opponents Field Goal Percentage: .458

Turnovers Per Game: 16.1

Opponents Turnovers Per Game: 15.7

Offensive Rebounding Percentage: .300

Defensive Rebounding Percentage: .673

Total Rebounding Percentage: .487

Scored Fewer Than 100 Points: 62

Opponents Scored Fewer Than 100 Points: 44

Mavericks Clipboard

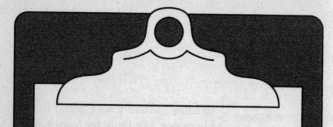

Why the Mavericks win: It takes a total effort for the Mavs to get a win. Bradley and Green have to control the boards, while Pack and Finley must take good shots and convert. Dallas can take some risks defensively with Bradley protecting the middle.

Why the Mavericks lose: The Mavs will turn the ball over if pressured. Bradley can be rendered ineffective when taken away from the basket. Dallas is one of the NBA's worst shooting teams.

1996–97 MVP: Michael Finley

Projected MVP: Shawn Bradley

Fast Fact: Dallas last year set a team record for fewest points allowed per game (97.0, 14th in the NBA)—down from 107.5, 29th in the league in 1995–96.

Shawn Bradley C

Age: 25
Seasons: 4
Height: 7-6
Weight: 248
College: Brigham Young

Bradley probably isn't going to alter the perceptions of his critics, but he is far from being a below-average NBA center. Nobody swats more shots, and his scoring and rebounding are statistically solid.

	G	MPG	FG%	3FG%	FT%	APG	RPG	PPG	BLK	STL
1996–97	73	31.3	.449	.000	.654	0.7	8.4	13.2	248	40
Career	283	29.6	.442	.056	.650	0.9	7.8	11.3	957	188

Sasha Danilovic G

Age: 27
Seasons: 2
Height: 6-6
Weight: 200
College: Serbia

Potentially a prolific NBA scorer, the European-born Danilovic began last season in Miami, then scored 16.6 ppg in 13 games with Dallas. He'll be playing in Italy this season.

	G	MPG	FG%	3FG%	FT%	APG	RPG	PPG	BLK	STL
1996–97	56	31.9	.435	.360	.801	1.8	2.4	12.5	9	54
Career	75	31.1	.439	.379	.789	2.0	2.4	12.8	12	69

Michael Finley   G/F

Age: 24
Seasons: 2
Height: 6-7
Weight: 215
College: Wisconsin

Finley has the raw tools and desire to be an All-Star. A much better shooter as a pro than he was in college, he has the versatility and athleticism to match up well at either the two or the three.

	G	MPG	FG%	3FG%	FT%	APG	RPG	PPG	BLK	STL
1996–97	83	33.6	.444	.361	.808	2.7	4.5	15.0	20	68
Career	165	36.4	.459	.348	.775	3.1	4.5	15.0	55	153

A.C. Green   F

Age: 34
Seasons: 12
Height: 6-9
Weight: 225
College: Oregon State

A true Iron Man, Green has played in 896 straight games, second on the all-time list. He plays tough defense, fights for every rebound, and gets his share of garbage buckets.

	G	MPG	FG%	3FG%	FT%	APG	RPG	PPG	BLK	STL
1996–97	83	30.0	.483	.050	.650	0.8	7.9	7.2	16	70
Career	982	30.2	.503	.263	.738	1.2	7.9	10.9	483	844

Derek Harper G

Age: 36
Seasons: 14
Height: 6-4
Weight: 206
College: Illinois

Returning to the franchise with which he began his career, Harper plans for this to be his final season before joining the Dallas front office. He currently ranks seventh on the NBA's all-time steals list.

	G	MPG	FG%	3FG%	FT%	APG	RPG	PPG	BLK	STL
1996–97	75	29.5	.444	.341	.742	4.3	1.8	10.0	12	92
Career	1088	32.1	.466	.353	.746	5.7	2.5	13.9	290	1841

Ed O'Bannon F

Age: 25
Seasons: 2
Height: 6-8
Weight: 220
College: UCLA

A terrific college player drafted ninth overall by New Jersey two years ago, O'Bannon has not made his mark at the NBA level but may still see legit minutes for the talent-short Mavericks.

	G	MPG	FG%	3FG%	FT%	APG	RPG	PPG	BLK	STL
1996–97	64	12.6	.333	.257	.886	0.6	2.3	3.7	12	29
Career	127	16.1	.367	.222	.755	0.8	2.5	5.0	23	73

Robert Pack   G

Age: 28
Seasons: 6
Height: 6-2
Weight: 190
College: Southern California

Pack is at his best when he pushes the ball in the open floor or drives to the rack in half-court sets. His assist totals have increased every season of his career, but his shooting has gone from so-so to awful.

	G	MPG	FG%	3FG%	FT%	APG	RPG	PPG	BLK	STL
1996–97	54	33.0	.392	.277	.807	8.4	2.7	14.3	6	94
Career	342	23.0	.431	.286	.790	5.3	2.3	10.6	36	419

Khalid Reeves   G

Age: 25
Seasons: 3
Height: 6-3
Weight: 201
College: Arizona

Reeves has played for four different teams in his brief career, and he has flip-flopped between the point and the two. He's a handful when his jumper is falling, but that doesn't happen very often.

	G	MPG	FG%	3FG%	FT%	APG	RPG	PPG	BLK	STL
1996–97	63	22.7	.391	.366	.747	3.6	1.9	8.2	9	34
Career	181	20.6	.418	.364	.729	3.5	2.1	7.8	22	148

Erick Strickland G

Age: 24
Seasons: 1
Height: 6-3
Weight: 210
College: Nebraska

Undrafted after a fine college career, Strickland was signed by the Mavericks, released, and then re-signed. He showed some ability as a scorer but struggled for consistency from the perimeter.

	G	MPG	FG%	3FG%	FT%	APG	RPG	PPG	BLK	STL
1996–97	28	27.1	.398	.304	.813	2.4	3.2	10.6	5	27
Career	28	27.1	.398	.304	.813	2.4	3.2	10.6	5	27

Samaki Walker F

Age: 21
Seasons: 1
Height: 6-9
Weight: 258
College: Louisville

Walker is raw, having played just two years of college ball, and he was dogged by foot injuries throughout his rookie campaign. He has the potential to be a dominant rebounder at the four.

	G	MPG	FG%	3FG%	FT%	APG	RPG	PPG	BLK	STL
1996–97	43	14.0	.444	.000	.649	0.4	3.4	5.0	22	15
Career	43	14.0	.444	.000	.649	0.4	3.4	5.0	22	15

Bobby Jackson

Denver
NUGGETS

Franchise History: One of the four ABA teams to merge with the NBA in 1976–77, the Nuggets are accustomed to winning plenty of games but no championships. They took the Midwest title in their first two years in the league, with high-flying David Thompson ranking among the top scorers. The Nuggets hung in the middle of the division pack until 1984–85, when they made it to the conference finals. Since winning the Midwest once more in 1987–88, Denver has slipped into mediocrity in the '90s.

1996–97 Review: The departure of Dikembe Mutombo via free agency, plus the trading of Mahmoud Abdul-Rauf, deprived Denver of its top defender and its leading scorer, opening the floodgates to a 60-loss season. Head coach Bernie Bickerstaff was fired after 13 games, replaced by Dick Motta, who was dumped at season's end. LaPhonso Ellis picked up some of the slack with 21.9 ppg, but he missed 27 games with injuries. The Nuggets lost 25 games in which they held a lead after the third quarter.

1997–98 Preview: The Nuggets have a new head coach, former Hawks assistant Bill Hanzlik. They've added three first-round rookies—Tony Battie, Bobby Jackson, and Danny Fortson. And forward Antonio McDyess is a rising star. That said, the Nuggets are probably in for another season of growing pains as part of the rebuilding process. It will take time for the youngsters to learn what it takes to win in the NBA (defense, shot selection, etc.), and 35 wins is the most that should be expected this year.

Nuggets Veteran Roster

No	Player	Pos	Ht	Wt	Exp
3	Dale Ellis	G/F	6-7	215	14
20	LaPhonso Ellis	F	6-8	240	5
21	Tom Hammonds	F	6-9	225	8
24	Antonio McDyess	F	6-9	220	2
—	Johnny Newman	G/F	6-7	200	11
23	Bryant Stith	G	6-5	208	5
—	Joe Wolf	F/C	6-11	260	9
25	George Zidek	C	7-0	266	2

Head Coach: Bill Hanzlik

Nuggets 1997 Draft Picks

Rookie	College	Position
Tony Battie (1-5)	Texas Tech	Forward
James Cotton (2-33)	Long Beach State	Guard
Jason Lawson (2-42)	Villanova	Center

The Nuggets will probably use Tony Battie at center if he can add some muscle to his 6-11, 225-pound frame. He sees himself as a four, but that isn't what Denver needs at the moment. He averaged a double-double as a senior, and his repertoire features a soft jumper from 17 feet. Denver sent James Cotton and a second-round pick to Seattle for the rights to Bobby Jackson, who appears to be a shooting guard in a point guard's body. The Nuggets will put him at the one and hope he develops. He was a major force as a scorer in college, his intangibles are first rate, and he chips in on the boards like few point guards can. The Nuggets also got Danny Fortson in a trade after Milwaukee picked him tenth overall, and they sent Jason Lawson to Orlando for guard Eric Washington.

Nuggets Scouting Report

Guard: It's likely that rookie Bobby Jackson, who few scouts consider a pure point guard, will be at the one for Denver this season. Anthony Goldwire, who took the spot after Mark Jackson was dealt, may return as a backup. The situation at shooting guard is more settled but hardly ideal. Bryant Stith will try to come back from foot problems that cost him 30 games last year. He reached a career high in point production but has shot just .416 for two years running. He is a superb defender when healthy. Veteran swingman Johnny Newman is also a solid defender, but his scoring skills have eroded in recent years. **Grade: D+**

Forward: LaPhonso Ellis is explosive, capable of putting up strong numbers in every aspect of the interior game. Unfortunately, he is never healthy for a full season. Dale Ellis (no relation) converted fewer than 40 percent of his three-point tries for the first time since 1990–91, yet took over 500 attempts to wind up scoring 16.6 ppg. Denver's best hope for the future is Antonio McDyess, who plays above the rim on both ends of the floor. Entering his third pro campaign, he is on the verge of All-Star status. Veteran backup Tom Hammonds had one of the better seasons of his career, snatching 400 boards and tossing in 500 points for the first time in his eight years as a pro. Danny Fortson figures to see limited action at the four in his initial NBA season. **Grade: B–**

Center: Denver traded last season's pivot, Ervin Johnson, so expect to see rookie Tony Battie playing significant minutes at center. He has finesse offensive skills—he calls himself a power forward—but will need to put on some bulk to handle NBA fives. He will need to develop quickly if the Nuggets are to avoid turning to Joe Wolf and/or George Zidek. **Grade: D**

Nuggets 1996–97 Player Statistics

	G	MIN	FG	FGA	FG%	FT	FTA	FT%	3FG	3FGA
L. Ellis	55	2002	445	1014	.439	218	282	.773	95	259
McDyess	74	2565	536	1157	.463	274	387	.708	6	35
D. Ellis	82	2940	477	1151	.414	215	263	.817	192	528
Stith	52	1788	251	603	.416	202	234	.863	70	182
Johnson	82	2599	243	467	.520	96	156	.615	0	2
Marciulionis	17	255	38	101	.376	29	36	.806	11	30
Thompson	67	1055	162	406	.399	24	38	.632	97	244
Goldwire	60	1188	131	330	.397	61	78	.782	64	153
Smith	48	765	101	239	.423	39	45	.867	59	135
Hammonds	81	1758	191	398	.480	124	172	.721	0	2
Askew	43	838	81	186	.435	70	88	.795	7	24
McInnis	13	117	23	49	.469	7	10	.700	12	26
Murdock	12	114	15	33	.455	11	12	.917	4	10
Allen	76	943	78	221	.353	42	72	.583	30	93
King	2	22	2	6	.333	2	4	.500	0	0
Zidek	52	376	49	118	.415	45	57	.789	0	2
Bennett	9	75	6	19	.316	7	10	.700	3	9

	ORB	REB	AST	STL	TO	BLK	PF	PTS	PPG
L Ellis	107	386	131	44	117	41	181	1203	21.9
McDyess	155	537	106	62	199	126	276	1352	18.3
D. Ellis	99	293	165	60	146	7	178	1361	16.6
Stith	74	217	133	60	101	20	119	774	14.9
Johnson	231	313	71	65	118	227	288	582	7.1
Marciulionis	12	30	25	12	40	1	38	116	6.8
Thompson	18	96	180	55	87	2	126	445	6.6
Goldwire	12	84	219	33	76	2	104	387	6.5
Smith	4	44	116	19	71	0	30	300	6.3
Hammonds	135	401	64	16	88	24	205	506	6.2
Askew	25	98	90	17	46	6	123	239	5.6
McInnis	2	6	18	2	13	1	16	65	5.0
Murdock	1	11	24	9	11	2	9	45	3.8
Allen	25	98	152	31	69	4	84	228	3.0
King	2	2	2	3	1	0	2	6	3.0
Zidek	35	86	14	5	27	3	61	143	2.8
Bennett	0	4	11	4	10	0	7	22	2.4

Nuggets 1996–97 Team Statistics

Final Record: 21–61

Home Record: 12–29

Road Record: 9–32

Division Record: 7–17

Conference Record: 13–39

Overtime Record: 3–7

Points Per Game: 97.8

Opponents Points Per Game: 104.1

Field Goal Percentage: .439

Opponents Field Goal Percentage: .467

Turnovers Per Game: 16.6

Opponents Turnovers Per Game: 12.9

Offensive Rebounding Percentage: .288

Defensive Rebounding Percentage: .693

Total Rebounding Percentage: .490

Scored Fewer Than 100 Points: 45

Opponents Scored Fewer Than 100 Points: 26

Nuggets Clipboard

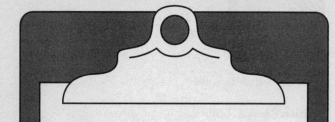

Why the Nuggets win: Bobby Jackson must think like a point guard, and Tony Battie needs to get strong enough to hold his own at center. If the oft-injured LaPhonso Ellis is healthy and McDyess goes to the next level, Denver might surprise some teams.

Why the Nuggets lose: Denver has put stock in two rookies who will probably be struggling to learn their positions. The Nuggets have too many players who score but don't defend or shoot but don't score. Denver's backcourt is weak and the bench is thin.

1996–97 MVP: Antonio McDyess

Projected MVP: Antonio McDyess

Fast Fact: Denver blew a 34-point lead in a loss to Utah and scored just 22 points in a half versus Portland.

Vincent Askew — G/F

Age: 31
Seasons: 8
Height: 6-6
Weight: 235
College: Memphis

Askew played just one game for New Jersey, was sent to Indiana for 41 games, then wound up in Denver for one game. He shot under .480 for the first time since his rookie season.

	G	MPG	FG%	3FG%	FT%	APG	RPG	PPG	BLK	STL
1996–97	43	19.5	.435	.292	.795	2.1	2.3	5.6	6	17
Career	437	20.4	.482	.303	.755	2.2	2.5	7.4	101	285

Dale Ellis — G/F

Age: 37
Seasons: 14
Height: 6-7
Weight: 215
College: Tennessee

The all-time leader in three-pointers converted, Ellis is a one-dimensional but prolific player. He launched a career-high 528 shots from beyond the arc last season.

	G	MPG	FG%	3FG%	FT%	APG	RPG	PPG	BLK	STL
1996–97	82	35.9	.414	.364	.817	2.0	3.6	16.6	7	60
Career	1040	29.8	.480	.398	.785	1.5	3.7	16.7	175	876

LaPhonso Ellis   F

Age: 27
Seasons: 5
Height: 6-8
Weight: 240
College: Notre Dame

Ellis would have ranked ninth in the NBA in scoring last season if he had played enough games to qualify. He has missed 140 contests over the past three seasons due to injuries.

	G	MPG	FG%	3FG%	FT%	APG	RPG	PPG	BLK	STL
1996–97	55	36.4	.439	.367	.773	2.4	7.0	21.9	41	44
Career	267	32.9	.474	.341	.712	2.0	8.1	15.4	270	216

Anthony Goldwire   G

Age: 26
Seasons: 2
Height: 6-2
Weight: 182
College: Houston

Goldwire came to the Nuggets from Charlotte as part of the Ricky Pierce trade. He knocks down his shots from long distance, but Denver went 3–19 in his starts at the point.

	G	MPG	FG%	3FG%	FT%	APG	RPG	PPG	BLK	STL
1996–97	60	19.8	.397	.418	.782	3.6	1.4	6.5	2	33
Career	102	17.7	.399	.411	.775	3.2	1.2	6.1	2	49

Tom Hammonds
F

Age: 30
Seasons: 8
Height: 6-9
Weight: 225
College: Georgia Tech

Hammonds was the ninth pick overall in 1989, yet he has never played more minutes than last year's 1,758. He works hard in the paint but is every inch a tweener.

	G	MPG	FG%	3FG%	FT%	APG	RPG	PPG	BLK	STL
1996–97	81	21.7	.480	.000	.721	0.8	5.0	6.2	24	16
Career	518	15.8	.480	.000	.701	0.6	3.3	5.7	109	136

Ervin Johnson
C

Age: 30
Seasons: 4
Height: 6-11
Weight: 245
College: New Orleans

Now playing in Milwaukee, Johnson joins his third team in three seasons. He does a great job on the boards, and he rates with the league's best shot blockers, but his offensive skills are primitive.

	G	MPG	FG%	3FG%	FT%	APG	RPG	PPG	BLK	STL
1996–97	82	31.7	.520	.000	.615	0.9	11.1	7.1	227	65
Career	272	19.5	.494	.167	.637	0.5	6.4	4.9	445	132

Antonio McDyess   F

Age: 23
Seasons: 2
Height: 6-9
Weight: 220
College: Alabama

Dice is a force in the low post, pouring in points on one end, swatting shots on the other, and attacking the boards on both. He has all the tools but is still refining his skills.

	G	MPG	FG%	3FG%	FT%	APG	RPG	PPG	BLK	STL
1996–97	74	34.7	.463	.171	.708	1.4	7.3	18.3	126	62
Career	150	32.3	.473	.154	.698	1.2	7.4	15.8	240	116

Kenny Smith   G

Age: 32
Seasons: 10
Height: 6-3
Weight: 170
College: North Carolina

Smith saw action for three teams last season after his release from Houston. He has dished out at least ten assists 101 times in his career, and he remains one of the league's best from long distance.

	G	MPG	FG%	3FG%	FT%	APG	RPG	PPG	BLK	STL
1996–97	48	15.9	.423	.437	.867	2.4	0.9	6.3	0	19
Career	737	30.1	.480	.399	.829	5.5	2.0	12.8	65	759

Bryant Stith   G

Age: 27
Seasons: 5
Height: 6-5
Weight: 208
College: Virginia

Stith uses above-average strength and tenacity to drive the lane and to defend on the perimeter. Usually durable, he was slowed by injuries last year but did have his best season in terms of points per game.

	G	MPG	FG%	3FG%	FT%	APG	RPG	PPG	BLK	STL
1996–97	52	34.4	.416	.385	.863	2.6	4.2	14.9	20	60
Career	336	31.7	.438	.324	.838	2.3	4.0	12.4	75	405

Brooks Thompson   G

Age: 27
Seasons: 3
Height: 6-4
Weight: 195
College: Oklahoma State

Thompson played twice the number of minutes last season as he had in the previous two years combined. He can shoot the rock, especially from downtown, but the rest of his game is pretty pedestrian.

	G	MPG	FG%	3FG%	FT%	APG	RPG	PPG	BLK	STL
1996–97	67	15.7	.399	.398	.632	2.7	1.4	6.6	2	55
Career	138	11.2	.409	.383	.662	1.8	1.0	5.1	4	77

Grant Hill

Detroit
PISTONS

Franchise History: Originally based in Fort Wayne, the Pistons joined the league in 1948–49. They made it to the Finals twice in the mid-'50s, losing both times. They moved to Detroit in 1957–58 and George Yardley paced the NBA in scoring, but the team struggled until Bob Lanier and Dave Bing helped generate a 52-win season in 1973–74. The Pistons won back-to-back championships in 1988–89 and 1989–90 with Isiah Thomas and Joe Dumars in the backcourt. The franchise has been rebuilding since then.

1996–97 Review: If the Pistons exceeded expectations by winning 46 games in 1995–96, they exploded them with a 54-victory performance last season. Playoff advancement again proved elusive—Detroit fell to the Hawks in five—but the fine coaching of Doug Collins and the outstanding play of Grant Hill was enough to inspire hope for a title when the other pieces come together. Detroit averaged a league-low 12.7 turnovers per game and finished as the NBA's second-best defense (88.9 ppg allowed).

1997–98 Preview: With the exception of Hill, Detroit is not exactly brimming with premier talent, but Collins has sold his players on the importance of protecting the ball, controlling tempo, and helping on defense. The payoff has come in the wins column. Hill's ability to get to the rack off the dribble almost makes up for the lack of a low-post scorer, but the absence of interior muscle can be a problem defensively, especially in the postseason. The Pistons are still a couple of parts short of championship contention.

Pistons Veteran Roster

No	Player	Pos	Ht	Wt	Exp
12	Michael Curry	G	6-5	210	3
4	Joe Dumars	G	6-3	195	12
33	Grant Hill	F	6-8	225	3
1	Lindsey Hunter	G	6-2	195	4
43	Grant Long	F	6-9	248	9
23	Aaron McKie	G	6-5	209	3
6	Terry Mills	F	6-10	250	7
42	Theo Ratliff	F/C	6-10	230	2
52	Don Reid	F/C	6-8	250	2
13	Jerome Williams	F	6-9	206	1

Head Coach: Doug Collins

Pistons 1997 Draft Picks

Rookie	College	Position
Scot Pollard (1-19)	Kansas	Forward
Charles O'Bannon (2-32)	UCLA	Forward

The Pistons raised a few eyebrows on draft day. Pollard was not expected to go in the first round, and O'Bannon is not likely to push Grant Hill for playing time. Pollard has good size (6-11, 255), mobility, and tenacity. As a senior, he posted roughly ten points and eight boards per game, plus a team-high 2.61 blocks. He missed eight games with a broken foot. O'Bannon, who has been called a poor man's Grant Hill, may have been downgraded by scouts because his brother, Ed, has been a disappointing pro. The younger O'Bannon can get up and down the floor and contribute in every aspect. He is the only player in Bruins history to register 1,700 points and 700 rebounds. Neither player is likely to be a star, but both could stick around.

Pistons Scouting Report

Guard: Statistically speaking, Lindsey Hunter is a disaster area. A 39-percent shooter in almost 2,900 career attempts from the field, he notched a career best last season with a tepid .404 mark. He has dished out 44 fewer assists in his four campaigns as a pro than Mark Jackson registered last year. Yet he was considered an invaluable part of Detroit's success last season, reaching personal highs in minutes, steals, and points. Joe Dumars is an enduring veteran with championship experience and a lingering reputation for solid defense. He was the team's second-leading scorer last season, and he also finished second in assists. Aaron McKie came over from Portland midway into 1996–97. He works hard and overachieves on both ends of the court, but he is not a great shooter or an explosive scorer. **Grade: C+**

Forward: Grant Hill does it all for the Pistons, liberating the team's role players to focus on what they do well, as Jordan and Pippen do for the Bulls. For the second straight season, he paced Detroit in minutes, assists, steals, points, and rebounds. Terry Mills, the league's most unlikely three-point specialist at 6-10 and 250 pounds, buried 42 percent of over 400 attempted triples. Grant Long found himself deep into the Detroit bench last year after having logged 3,000 minutes for Atlanta in 1995–96. He is a so-so scorer who can be a difference maker on defense. **Grade: A**

Center: The Pistons are banking on Theo Ratliff's further development at center. He is undersized but athletic, with the timing, extension, and quick ups of a top shot blocker. He doesn't have the bulk to be a great low-post stopper, and his career-best 5.8 ppg last season speaks for itself. Don Reid made 14 starts at the five but also sat out 23 games due to coach's decisions. He works like a dog but is too short for the pivot. **Grade: D+**

Pistons 1996–97 Player Statistics

	G	MIN	FG	FGA	FG%	FT	FTA	FT%	3FG	3FGA
Hill	80	3147	625	1259	.496	450	633	.711	10	33
Dumars	79	2923	385	875	.440	222	256	.867	166	384
Hunter	82	3023	421	1042	.404	158	203	.778	166	468
Thorpe	79	2661	419	787	.532	198	303	.653	0	2
Mills	79	1997	312	702	.444	58	70	.829	175	415
Ratliff	76	1292	179	337	.531	81	116	.698	0	0
McKie	83	1625	150	365	.411	92	110	.836	41	103
Long	65	1166	123	275	.447	63	84	.750	17	47
Curry	81	1217	99	227	.448	97	108	.898	23	77
Reid	47	462	54	112	.482	24	32	.750	0	1
Mahorn	22	218	20	54	.370	16	22	.727	0	1
Green	45	311	30	64	.469	30	47	.638	0	10
Childress	23	155	14	40	.350	6	8	.750	5	19
Williams	33	177	20	51	.392	9	17	.529	0	0

	ORB	REB	AST	STL	TO	BLK	PF	PTS	PPG
Hill	123	721	583	144	259	48	186	1710	21.4
Dumars	38	191	318	57	128	1	97	1158	14.7
Hunter	59	233	154	129	96	24	206	1166	14.2
Thorpe	226	622	133	59	145	17	298	1036	13.1
Mills	68	377	99	35	85	27	161	857	10.8
Ratliff	109	256	13	29	56	111	181	439	5.8
McKie	40	221	161	77	90	22	130	433	5.2
Long	88	222	39	43	48	6	106	326	5.0
Curry	23	119	43	31	28	12	128	318	3.9
Reid	36	101	14	16	23	15	105	132	2.8
Mahorn	19	53	6	4	10	3	34	56	2.5
Green	6	22	41	16	15	1	27	90	2.0
Childress	1	6	17	9	18	0	16	39	1.7
Williams	22	50	7	13	13	1	18	49	1.5

Pistons 1996–97 Team Statistics

Final Record: 54–28

Home Record: 30–11

Road Record: 24–17

Division Record: 16–11

Conference Record: 34–20

Overtime Record: 4–1

Points Per Game: 94.2

Opponents Points Per Game: 88.9

Field Goal Percentage: .464

Opponents Field Goal Percentage: .444

Turnovers Per Game: 12.7

Opponents Turnovers Per Game: 14.6

Offensive Rebounding Percentage: .275

Defensive Rebounding Percentage: .704

Total Rebounding Percentage: .489

Scored Fewer Than 100 Points: 63

Opponents Scored Fewer Than 100 Points: 71

Pistons Clipboard

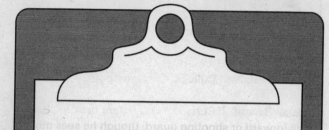

Why the Pistons win: When the ball is in Grant Hill's hands, good things happen. His ability to get to the basket almost makes up for the lack of a post-up scorer. The Pistons play terrific team defense and rarely waste a trip downcourt.

Why the Pistons lose: Detroit doesn't have the explosiveness or the multiple offensive weapons to shoot it out with the league's elite. The Pistons play great perimeter defense but are a little soft in the paint. Hill and the Pistons seemed to tire in the latter part of last season.

1996–97 MVP: Grant Hill

Projected MVP: Grant Hill

Fast Fact: Detroit held 24 consecutive opponents to under 100 points, marking the second-longest streak in NBA history.

MICHAEL CURRY

Michael Curry   G

Age: 29
Seasons: 3
Height: 6-5
Weight: 210
College: Georgia Southern

Curry is a competent backup at either small forward or shooting guard, though he sees most of his minutes at the two. He missed just 11 of 108 free throws last season.

	G	MPG	FG%	3FG%	FT%	APG	RPG	PPG	BLK	STL
1996–97	81	15.0	.448	.299	.898	0.5	1.5	3.9	12	31
Career	137	14.9	.442	.326	.833	0.5	1.5	3.9	14	56

Joe Dumars   G

Age: 34
Seasons: 12
Height: 6-3
Weight: 195
College: McNeese State

The venerable Dumars ranked fourth in the league in three-point accuracy last season while contributing his trademark on-ball defense. He tallied more minutes than in any campaign since 1992–93.

	G	MPG	FG%	3FG%	FT%	APG	RPG	PPG	BLK	STL
1996–97	79	37.0	.440	.432	.867	4.0	2.4	14.7	1	57
Career	908	34.9	.465	.382	.844	4.7	2.2	16.6	79	835

Grant Hill   F

Age: 25
Seasons: 3
Height: 6-8
Weight: 225
College: Duke

Like a young M.J., Hill does most of his scoring damage on drives. He is arguably already one of the five best players in the NBA. He posted six triple-doubles in the final 11 games last year, 13 for the season.

	G	MPG	FG%	3FG%	FT%	APG	RPG	PPG	BLK	STL
1996–97	80	39.3	.496	.303	.711	7.5	9.0	21.4	48	144
Career	230	39.5	.479	.221	.731	6.5	8.5	20.5	158	368

Lindsey Hunter   G

Age: 27
Seasons: 4
Height: 6-2
Weight: 195
College: Jackson State

Hunter takes a lot of risks on defense, many of which pay off. He is a decent scorer when not responsible for running the offense, but his shooting is deeply inconsistent.

	G	MPG	FG%	3FG%	FT%	APG	RPG	PPG	BLK	STL
1996–97	82	36.9	.404	.355	.778	1.9	2.8	14.2	24	129
Career	286	28.9	.387	.362	.742	3.1	2.4	10.5	59	385

Grant Long   F

Age: 31
Seasons: 9
Height: 6-9
Weight: 248
College: Eastern Michigan

In his first season with the Pistons, Long registered a career low in minutes, rebounds, and points. An intense worker, he can be a stopper on defense but is prone to fouls.

	G	MPG	FG%	3FG%	FT%	APG	RPG	PPG	BLK	STL
1996–97	65	17.9	.447	.362	.750	0.6	3.4	5.0	6	43
Career	698	31.0	.477	.315	.766	1.9	7.0	11.2	300	925

Aaron McKie   G

Age: 25
Seasons: 3
Height: 6-5
Weight: 209
College: Temple

McKie exceeded expectations his first two seasons with Portland, but last year his field-goal percentage plunged by 58 points from 1995–96, while his scoring average was cut by half.

	G	MPG	FG%	3FG%	FT%	APG	RPG	PPG	BLK	STL
1996–97	83	19.6	.411	.398	.836	1.9	2.7	5.2	22	77
Career	209	22.4	.447	.363	.770	2.2	3.1	7.6	59	205

Terry Mills   F

Age: 30
Seasons: 7
Height: 6-10
Weight: 250
College: Michigan

A soft defender who primarily spots up on the perimeter, Mills put together a stellar season from beyond the arc. He knocked down 13 straight triples during one stretch.

	G	MPG	FG%	3FG%	FT%	APG	RPG	PPG	BLK	STL
1996–97	79	25.2	.444	.422	.829	4.3	4.7	10.8	27	35
Career	531	25.7	.462	.391	.783	1.4	5.9	12.0	262	336

Theo Ratliff   F/C

Age: 24
Seasons: 2
Height: 6-10
Weight: 230
College: Wyoming

Ratliff paced the Pistons in swats in each of the past two seasons, despite averaging only about 1,300 minutes per campaign. He makes the shots he takes but is not much of a scoring threat.

	G	MPG	FG%	3FG%	FT%	APG	RPG	PPG	BLK	STL
1996–97	76	17.0	.531	.000	.698	0.2	3.4	5.8	111	29
Career	151	17.2	.541	.000	.703	0.2	3.7	5.2	227	45

Don Reid F/C

Age: 24
Seasons: 2
Height: 6-8
Weight: 250
College: Georgetown

Knee problems and coach's decisions reduced Reid's playing time by half from his rookie year. He is offensively inept and not tall enough to match up at center, where Detroit has been desperate for help.

	G	MPG	FG%	3FG%	FT%	APG	RPG	PPG	BLK	STL
1996–97	47	9.8	.482	.000	.750	0.3	2.1	2.8	15	16
Career	116	12.6	.535	.000	.688	0.2	2.6	3.4	55	63

Otis Thorpe F

Age: 35
Seasons: 13
Height: 6-10
Weight: 246
College: Providence

Usually good for 14 points and eight caroms per game, Thorpe has a nose for the basket and is physical under the boards. He has played all 82 games in nine of his 13 seasons.

	G	MPG	FG%	3FG%	FT%	APG	RPG	PPG	BLK	STL
1996–97	79	33.7	.532	.000	.653	1.7	7.9	13.1	17	59
Career	1034	33.5	.552	.056	.687	2.3	8.9	15.4	436	712

Latrell Sprewell

Golden State
WARRIORS

Franchise History: The Philadelphia Warriors won the first BAA title in 1946–47, with Joe Fulks leading the league in scoring. The team won another championship (1955–56) before moving to the West Coast for the 1962–63 season. The Warriors made it to the Finals a couple of times in the 1960s, then broke through for a ring in 1974–75 behind the scoring prowess of Rick Barry. The franchise enjoyed some success in the late '80s, but the talent base deteriorated and the Warriors dove headfirst into a rebuilding phase.

1996–97 Review: Golden State sank to the bottom of the division standings last year, allowing more points per game than any other team in the conference. Latrell Sprewell put up huge numbers in every category (including turnovers), but the Warriors had no interior presence, no consistency, and no direction. They claimed only four victories within the Pacific Division—only the Celtics fared worse versus division rivals—and head coach Rick Adelman was fired at season's end.

1997–98 Preview: P.J. Carlesimo, fresh off a 49-win season with Portland, is in as Golden State's head coach. He'll be doing the usual talk about cleaning house, but the Warriors might not be able to come up with anything more than change for its own sake at this stage. It may take a trip to rock bottom—as with the Celtics—so that the franchise can acquire the Fab Five draft picks that turn current losers into future champions. In the meantime, the Warriors should play with more intensity than they did last year.

Warriors Veteran Roster

No	Player	Pos	Ht	Wt	Exp
11	B.J. Armstrong	G	6-2	185	8
23	Scott Burrell	F	6-7	218	4
12	Bimbo Coles	G	6-2	182	7
55	Andrew DeClercq	F	6-10	230	2
52	Todd Fuller	C	6-11	255	1
3	Donyell Marshall	F	6-9	230	3
17	Chris Mullin	F	6-7	215	12
25	Mark Price	G	6-0	180	11
32	Joe Smith	F	6-10	225	2
50	Felton Spencer	C	7-0	265	7
15	Latrell Sprewell	G	6-5	190	5

Head Coach: P.J. Carlesimo

Warriors 1997 Draft Picks

Rookie	College	Position
Adonal Foyle (1-8)	Colgate	Forward
Marc Jackson (2-38)	Temple	Forward

A center in college, Adonal Foyle lists at 6-10 (he might be an inch or two smaller), the size of an NBA power forward. He towered above most of his competition in the Patriot League, but he does have the quick ups and timing to swat shots at any level. He ranked second and first in the nation in rebounding (13.1) and blocks per game (6.4) as a junior last season. Intelligent and hard-working, Foyle has defensive abilities that are worlds ahead of his offensive skills, but he still finished among the country's top five in scoring (24.4). He is only the third player in NCAA history to record 1,700 points, 1,000 caroms, and 450 rejections. Marc Jackson is expected to play in Europe this season.

Warriors Scouting Report

Guard: Mark Price is an experienced point guard who can shoot from outside and score in double figures without hoisting up bad shots. His recent history of injuries and a general lack of quickness keep him from being the All-Star he once was. Bimbo Coles is an adequate backup, but he struggles to shoot 40 percent from the field. At the two, Latrell Sprewell has had an up-and-down five years for the Warriors. A change of scenery would probably work wonders for his career while plunging Golden State into total darkness. A complete talent who passes the ball, gets to the basket, converts his free throws, and defends like a demon. His weaknesses are turnovers—a whopping 322 last season—and a perimeter stroke that has improved but is still inconsistent. **Grade: B–**

Forward: Power forward Joe Smith, the top pick overall in 1995, brings fine mobility and range to the position, but he has been the subject of extensive trade talks. Despite having the ups and timing of a shot blocker, he doesn't have the bulk to be a great low-post defender. Chris Mullin stayed healthy for the first time in five years, missing only three games. A textbook shooter with rare court sense and savvy, he makes plenty of steals but is too slow to qualify as a defensive standout. Donyell Marshall hasn't got much game, but he figures to keep getting chances to justify his status as 1994's fourth pick overall. Athleticism and a long wingspan can't make up for his lack of muscle and a poor shooting touch. **Grade: B–**

Center: Felton Spencer doesn't contribute scoring in the low post, and he is extremely prone to fouls and injuries, but he brings size, smarts, and a solid work ethic to the pivot. Todd Fuller had an uneventful rookie season and is not expected to be a major factor at the five. **Grade: D+**

Warriors 1996–97 Player Statistics

	G	MIN	FG	FGA	FG%	FT	FTA	FT%	3FG	3FGA
Sprewell	80	3353	649	1444	.449	493	585	.843	147	415
Smith	80	3086	587	1293	.454	307	377	.814	12	46
Mullin	79	2733	438	792	.553	184	213	.864	83	202
Price	70	1876	263	589	.447	155	171	.906	112	283
Armstrong	49	1020	148	327	.453	68	79	.861	25	90
Marshall	61	1022	174	421	.413	61	98	.622	35	111
Coles	51	1183	122	314	.389	37	49	.755	30	102
Booker	21	430	46	105	.438	18	20	.900	12	37
DeClercq	71	1065	142	273	.520	91	151	.603	0	0
Burrell	57	939	98	871	.362	57	76	.750	41	116
Spencer	73	1558	139	284	.489	94	161	.584	0	0
Fuller	75	949	114	266	.429	76	110	.691	0	0
Owes	57	592	75	180	.417	26	46	.565	1	5
Roe	17	107	14	48	.292	9	19	.474	3	11

	ORB	REB	AST	STL	TO	BLK	PF	PTS	PPG
Sprewell	58	366	507	132	322	45	153	1938	24.2
Smith	261	679	125	74	192	86	244	1493	18.7
Mullin	75	317	322	130	192	33	155	1143	14.5
Price	36	179	342	67	161	3	100	793	11.3
Armstrong	7	74	126	25	53	2	56	389	7.9
Marshall	92	276	54	25	55	46	96	444	7.3
Coles	39	118	149	35	59	7	96	311	6.1
Booker	7	29	53	3	27	2	28	122	5.8
DeClercq	122	298	32	33	76	27	229	375	5.3
Burrell	49	158	74	28	53	19	120	294	5.2
Spencer	157	416	22	34	88	50	275	372	5.1
Fuller	108	249	24	10	52	20	146	304	4.1
Owes	64	163	15	15	23	20	86	177	3.1
Roe	7	14	6	3	11	1	10	40	2.4

Warriors 1996–97 Team Statistics

Final Record: 30–52

Home Record: 19–23

Road Record: 11–29

Division Record: 4–20

Conference Record: 19–33

Overtime Record: 3–6

Points Per Game: 99.6

Opponents Points Per Game: 104.4

Field Goal Percentage: .456

Opponents Field Goal Percentage: .475

Turnovers Per Game: 17.2

Opponents Turnovers Per Game: 15.7

Offensive Rebounding Percentage: .323

Defensive Rebounding Percentage: .675

Total Rebounding Percentage: .499

Scored Fewer Than 100 Points: 39

Opponents Scored Fewer Than 100 Points: 28

Warriors Clipboard

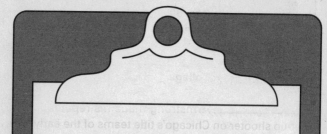

Why the Warriors win: Mullin and Spree must be hitting from the perimeter for the Warriors to have a prayer. If the duo of Foyle and Spencer provide some help on the boards, the Warriors may be able to outscore their opponent.

Why the Warriors lose: Golden State is undersized at most positions, so they have trouble matching up on defense. The problem is compounded by a lack of defensive intensity and teamwork. The Warriors have no interior presence and are not a great perimeter shooting team.

1996–97 MVP: Latrell Sprewell

Projected MVP: Latrell Sprewell

Fast Fact: Spree knocked down 22 free throws, the NBA single-game high for the year, versus the Clippers on March 10.

B.J. Armstrong   G

Age: 30
Seasons: 8
Height: 6-2
Weight: 185
College: Iowa

Armstrong made his reputation as a spot-up shooter on Chicago's title teams of the early '90s, when Jordan and Pippen fed him a steady diet of open shots. Nowadays, he's just another two in a one's body.

	G	MPG	FG%	3FG%	FT%	APG	RPG	PPG	BLK	STL
1996–97	49	20.8	.453	.278	.861	2.6	1.5	7.9	2	25
Career	622	25.8	.477	.429	.856	3.5	1.9	10.9	46	485

Scott Burrell   F

Age: 26
Seasons: 4
Height: 6-7
Weight: 218
College: Connecticut

Burrell was drafted for his defensive potential, but he has shown flashes of shooting ability. The problems are that he can't create for himself and has never stayed healthy enough to play more than 65 games.

	G	MPG	FG%	3FG%	FT%	APG	RPG	PPG	BLK	STL
1996–97	57	16.5	.362	.353	.750	1.3	2.8	5.2	19	28
Career	193	22.9	.434	.387	.708	1.8	3.9	8.0	88	167

Bimbo Coles G

Age: 29
Seasons: 7
Height: 6-2
Weight: 182
College: Virginia Tech

One of those players who does a little of everything but nothing exceptionally well, Coles is not a great playmaker or a reliable shooter. He understands his role and can be a catalyst off the bench.

	G	MPG	FG%	3FG%	FT%	APG	RPG	PPG	BLK	STL
1996–97	51	23.2	.389	.294	.755	2.9	2.3	6.1	7	35
Career	520	25.6	.433	.281	.799	4.3	2.4	8.7	85	521

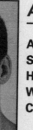

Andrew DeClercq F

Age: 24
Seasons: 2
Height: 6-10
Weight: 230
College: Florida

A serviceable backup power forward, DeClercq hits better than half his shots and chips in on the boards. He scored in double figures over the season's final month.

	G	MPG	FG%	3FG%	FT%	APG	RPG	PPG	BLK	STL
1996–97	71	15.0	.520	.000	.603	0.5	4.2	5.3	27	33
Career	93	13.6	.514	.000	.600	0.4	3.6	4.7	32	40

DONYELL MARSHALL

Donyell Marshall F

Age: 24
Seasons: 3
Height: 6-9
Weight: 230
College: Connecticut

Marshall is fluid and explosive, which is enough to keep him in the league for a while, but he had no business launching 111 three-point shots last year, and his defense is flat awful.

	G	MPG	FG%	3FG%	FT%	APG	RPG	PPG	BLK	STL
1996–97	61	16.8	.413	.315	.622	0.9	4.5	7.3	46	25
Career	195	20.7	.400	.295	.675	1.1	4.6	8.7	165	92

Chris Mullin G/F

Age: 34
Seasons: 12
Height: 6-7
Weight: 215
College: St. John's

Mullin, who ranked fifth in the league in field-goal accuracy and 12th from three-point range, is a crafty veteran who sees the entire floor and rarely makes a wrong decision.

	G	MPG	FG%	3FG%	FT%	APG	RPG	PPG	BLK	STL
1996–97	79	34.6	.553	.411	.864	4.1	4.0	14.5	33	130
Career	787	35.4	.514	.366	.862	4.0	4.5	20.5	478	1344

Mark Price G

Age: 33
Seasons: 11
Height: 6-0
Weight: 180
College: Georgia Tech

A four-time All-Star with Cleveland, the oft-injured Price can still fill it up from outside and is money at the charity stripe. Not very quick or strong, he isn't a top-notch penetrator or defender.

	G	MPG	FG%	3FG%	FT%	APG	RPG	PPG	BLK	STL
1996–97	70	26.8	.447	.396	.906	4.9	2.6	11.3	3	67
Career	659	30.5	.475	.407	.907	6.9	2.6	15.8	71	807

Joe Smith F

Age: 22
Seasons: 2
Height: 6-10
Weight: 225
College: Maryland

The number-one pick in the 1995 draft, Smith is a terrific young player with vast potential. He ranked among the NBA's top 30 in both rebounding and blocked shots in what would have been his senior year.

	G	MPG	FG%	3FG%	FT%	APG	RPG	PPG	BLK	STL
1996–97	80	38.6	.454	.261	.814	1.6	8.5	18.7	86	74
Career	162	36.5	.456	.297	.793	1.3	8.6	16.9	220	159

Felton Spencer   C

Age: 29
Seasons: 7
Height: 7-0
Weight: 265
College: Louisville

Spencer's game has holes—he can't pass or score in the low post, and he is susceptible to fouls and injuries—but he holds his position in the paint and plays within his limits.

	G	MPG	FG%	3FG%	FT%	APG	RPG	PPG	BLK	STL
1996–97	73	21.3	.489	.000	.584	0.3	5.7	5.1	50	34
Career	470	23.0	.489	.000	.672	0.4	6.5	6.5	469	205

Latrell Sprewell   G

Age: 27
Seasons: 5
Height: 6-5
Weight: 190
College: Alabama

Spree topped all NBA twos in assists last season, but frequent turnovers amounted to a spotty three-to-two ratio. He ranked fifth in the league in scoring, third in minutes.

	G	MPG	FG%	3FG%	FT%	APG	RPG	PPG	BLK	STL
1996–97	80	41.9	.449	.354	.843	6.3	4.6	24.2	45	132
Career	386	40.1	.438	.336	.793	4.6	4.3	20.0	261	677

Hakeem Olajuwon

Houston
ROCKETS

Franchise History: The Rockets originated in San Diego for the 1967–68 season, then transferred to Houston in 1971–72. The franchise has historically featured big men, from Elvin Hayes to Moses Malone to Ralph Sampson to Hakeem Olajuwon. Houston made it to the Finals in 1980–81, but lost to Boston in six. The Rockets played for a championship again in 1985-86, only to fall again to the Celtics in six. They broke through with back-to-back titles in 1993–94 and 1994–95.

1996–97 Review: It was a confluence of three players who are destined for the Hall of Fame, and it was to be the best (and perhaps last) chance at a championship for Charles Barkley. Houston management managed to put Clyde Drexler, Hakeem Olajuwon, and Sir Charles on the same team, but it wasn't enough to bring the Rockets a third title in four years. The titanic trio struggled to stay healthy during the regular season, then fell to the methodical Jazz in the conference finals.

1997–98 Preview: When the terrific threesome is intact, they present match-up problems for most opponents. The weak link is at the point, Matt Maloney notwithstanding. It can be argued that the Rockets were hurt more by the loss of Sam Cassell and Kenny Smith at the one than they were helped by the de facto swap of Barkley for Robert Horry at the four. The experience-versus-athleticism factor could be at issue in possible playoff tussles with the Spurs, the Sonics, and/or the Lakers.

Rockets Veteran Roster

No	Player	Pos	Ht	Wt	Exp
4	Charles Barkley	F	6-6	252	13
50	Matt Bullard	F	6-10	235	6
22	Clyde Drexler	G	6-7	222	14
32	Othella Harrington	F	6-9	235	1
8	Eddie Johnson	G	6-7	215	15
3	Randy Livingston	G	6-4	209	1
5	Sam Mack	G	6-7	220	3
12	Matt Maloney	G	6-3	200	1
34	Hakeem Olajuwon	C	7-0	255	13
20	Brent Price	G	6-1	185	4
2	Sedale Threatt	G	6-2	185	14
42	Kevin Willis	F/C	7-0	245	13

Head Coach: Rudy Tomjanovich

Rockets 1997 Draft Picks

Rookie	College	Position
Rodrick Rhodes (1-24)	Southern Calif.	Guard
Serge Zwikker (2-30)	North Carolina	Center

Rodrick Rhodes spent his first three years at Kentucky, then finished at USC. Versatile enough to handle the point, the two, or small forward, he paced the Trojans in assists, wound up second in scoring, and was third in rebounding. The leadoff pick of the second round, Serge Zwikker, has the size of an Ostertag to go with a midrange set shot that is almost automatic. He is a willing pupil when it comes to the finer points of the game, and his progress while at Carolina was impressive. He was utterly out of his element as a freshman but recorded the second 20-point, 20-rebound performance in school history as a senior.

Rockets Scouting Report

Guard: Matt Maloney, who was undrafted out of Penn and spent a season in the CBA, stepped in at the point and was the only Rockets player to appear in every game last year. He plays within his limits, protects the ball, feeds the post, and converts 40 percent of his three-point attempts. He lacks the quickness needed for drive-and-dish offense and one-on-one defense. At the off-guard spot, Clyde Drexler still has too much height and explosiveness for most of his matchups. Though he is not particularly durable at this stage of his career and his perimeter shooting is erratic, the Glide can score, rebound, pass, and defend at an All-Star level. Off the bench, Eddie Johnson put together a solid regular season in his 15th NBA campaign, then exploded in the conference finals. He is a streak shooter who can drive and finish or bury the trifecta. **Grade: B**

Forward: Charles Barkley returns for another campaign, and the league is better for it. Still defying preconceptions about what physical traits are required to be an NBA four, he scores on jumpers from all over the court, plus the best up-and-under move in the business. He still follows his own "go get the damn ball" philosophy, and he remains one of the game's great rebounders. The lack of durability and defensive prowess are his primary weaknesses. At the three, Mario Elie is tough and smart, a good defender who can hit the open jumper and distribute the ball. **Grade: B+**

Center: Hakeem Olajuwon continues to baffle opposition centers with his infinite repertoire of fakes and his deadly turnaround jumper. One of the league's top defenders, he annually registers 100-plus steals and roughly 200 blocks. Kevin Willis is a physically overpowering low-post scorer and rebounder who is comfortable at power forward or in the pivot. **Grade: A+**

Rockets 1996–97 Player Statistics

	G	MIN	FG	FGA	FG%	FT	FTA	FT%	3FG	3FGA
Olajuwon	78	2852	727	1426	.510	351	446	.787	5	16
Barkley	53	2009	335	692	.484	288	415	.694	58	205
Drexler	62	2271	397	899	.442	201	268	.750	119	335
Elie	78	2687	291	585	.497	207	231	.896	120	286
Willis	75	1964	350	728	.481	140	202	.693	2	14
Maloney	82	2386	271	615	.441	71	93	.763	154	381
Johnson	52	913	160	362	.442	55	68	.809	49	131
Mack	52	904	105	262	.401	35	42	.833	47	142
Price	25	390	44	105	.419	21	21	1.000	17	53
Davis	13	230	24	54	.444	5	8	.625	12	27
Harrington	57	860	112	204	.549	49	81	.605	0	3
Bullard	71	1025	114	284	.401	25	34	.735	67	183
Livingston	64	981	100	229	.437	42	65	.646	9	22
Moore	27	237	33	85	.388	22	31	.710	11	43
Threatt	21	334	28	74	.378	6	8	.750	8	20
Stephens	2	9	1	5	.200	0	0	.000	1	3
Jones	12	93	2	5	.400	0	0	.000	0	0

	ORB	REB	AST	STL	TO	BLK	PF	PTS	PPG
Olajuwon	173	716	236	117	281	173	249	1810	23.2
Barkley	212	716	248	69	151	25	153	1016	19.2
Drexler	118	373	354	119	156	36	151	1114	18.0
Elie	60	235	310	92	135	12	200	909	11.7
Willis	146	561	71	42	119	32	216	842	11.2
Maloney	19	160	303	82	122	1	125	767	9.4
Johnson	27	138	52	15	47	2	81	424	8.2
Mack	20	106	58	29	42	6	67	292	5.6
Price	10	29	65	17	32	0	34	126	5.0
Davis	2	22	26	9	17	2	20	65	5.0
Harrington	75	198	18	12	57	22	112	273	4.8
Bullard	13	117	67	21	38	18	68	320	4.5
Livingston	32	94	155	39	102	12	107	251	3.9
Moore	11	26	20	5	14	0	19	99	3.7
Threatt	5	24	40	15	13	3	29	70	3.3
Stephens	2	3	0	3	3	0	3	3	1.5
Jones	5	13	3	2	0	4	8	4	0.3

Rockets 1996–97 Team Statistics

Final Record: 57–25

Home Record: 30–11

Road Record: 27–14

Division Record: 18–5

Conference Record: 40–12

Overtime Record: 4–2

Points Per Game: 100.6

Opponents Points Per Game: 96.1

Field Goal Percentage: .468

Opponents Field Goal Percentage: .443

Turnovers Per Game: 16.6

Opponents Turnovers Per Game: 14.3

Offensive Rebounding Percentage: .284

Defensive Rebounding Percentage: .714

Total Rebounding Percentage: .499

Scored Fewer Than 100 Points: 38

Opponents Scored Fewer Than 100 Points: 51

Rockets Clipboard

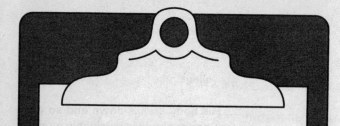

Why the Rockets win: When healthy, the Rockets have three of the top 50 players in league history, including two go-to scorers in the low post. Houston passes the ball well as a team, dominates the defensive boards, and has a plethora of playoff-proven veterans.

Why the Rockets lose: Always among the poorest offensive rebounding teams in the league, statistically speaking, the Rockets followed suit last year. They also commit turnovers more often than most teams, while forcing fewer.

1996–97 MVP: Hakeem Olajuwon

Projected MVP: Hakeem Olajuwon

Fast Fact: The Rockets logged 20 fourth-quarter comeback victories last year—more than one-third of their total wins.

Charles Barkley   F

Age: 34
Seasons: 13
Height: 6-6
Weight: 252
College: Auburn

His body breaks down and so does his defense, but Sir Charles provides invaluable on-court leadership and point production. He has a rare knack for finishing shots when fouled.

	G	MPG	FG%	3FG%	FT%	APG	RPG	PPG	BLK	STL
1996–97	53	37.9	.484	.283	.694	4.7	13.5	19.2	25	69
Career	943	37.1	.547	.271	.736	4.0	11.7	23.1	843	1520

Matt Bullard   F

Age: 30
Seasons: 6
Height: 6-10
Weight: 235
College: Iowa

Bullard is a big guy who is far more familiar with the perimeter than the paint. He launched 183 three-point attempts last season while snagging just 117 caroms.

	G	MPG	FG%	3FG%	FT%	APG	RPG	PPG	BLK	STL
1996–97	71	14.4	.401	.366	.735	0.9	1.6	4.5	18	21
Career	359	13.7	.420	.363	.760	0.9	2.0	5.1	67	111

Clyde Drexler   **G**

Age: 35
Seasons: 14
Height: 6-7
Weight: 222
College: Houston

Drexler is unstoppable in the open floor and can be devastating off the dribble. On the other hand, his perimeter stroke comes and goes and he has missed 50 games in the past two years.

	G	MPG	FG%	3FG%	FT%	APG	RPG	PPG	BLK	STL
1996–97	62	36.6	.442	.355	.750	5.7	6.0	18.0	36	119
Career	1016	34.5	.474	.318	.787	5.7	6.2	20.6	677	2081

Mario Elie   **G/F**

Age: 34
Seasons: 7
Height: 6-5
Weight: 210
College: American International

Elie has modest physical gifts but all the savvy and mettle of a two-time NBA champion. He plays tenacious defense and understands when to shoot, drive, or pass.

	G	MPG	FG%	3FG%	FT%	APG	RPG	PPG	BLK	STL
1996–97	78	34.4	.497	.420	.896	4.0	3.0	11.7	12	92
Career	465	25.1	.487	.373	.860	2.7	2.8	9.3	88	413

Othella Harrington   F

Age: 23
Seasons: 1
Height: 6-9
Weight: 235
College: Georgetown

Harrington, the first pick of the 1996 second round, saw limited action in the regular season and was a nonentity during the playoffs, but he wasn't a washout when given minutes.

	G	MPG	FG%	3FG%	FT%	APG	RPG	PPG	BLK	STL
1996–97	57	15.1	.549	.000	.605	0.3	3.5	4.8	22	12
Career	57	15.1	.549	.000	.605	0.3	3.5	4.8	22	12

Eddie Johnson   G

Age: 38
Seasons: 15
Height: 6-7
Weight: 215
College: Illinois

A former Kansas City Kings draftee who is still in the league, Johnson is the only player in history to score 18,000 points but never be selected to the All-Star team.

	G	MPG	FG%	3FG%	FT%	APG	RPG	PPG	BLK	STL
1996–97	52	17.6	.442	.374	.809	1.0	2.7	8.2	2	15
Career	1121	27.7	.474	.335	.841	2.2	4.2	16.6	177	707

Sam Mack   G

Age: 27
Seasons: 3
Height: 6-7
Weight: 220
College: Houston

Mack has toiled for five different CBA franchises, plus the Spurs and Rockets. A tweener who makes his living from the perimeter, he missed almost 35 percent of last season due to foot injuries.

	G	MPG	FG%	3FG%	FT%	APG	RPG	PPG	BLK	STL
1996–97	52	17.4	.401	.331	.833	1.1	2.0	5.6	6	29
Career	123	16.6	.409	.348	.815	1.2	2.0	6.3	20	65

Matt Maloney   G

Age: 26
Seasons: 1
Height: 6-3
Weight: 200
College: Pennsylvania

Houston's answer to Rex Walters, Maloney is a terrific spot-up shooter and a mediocre everything else. He played a key role in the postseason but was abused by John Stockton in the Utah series.

	G	MPG	FG%	3FG%	FT%	APG	RPG	PPG	BLK	STL
1996–97	82	29.1	.441	.404	.763	3.7	2.0	9.4	1	82
Career	82	29.1	.441	.404	.763	3.7	2.0	9.4	1	82

Hakeem Olajuwon   C

Age: 34
Seasons: 13
Height: 7-0
Weight: 255
College: Houston

The league's all-time leader in blocks, Olajuwon has failed to make the All-Star team just once in his career. He is the best center in the business until further notice.

	G	MPG	FG%	3FG%	FT%	APG	RPG	PPG	BLK	STL
1996–97	78	36.6	.510	.313	.787	3.0	9.2	23.2	173	117
Career	978	37.7	.516	.204	.716	2.7	12.0	24.2	3363	1811

Kevin Willis   F/C

Age: 35
Seasons: 13
Height: 7-0
Weight: 245
College: Michigan State

Willis can be a powerhouse on the boards, and his baby hook is a go-to move in the post. His total minutes dropped for the fifth straight season last year, but he is a quality backup at the four or the five.

	G	MPG	FG%	3FG%	FT%	APG	RPG	PPG	BLK	STL
1996–97	75	26.2	.481	.143	.693	0.9	7.5	11.2	32	42
Career	939	30.5	.497	.223	.695	1.1	9.7	14.1	524	706

Rik Smits

Indiana
PACERS

Franchise History: Representing the very best of the old ABA, the Pacers were three-time champions and two-time runners-up from 1968–69 through 1974–75. Great players from those early days of the franchise included Mel Daniels and George McGinnis. Indiana joined the NBA in 1976–77, but the team was never very good until Larry Brown took over as head coach in the mid-'90s. Paced by Reggie Miller and Rik Smits, Indiana made trips to the conference finals in 1993–94 and 1994–95.

1996–97 Review: The Pacers shot themselves in the feet by trading point guard Mark Jackson to Denver before the season began. That move, plus the loss of forward Derrick McKey and center Rik Smits for roughly 30 games apiece due to injuries, put the team on a slow ride to the draft lottery. Reggie Miller contributed his usual 20 points per game, but the team understandably lacked cohesiveness, and the situation only worsened amid speculation that Brown was working his final season in Indiana.

1997–98 Preview: The signing of Larry Bird as head coach will generate peak interest in the Pacers among residents of Indiana, which should give the players an emotional boost. The injuries and upheaval, mixed with the memory of twice being within one win of the Finals, seemed to dull the team's spirit last season. In the best of times, the Pacers won with interior size and intimidating defense. Miller and Smits will usually score in double figures, but the team could really use a reliable third option.

Pacers Veteran Roster

No	Player	Pos	Ht	Wt	Exp
4	Travis Best	G	5-11	182	2
25	Erick Dampier	C	6-11	265	1
33	Antonio Davis	F/C	6-9	230	4
32	Dale Davis	F	6-11	230	6
27	Duane Ferrell	F	6-7	215	9
24	Darvin Ham	F	6-7	220	1
20	Fred Hoiberg	G	6-4	203	2
13	Mark Jackson	G	6-3	185	10
9	Derrick McKey	F	6-10	225	10
31	Reggie Miller	G	6-7	185	10
5	Jalen Rose	G	6-8	210	3
45	Rik Smits	C	7-4	265	9
41	LaSalle Thompson	F/C	6-10	260	15
3	Haywoode Workman	G	6-3	180	6

Head Coach: Larry Bird

Pacers 1997 Draft Picks

Rookie	College	Position
Austin Croshere (1-12)	Providence	Forward

Croshere has quality face-up skills and can usually get his shot with pump fakes and decent ballhandling for his size (6-8, 235). He is a major tweener defensively, lacking the strength to body up against fours and the quickness to check threes on the perimeter. He improved immensely in his four seasons with the Friars and was a unanimous All–Big East selection as a senior. He was arguably the best shooter among forwards from this draft class, and he is clean money from the charity stripe. For a possible pro comparison, see Don MacLean (sans injuries).

Pacers Scouting Report

Guard: Four games after his return to the Pacers, point guard Mark Jackson handed out 19 assists. The next game, he posted his first triple-double. Always a fine distributor, he beat John Stockton for the league assist title, handing out 11.4 per contest. Travis Best handled the one while Jackson was with Denver, but it appears that he'll be best suited to an off-the-bench role. He is a better shooter than Jackson but an inferior playmaker. Indiana's biggest star is, of course, shooting guard Reggie Miller. His knack for coming up big against the Knicks—plus his penchant for talking about it—has made him a minor media icon. He is one of the league's purest catch-and-shoot scorers, able to wind defenders through a plethora of screens, then stick the long-distance jumper. His slender frame isn't built for defense or rebounding. Jalen Rose hasn't found a steady role; he wants to be a one but has the skills and build of a two-three tweener. **Grade: B**

Forward: Small forward Derrick McKey is Indiana's most complete player, but he's a classic "good at everything but not great at anything" case. The Pacers would love to see him become a consistently aggressive scorer, but it just doesn't seem to be in his makeup. He is one of the better passers and defenders among NBA threes. The Pacers have a good thing going at power forward, where Dale and Antonio Davis rule the boards. Both are most effective near the basket, where they can pound the offensive glass and score on putbacks. **Grade: B–**

Center: Rik Smits has one of the smoothest releases in the NBA—at any position. His rebounding and defense are not exceptional, considering his size, but he isn't exactly a liability on either end of the floor. Erick Dampier is a raw but promising young pivot. **Grade: B**

Pacers 1996–97 Player Statistics

	G	MIN	FG	FGA	FG%	FT	FTA	FT%	3FG	3FGA
Miller	81	2966	552	1244	.444	418	475	.880	229	536
Smits	52	1518	356	733	.486	173	217	.797	2	8
A. Davis	82	2335	308	641	.480	241	362	.666	1	14
D. Davis	80	2589	370	688	.538	92	215	.428	0	0
Best	76	2064	274	620	.442	149	197	.756	57	155
Jackson	82	3054	289	679	.426	168	213	.789	66	178
McKey	50	1449	148	379	.391	89	123	.724	15	58
Rose	66	1188	172	377	.456	117	156	.750	21	72
Ferrell	62	1115	159	337	.472	58	94	.617	18	44
Workman	4	81	11	20	.550	0	1	.000	0	3
Dampier	72	1052	131	336	.390	107	168	.637	1	1
Hoiberg	47	572	67	156	.429	61	77	.792	29	70
Ham	36	318	33	62	.532	17	35	.486	0	0
Scott	16	55	8	17	.471	3	6	.500	0	0
Thompson	26	140	3	19	.158	4	6	.667	0	0

	ORB	REB	AST	STL	TO	BLK	PF	PTS	PPG
Miller	53	286	273	75	166	25	172	1751	21.6
Smits	105	361	67	22	126	59	175	887	17.1
A. Davis	190	598	65	42	141	84	260	858	10.5
D. Davis	301	772	59	60	108	77	233	832	10.4
Best	36	166	318	98	153	5	221	754	9.9
Jackson	91	395	935	97	274	12	161	812	9.9
McKey	80	241	135	47	83	30	141	400	8.0
Rose	27	121	155	57	107	18	136	482	7.3
Ferrell	57	141	66	38	55	6	120	394	6.4
Workman	4	7	11	3	5	0	10	22	5.5
Dampier	96	294	43	19	84	73	153	370	5.1
Hoiberg	13	81	41	27	22	6	51	224	4.8
Ham	29	56	14	9	22	8	57	83	2.3
Scott	3	9	3	1	4	1	14	19	1.2
Thompson	7	34	2	3	9	6	33	10	0.4

Pacers 1996–97 Team Statistics

Final Record: 39–43

Home Record: 21–20

Road Record: 18–23

Division Record: 11–16

Conference Record: 22–32

Overtime Record: 6–3

Points Per Game: 95.4

Opponents Points Per Game: 94.4

Field Goal Percentage: .456

Opponents Field Goal Percentage: .440

Turnovers Per Game: 16.3

Opponents Turnovers Per Game: 15.7

Offensive Rebounding Percentage: .313

Defensive Rebounding Percentage: .704

Total Rebounding Percentage: .508

Scored Fewer Than 100 Points: 54

Opponents Scored Fewer Than 100 Points: 54

Pacers Clipboard

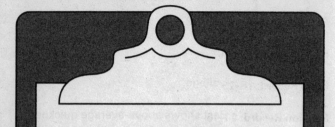

Why the Pacers win: Indiana will put the clamps on opposition offenses, stake permanent claim on the boards, and take control of the tempo. Smits is a superb shooter, and Miller can outscore entire teams for significant stretches. The Pacers have superior height in the frontcourt.

Why the Pacers lose: The Pacers lack an off-the-dribble creator, and they rarely run in the open floor. If they don't set good screens for Miller, or if he goes cold from the perimeter, the team struggles.

1996–97 MVP: Reggie Miller

Projected MVP: Reggie Miller

Fast Fact: The Pacers had 14 different players miss 265 games due to injury or illness last season. Only one player saw action in all 82 games.

Travis Best G

Age: 25
Seasons: 2
Height: 5-11
Weight: 182
College: Georgia Tech

Best shows above-average quickness and is good at breaking down defenses with penetration, but he has yet to demonstrate top-notch leadership and distribution skills.

	G	MPG	FG%	3FG%	FT%	APG	RPG	PPG	BLK	STL
1996–97	76	27.2	.442	.368	.756	4.2	2.2	9.9	5	98
Career	136	19.5	.438	.361	.780	3.1	1.6	7.2	8	118

Erick Dampier C

Age: 23
Seasons: 1
Height: 6-11
Weight: 265
College: Mississippi State

Dampier, the tenth pick overall in the 1996 draft, logged 20-odd starts because of injuries to Rik Smits. He has some defensive potential but is a major project on offense.

	G	MPG	FG%	3FG%	FT%	APG	RPG	PPG	BLK	STL
1996–97	72	14.6	.390	1.000	.637	0.6	4.1	5.1	73	19
Career	72	14.6	.390	1.000	.637	0.6	4.1	5.1	73	19

Antonio Davis   F/C

Age: 29
Seasons: 4
Height: 6-9
Weight: 230
College: Texas–El Paso

The shorter, bulkier of the Davis boys, Antonio will swing to the five in a pinch, but his natural spot is power forward. He registered career highs in both scoring and rebounding last year.

	G	MPG	FG%	3FG%	FT%	APG	RPG	PPG	BLK	STL
1996–97	82	28.5	.480	.071	.666	0.8	7.3	10.5	84	42
Career	289	24.9	.485	.118	.675	0.7	6.5	8.8	263	139

Dale Davis   F

Age: 28
Seasons: 6
Height: 6-11
Weight: 230
College: Clemson

Dale is a force on the boards, and he gives opponents fits with his tenacious defense, but few players in the league are more limited offensively or as pathetic at the charity stripe.

	G	MPG	FG%	3FG%	FT%	APG	RPG	PPG	BLK	STL
1996–97	80	32.4	.538	.000	.428	0.7	9.7	10.4	77	60
Career	444	30.2	.550	.000	.506	0.9	9.1	9.7	633	326

Duane Ferrell — F

Age: 32
Seasons: 9
Height: 6-7
Weight: 215
College: Georgia Tech

Not drafted out of college, Ferrell was with Atlanta for six seasons before joining the Pacers in 1994–95. He usually doesn't see a starter's minutes but does provide a scoring spark off the bench.

	G	MPG	FG%	3FG%	FT%	APG	RPG	PPG	BLK	STL
1996–97	62	18.0	.472	.409	.617	1.1	2.3	6.4	6	38
Career	525	15.7	.486	.300	.754	0.9	2.1	6.9	98	280

Mark Jackson — G

Age: 32
Seasons: 10
Height: 6-3
Weight: 185
College: St. John's

Jackson is one of the league's all-time assist leaders, currently sitting at number nine. He isn't particularly quick, and his shooting is erratic, but he will invariably deliver the ball where it's supposed to be.

	G	MPG	FG%	3FG%	FT%	APG	RPG	PPG	BLK	STL
1996–97	82	37.2	.426	.371	.789	11.4	4.8	9.9	12	97
Career	795	32.9	.458	.319	.766	8.6	4.2	11.3	90	1183

Derrick McKey   *F*

Age: 31
Seasons: 10
Height: 6-10
Weight: 225
College: Alabama

McKey may be remembered as the player for whom the Pacers traded Detlef Schrempf, but his game has slipped a bit, due in part to injuries. He has never been the scorer Indiana lacks at the three.

	G	MPG	FG%	3FG%	FT%	APG	RPG	PPG	BLK	STL
1996–97	50	29.0	.391	.259	.724	2.7	4.8	8.0	30	47
Career	728	32.0	.490	.316	.781	2.7	5.1	13.0	547	885

Reggie Miller   *G*

Age: 32
Seasons: 10
Height: 6-7
Weight: 185
College: UCLA

Miller can take over a game with his shooting, and he'll be happy to tell you all about it. His release is quick and consistent, but the same cannot be said of his defensive assets.

	G	MPG	FG%	3FG%	FT%	APG	RPG	PPG	BLK	STL
1996–97	81	36.6	.444	.427	.880	3.4	3.5	21.6	25	75
Career	801	34.3	.486	.401	.878	3.2	3.2	19.8	209	959

Jalen Rose G

Age: 24
Seasons: 3
Height: 6-8
Weight: 210
College: Michigan

Rose is an almost too perfect example of a player who dominates the college game but doesn't have a position to play when he gets to the NBA. Is he a one, a two, or a three? Answer: none of the above.

	G	MPG	FG%	3FG%	FT%	APG	RPG	PPG	BLK	STL
1996–97	66	18.0	.456	.292	.750	2.3	1.8	7.3	18	57
Career	227	22.6	.465	.303	.721	4.6	2.6	8.6	79	175

Rik Smits C

Age: 31
Seasons: 9
Height: 7-4
Weight: 265
College: Marist

The Dunking Dutchman was hobbled by bad feet last season, but he still finished second on the team in scoring. When healthy, he is one of the NBA's most accomplished low-post shooters.

	G	MPG	FG%	3FG%	FT%	APG	RPG	PPG	BLK	STL
1996–97	52	29.2	.486	.250	.797	1.3	6.9	17.1	59	22
Career	666	26.9	.512	.150	.772	1.5	6.2	14.9	871	294

Rodney Rogers

Los Angeles
CLIPPERS

Franchise History: Beginning as the Buffalo Braves in 1970–71, the franchise had some early success, peaking with a 49-win campaign in 1974–75. Bob McAdoo was an MVP and scoring champion that year. The team moved to San Diego for the 1978–79 season and was renamed the Clippers. Five straight sub-.500 records prompted another move, this time to Los Angeles. The Clippers occasionally nosed into the playoffs, but they have generally been one of the league's poor cousins.

1996–97 Review: Bill Fitch brought a reputation for being able to mold modestly talented young teams into playoff contenders, and Lo (Wright) and behold, he did it again. Veteran forward Loy Vaught snatched over 800 rebounds, rookie Lorenzen Wright exceeded expectations at center, and L.A. put together a winning record at home for the first time in four years of playing at the Pond in Anaheim. In the first round of the playoffs, the Clippers were sunk 3–0 by Utah.

1997–98 Preview: The last time the Clippers were playoff participants, they wound up in the division dungeon the following season. That could easily happen again, but it is less likely with Fitch at the controls. L.A.'s top scorer (Vaught) registered just 14.9 points per game, worst in the league for a team leader. This is a team that can win with below-average talent if the players continue to follow the mandates of their head coach. It wouldn't be a shock to see the Clippers either sink or sail this season.

Clippers Veteran Roster

No	Player	Pos	Ht	Wt	Exp
31	Brent Barry	G	6-6	185	2
15	Darrick Martin	G	5-11	170	3
7	Lamond Murray	F	6-7	236	3
45	Bo Outlaw	F	6-8	210	4
52	Eric Piatkowski	G/F	6-7	215	3
2	Pooh Richardson	G	6-1	180	8
54	Rodney Rogers	F	6-7	255	4
21	Malik Sealy	G/F	6-8	190	5
35	Loy Vaught	F	6-9	240	7
—	Stojko Vrankovic	C	7-2	260	3
55	Lorenzen Wright	C/F	6-11	225	1

Head Coach: Bill Fitch

Clippers 1997 Draft Picks

Rookie	College	Position
Maurice Taylor (1-14)	Michigan	Forward

L.A. dealt a 1998 second-round pick to Philadelphia for James Collins, this year's 37th selection. He underachieved somewhat as a senior at Florida State but was impressive at the pre-draft camps. A streaky shooter and a mediocre ball handler, he chips in on the boards and can score points in bunches. Maurice Taylor didn't have overwhelming numbers for the Wolverines (12.3 ppg, 6.2 rpg) last year, and he didn't attend the pre-draft camps. He did flash a surprising touch from 16 feet in personal workouts, and he has NBA size (6-8, 245) and leaping ability. His low-post game has gotten mixed reviews, and he may be more of a face-up scorer than a back-to-the-basket type. He can play small forward in a pinch but is slated for the four.

Clippers Scouting Report

Guard: Darrick Martin has bounced around the NBA and the CBA, but he found a home as L.A.'s starting point guard last year. A waterbug who can swipe the ball and push it up the court, he has improved his decision making but not his perimeter shooting. Pooh Richardson wound up on the bench, thanks to Martin's emergence and his own 38-percent accuracy from the field. Malik Sealy also shot under 40 percent, yet he posted a career high in starts and scoring. A rugged defender, he paced the Clippers in steals by a wide margin. This could be a breakthrough year for Brent Barry, who shows flashes of brilliance blended with periods of injury and ice-cold shooting. **Grade: C–**

Forward: Toiling in obscurity for the lowly Clippers, Loy Vaught has put together three All-Star-worthy seasons in a row. He logs ten boards and 15 points on a nightly basis. He also makes a lot of steals but tends to reach rather than play strong defense. At small forward, Rodney Rogers registered career-best numbers in points, blocks, rebounds, and assists. His feel for the game isn't great, but excellent inside-outside explosiveness makes him an all-around threat. Inch for inch, Bo Outlaw is arguably the NBA's best shot blocker. He brings energy and hustle to the defensive effort, and his versatility is also an asset. Strictly a warm body on offense, his range extends to two feet. He hit 61 percent of his attempts last season. **Grade: B–**

Center: Lorenzen Wright got off to a slow start in his debut campaign but came on to average roughly nine points and eight caroms per game in the final three months. He is a tad undersized for the pivot, but nobody is arguing with his production. Stojko Vrankovic opened last season as a starter in Minnesota but played just 90 minutes total in the final 44 contests. **Grade: C–**

Clippers 1996–97 Player Statistics

	G	MIN	FG	FGA	FG%	FT	FTA	FT%	3FG	3FGA
Vaught	82	2838	542	1084	.500	134	191	.702	2	12
Sealy	80	2456	373	942	.396	254	290	.876	79	222
Rogers	81	2480	408	884	.462	191	288	.663	65	180
Martin	82	1820	292	718	.407	218	250	.872	91	234
Roberts	18	378	63	148	.426	45	64	.703	0	0
Outlaw	82	2185	254	417	.609	117	232	.504	0	8
Barry	59	1094	155	379	.409	76	93	.817	56	173
Murray	74	1295	181	435	.416	156	211	.739	31	91
Wright	77	1936	236	491	.481	88	150	.587	1	4
Dehere	73	1053	148	383	.386	122	148	.824	52	160
Piatkowski	65	747	134	298	.450	69	84	.821	51	120
Richardson	59	1065	131	344	.381	26	43	.605	42	128
Duckworth	26	384	45	103	.437	11	16	.688	3	4
Manning	26	201	32	82	.390	9	14	.643	2	4
Schintzius	15	116	13	36	.361	7	8	.875	1	2

	ORB	REB	AST	STL	TO	BLK	PF	PTS	PPG
Vaught	222	817	110	85	137	25	241	1220	14.9
Sealy	59	238	165	124	154	45	185	1079	13.5
Rogers	137	411	222	88	221	61	272	1072	13.2
Martin	26	113	339	57	127	2	165	893	10.9
Roberts	24	91	9	8	23	23	57	171	9.5
Outlaw	174	454	157	94	107	142	227	625	7.6
Barry	30	110	154	51	76	15	88	442	7.5
Murray	85	233	57	53	86	29	113	549	7.4
Wright	206	471	49	48	79	60	211	561	7.3
Dehere	15	95	158	27	96	3	142	470	6.4
Piatkowski	49	105	52	33	46	10	85	388	6.0
Richardson	25	98	169	54	62	5	82	330	5.6
Duckworth	23	60	16	9	33	11	63	104	4.0
Manning	16	39	3	4	7	7	29	75	2.9
Schintzius	9	22	4	1	7	9	22	34	2.3

Clippers 1996–97 Team Statistics

Final Record: 36–46

Home Record: 21–20

Road Record: 15–26

Division Record: 10–14

Conference Record: 26–26

Overtime Record: 3–5

Points Per Game: 97.2

Opponents Points Per Game: 99.5

Field Goal Percentage: .446

Opponents Field Goal Percentage: .462

Turnovers Per Game: 16.0

Opponents Turnovers Per Game: 16.7

Offensive Rebounding Percentage: .308

Defensive Rebounding Percentage: .681

Total Rebounding Percentage: .495

Scored Fewer Than 100 Points: 55

Opponents Scored Fewer Than 100 Points: 40

Clippers Clipboard

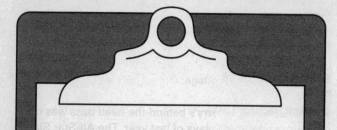

Why the Clippers win: The Clippers don't excel in any crucial statistical area (they were the only playoff team to be outscored by their opponents on average), but Fitch makes the most of the available talent. The Clippers play playoff-style ball versus weaker, less motivated teams.

Why the Clippers lose: L.A. simply does not have enough good players. The Clips were 8–20 against 1996–97 conference playoff participants.

1996–97 MVP: Loy Vaught

Projected MVP: Loy Vaught

Fast Fact: Bill Fitch, who is entering his 25th season and has been at the helm for more games than any individual in NBA history, is the first head coach ever to record 1,000 losses.

Brent Barry G

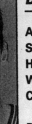

Age: 26
Seasons: 2
Height: 6-6
Weight: 185
College: Oregon State

Barry's behind-the-head pass was one of the most replayed plays of last year. The All-Star Slam Dunk champion as a rookie in 1995–96, he's exciting but inconsistent—the curse of most would-be starters.

	G	MPG	FG%	3FG%	FT%	APG	RPG	PPG	BLK	STL
1996–97	59	18.5	.409	.324	.817	2.6	1.9	7.5	15	51
Career	138	21.7	.449	.382	.813	2.8	2.0	9.0	37	146

Terry Dehere G

Age: 26
Seasons: 4
Height: 6-4
Weight: 190
College: Seton Hall

Dehere has made more three-pointers than any other player in Clippers history, but his minutes have been in steady decline. He is quick and versatile, but his shooting and defense are unreliable.

	G	MPG	FG%	3FG%	FT%	APG	RPG	PPG	BLK	STL
1996–97	73	14.4	.386	.325	.824	2.2	1.3	6.4	3	27
Career	299	18.7	.416	.376	.777	2.7	1.5	8.9	29	154

Darrick Martin   G

Age: 26
Seasons: 3
Height: 5-11
Weight: 170
College: UCLA

Martin has seen action with three NBA franchises and been released by a couple of CBA teams since coming out of college five years ago. His game is all about quickness.

	G	MPG	FG%	3FG%	FT%	APG	RPG	PPG	BLK	STL
1996–97	82	22.2	.407	.389	.872	4.1	1.4	10.9	2	57
Career	175	21.6	.407	.346	.864	3.9	1.5	8.9	5	144

Lamond Murray   F

Age: 24
Seasons: 3
Height: 6-7
Weight: 236
College: California

The seventh selection overall in 1994, Murray hasn't made much progress in the two seasons since his promising rookie campaign (14.1 ppg). He has the talent but hasn't put it to use.

	G	MPG	FG%	3FG%	FT%	APG	RPG	PPG	BLK	STL
1996–97	74	17.5	.416	.341	.739	0.8	3.1	7.4	29	53
Career	232	24.4	.417	.313	.748	1.2	3.6	10.1	109	186

Bo Outlaw F

Age: 26
Seasons: 4
Height: 6-8
Weight: 210
College: Houston

Not many 6-8 players swat shots like Outlaw. He has great springs and perfect timing. He can't do anything imaginative on offense, but he plays within his limits and shoots for a terrific percentage.

	G	MPG	FG%	3FG%	FT%	APG	RPG	PPG	BLK	STL
1996–97	82	26.8	.609	.000	.504	1.9	5.5	7.6	142	94
Career	280	20.4	.574	.000	.486	1.2	4.2	5.7	421	264

Pooh Richardson G

Age: 31
Seasons: 8
Height: 6-1
Weight: 180
College: UCLA

Pooh failed to register a double-figure scoring average last season for the first time in his career. He sprained an ankle in mid-December and never got his starting job back.

	G	MPG	FG%	3FG%	FT%	APG	RPG	PPG	BLK	STL
1996–97	59	18.1	.381	.328	.605	2.9	1.7	5.6	5	54
Career	559	32.2	.448	.339	.648	7.0	3.0	12.1	108	769

Rodney Rogers   F

Age: 26
Seasons: 4
Height: 6-7
Weight: 255
College: Wake Forest

Rogers is a legit low-post scorer who can also bury the jumper. He doesn't have a perfect grasp of the game's subtleties, but his output improved across the board last year.

	G	MPG	FG%	3FG%	FT%	APG	RPG	PPG	BLK	STL
1996–97	81	30.6	.462	.361	.663	2.7	5.1	13.2	61	88
Career	307	26.0	.468	.347	.655	2.1	4.3	11.3	190	321

Malik Sealy   F

Age: 27
Seasons: 5
Height: 6-8
Weight: 190
College: St. John's

Sealy is an underrated defender, and he knows how to get to the basket. He paced the Clippers in free throws last season and finished seventh in the NBA in accuracy from the stripe.

	G	MPG	FG%	3FG%	FT%	APG	RPG	PPG	BLK	STL
1996–97	80	30.7	.396	.356	.876	2.1	3.0	13.5	45	124
Career	303	23.0	.414	.301	.798	1.6	3.0	10.5	113	347

Loy Vaught F

Age: 29
Seasons: 7
Height: 6-9
Weight: 240
College: Michigan

The closest thing the Clippers have to a star, Vaught is the franchise's all-time leading rebounder. He has a baseline jump shot that is automatic, and he has paced the team in scoring for three straight seasons.

	G	MPG	FG%	3FG%	FT%	APG	RPG	PPG	BLK	STL
1996–97	82	34.6	.500	.167	.702	1.3	10.0	14.9	25	85
Career	548	28.1	.512	.263	.721	1.1	8.0	11.9	209	464

Lorenzen Wright F/C

Age: 22
Seasons: 1
Height: 6-11
Weight: 225
College: Memphis

One magazine said of Wright, "He doesn't have an offensive game." It may be true, but he did score in double figures 25 times as a rookie while playing out of position for a playoff team.

	G	MPG	FG%	3FG%	FT%	APG	RPG	PPG	BLK	STL
1996–97	77	25.1	.481	.250	.587	0.6	6.1	7.3	60	48
Career	77	25.1	.481	.250	.587	0.6	6.1	7.3	60	48

Shaquille O'Neal

Los Angeles
LAKERS

Franchise History: Born in Minneapolis, the Lakers won five league championships from 1948–49 through 1953–54, led by three-time scoring leader George Mikan. Moving to Los Angeles in 1960, the franchise became basketball's bridesmaid, losing in the Finals seven times during the decade. Wilt Chamberlain and Jerry West finally brought L.A. an NBA title in 1971–72. In the 1980s, Magic Johnson and Kareem Abdul-Jabbar earned five rings for Pat Riley's star-laden Showtime cast.

1996–97 Review: Guru of basketball operations Jerry West made several impact additions, including free-agent gem Shaquille O'Neal, to a squad that had won 53 games the previous season. A trio of rookies, youngster Kobe Bryant premier among them, logged 900-plus minutes apiece, while returning starters Eddie Jones, Nick Van Exel, and Elden Campbell kept the team winning when O'Neal was out with a knee injury. Expectations were high entering the playoffs, but Utah dashed them in the conference semis.

1997–98 Preview: L.A. is loaded with young guns thanks to West's work in the front office, but inconsistency and injuries kept the team from turning its potential into a title last year. Each of the NBA's elite have at least one veteran All-Star who consistently steps up under playoff pressure, but Shaq, Kobe, E.J., etc. are still learning what it takes to win a championship, and the Lakers lacked go-to options when the postseason stakes were high. Inexperience is the only element delaying an L.A. dynasty.

Lakers Veteran Roster

No	Player	Pos	Ht	Wt	Exp
43	Corie Blount	F	6-10	242	4
8	Kobe Bryant	G	6-6	200	1
41	Elden Campbell	F/C	6-11	250	7
2	Derek Fisher	G	6-1	200	1
5	Robert Horry	F	6-10	220	5
6	Eddie Jones	G/F	6-6	190	3
12	Jerome Kersey	F	6-7	240	13
24	George McCloud	G/F	6-8	225	7
34	Shaquille O'Neal	C	7-1	300	5
45	Sean Rooks	C	6-10	260	5
9	Nick Van Exel	G	6-1	183	4

Head Coach: Del Harris

Lakers 1997 Draft Picks

Rookie	College	Position
DeJuan Wheat (2-52)	Louisville	Guard
Paul Rogers (2-54)	Gonzaga	Center

The Lakers dealt their first-round pick to Dallas in the trade for George McCloud, and they picked up the 54th selection in a 1994 exchange with New York for Doug Christie. DeJuan Wheat started 136 consecutive games at Louisville, a school record. A complete point guard, he is the only player in Division I history to register 2,000 points, 450 assists, 300 triples and 200 steals. Paul Rogers was a medical redshirt after breaking his foot four games into his senior season. He has the height and touch of an NBA pivot but is not a dominant rebounder. His injury history and the level of competition he faced at Gonzaga make him tough to evaluate.

Lakers Scouting Report

Guard: Eddie Jones, a first-time All-Star in his third pro season, is a versatile scorer who can drill the three, finish in transition, and beat defenders off the dribble. He finished fourth in the league in steals per game last year and was tenth in theft-to-turnover ratio. At the point, Nick Van Exel was one of only five players last season to average at least 15 points and eight assists, but he can be very streaky and is often a defensive liability. Fresh out of high school, Kobe Bryant has incredible one-on-one skills but is raw as sushi. Derek Fisher also had a solid rookie campaign, backing up Van Exel at the one. **Grade: B+**

Forward: Traded from Houston to Phoenix to L.A., Robert Horry missed 25 games due to injuries after joining the Lakers. A terrific defender, he creates matchup problems with his postup ability and perimeter shooting. Elden Campbell improved his scoring average for the seventh straight year and played the best ball of his career during the 30-game span in which Shaquille O'Neal was injured. One of the league's biggest forwards, Campbell swats shots, pounds the boards, and scores in the paint. The Lakers dealt a first-round pick to acquire three-point sharpshooter George McCloud, who has an underrated all-around game. Thirteen-year veteran Jerome Kersey provided a defensive spark off the bench. **Grade: B–**

Center: Shaq was the only NBA player to average at least 25 points and ten rebounds last season, but he saw action in fewer than 55 contests for the second year in a row. Physically dominant when healthy, he weighs 20 to 50 pounds more than most centers and doesn't lack mobility or skills. Of course, he's also a sub-.500 shooter from the charity stripe, and non-L.A. fans feel that he commits an offensive foul every time he lowers his shoulder. **Grade: A+**

Lakers 1996–97 Player Statistics

	G	MIN	FG	FGA	FG%	FT	FTA	FT%	3FG	3FGA
O'Neal	51	1941	552	991	.557	232	479	.484	0	4
Jones	80	2998	473	1081	.438	276	337	.819	152	389
Van Exel	79	2937	432	1075	.402	165	200	.825	177	468
Campbell	77	2576	442	942	.469	263	370	.711	1	4
McCloud	64	1493	238	578	.412	83	101	.822	99	254
Horry	54	1395	157	360	.436	60	90	.667	49	154
Bryant	71	1103	176	422	.417	136	166	.819	51	136
Kersey	70	1766	194	449	.432	71	118	.602	17	65
Scott	79	1440	163	379	.430	127	151	.841	73	188
Knight	71	1156	140	275	.509	62	100	.620	0	0
Blount	58	1009	92	179	.514	56	83	.675	1	3
Fisher	80	921	104	262	.397	79	120	.658	22	73
Rooks	69	735	87	185	.470	91	130	.700	0	1
Krystkowiak	3	11	1	2	.500	1	2	.500	0	0

	ORB	REB	AST	STL	TO	BLK	PF	PTS	PPG
O'Neal	195	640	159	46	146	147	180	1336	26.2
Jones	90	326	270	189	169	49	226	1374	17.2
Van Exel	44	226	672	75	212	10	110	1206	15.3
Campbell	207	615	126	46	130	117	276	1148	14.9
McCloud	36	179	109	61	61	8	126	658	10.3
Horry	68	237	110	66	72	55	153	423	7.8
Bryant	47	132	91	49	112	23	102	539	7.6
Kersey	112	363	89	119	74	49	219	476	6.8
Scott	21	118	99	46	53	16	72	526	6.7
Knight	130	319	39	31	49	58	170	342	4.8
Blount	113	276	35	22	50	26	121	241	4.2
Fisher	25	97	119	41	71	5	87	309	3.9
Rooks	56	163	42	17	51	38	123	265	3.8
Krystkowiak	2	5	3	2	1	0	3	3	1.0

Lakers 1996–97 Team Statistics

Final Record: 56–26

Home Record: 31–10

Road Record: 25–16

Division Record: 18–5

Conference Record: 37–15

Overtime Record: 4–3

Points Per Game: 100.0

Opponents Points Per Game: 95.7

Field Goal Percentage: .454

Opponents Field Goal Percentage: .441

Turnovers Per Game: 14.9

Opponents Turnovers Per Game: 16.4

Offensive Rebounding Percentage: .316

Defensive Rebounding Percentage: .685

Total Rebounding Percentage: .500

Scored Fewer Than 100 Points: 43

Opponents Scored Fewer Than 100 Points: 52

Lakers Clipboard

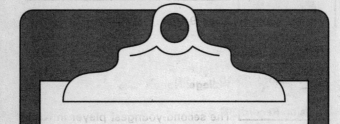

Why the Lakers win: Young superstars and a deep bench give L.A. the ability to run most teams off the court. The power of O'Neal and Campbell provides an ideal complement to the athleticism and outside shooting of Jones and Bryant.

Why the Lakers lose: Injuries to Shaq are an obvious factor, as are his foibles at the free throw line. Those nights when Van Exel is distracted or shooting poorly, the team as a whole can look completely out of synch.

1996–97 MVP: Eddie Jones

Projected MVP: Shaquille O'Neal

Fast Fact: The Lakers joined Chicago as the only two teams not to lose more than two straight games at any point during the 1996–97 season.

Kobe Bryant G

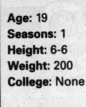

Age: 19
Seasons: 1
Height: 6-6
Weight: 200
College: None

The second-youngest player in NBA history, Bryant has the height, quickness, and creativity to become a megastar before he's old enough to quaff championship champagne.

	G	MPG	FG%	3FG%	FT%	APG	RPG	PPG	BLK	STL
1996–97	71	15.5	.417	.375	.819	1.3	1.9	7.6	23	49
Career	71	15.5	.417	.375	.819	1.3	1.9	7.6	23	49

Elden Campbell F/C

Age: 29
Seasons: 7
Height: 6-11
Weight: 250
College: Clemson

One of the few players who swings from the four to the five without much dropoff, Campbell protects the basket and has developed into a consistent scoring threat.

	G	MPG	FG%	3FG%	FT%	APG	RPG	PPG	BLK	STL
1996–97	77	32.7	.469	.250	.711	1.6	8.0	14.9	117	46
Career	520	25.7	.469	.059	.679	1.2	5.9	10.5	903	390

Robert Horry   F

Age: 27
Seasons: 5
Height: 6-10
Weight: 220
College: Alabama

Often knocked for not attacking the basket with regularity, Horry won two NBA titles while in Houston and is arguably the league's best shot blocker among small forwards.

	G	MPG	FG%	3FG%	FT%	APG	RPG	PPG	BLK	STL
1996–97	54	25.8	.436	.318	.667	2.1	4.5	7.8	55	66
Career	349	31.0	.446	.349	.733	3.0	5.2	10.1	398	475

Eddie Jones   G/F

Age: 26
Seasons: 3
Height: 6-6
Weight: 190
College: Temple

A steady demeanor and highlight-film skills make Jones a fan favorite. He's solid from beyond the arc, reliable from the free throw line, dynamite in the open floor, and a stopper on defense.

	G	MPG	FG%	3FG%	FT%	APG	RPG	PPG	BLK	STL
1996–97	80	37.6	.438	.391	.819	3.4	4.1	17.2	49	189
Career	214	33.5	.460	.379	.774	3.0	3.8	14.8	135	449

Jerome Kersey F

Age: 35
Seasons: 13
Height: 6-7
Weight: 240
College: Longwood

A small-college success story, Kersey has made a fine career out of running the floor and doing the dirty work on defense. At this point, his game is more effective than attractive.

	G	MPG	FG%	3FG%	FT%	APG	RPG	PPG	BLK	STL
1996–97	70	25.2	.432	.262	.602	1.3	5.2	6.8	49	119
Career	977	25.7	.470	.213	.694	2.0	5.9	11.3	716	1269

Travis Knight C

Age: 23
Seasons: 1
Height: 7-0
Weight: 235
College: Connecticut

Now playing for Boston, Knight had a better-than-expected rookie season and was invaluable when O'Neal got hurt. Skinny but mobile, he has a soft shooting touch and keen instincts.

	G	MPG	FG%	3FG%	FT%	APG	RPG	PPG	BLK	STL
1996–97	71	16.4	.509	.000	.620	0.5	4.5	4.8	58	31
Career	71	16.4	.509	.000	.620	0.5	4.5	4.8	58	31

George McCloud　　　　　G/F

Age: 30
Seasons: 7
Height: 6-8
Weight: 225
College: Florida State

A former lottery bust, McCloud came back to the NBA after a stint in Italy and put up 18.9 ppg for Dallas in 1995–96. He has decent overall skills but is primarily a designated three-point bomber.

	G	MPG	FG%	3FG%	FT%	APG	RPG	PPG	BLK	STL
1996–97	64	23.3	.412	.390	.822	1.7	2.8	10.3	8	61
Career	432	20.9	.407	.367	.795	2.0	2.8	9.1	91	335

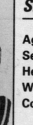

Shaquille O'Neal　　　　　C

Age: 25
Seasons: 5
Height: 7-1
Weight: 300
College: Louisiana State

All the hype mongers and knee-jerk critics aside, O'Neal is the first Laker since Abdul-Jabbar to average more than 20 points and ten rebounds in a year, a trick Shaq has turned each season of his career.

	G	MPG	FG%	3FG%	FT%	APG	RPG	PPG	BLK	STL
1996–97	51	38.1	.557	.000	.484	3.1	12.5	26.2	147	46
Career	346	37.9	.577	.067	.537	2.5	12.5	27.0	971	289

Byron Scott G

Age: 36
Seasons: 14
Height: 6-4
Weight: 205
College: Arizona State

Although he failed to score in double figures for the first time in his career, it was nice to see Scott back in an L.A. uniform after a three-year absence. Not re-signed, he'll be playing in Greece this season.

	G	MPG	FG%	3FG%	FT%	APG	RPG	PPG	BLK	STL
1996–97	79	18.2	.430	.388	.841	1.3	1.5	6.7	16	46
Career	1073	28.1	.482	.370	.833	2.5	2.8	14.1	276	1224

Nick Van Exel G

Age: 26
Seasons: 4
Height: 6-1
Weight: 183
College: Cincinnati

A talented but erratic point guard, Van Exel is capable of sparking the Lakers one night and making them blow up the next. He finished seventh in the league in assist-to-turnover ratio last year.

	G	MPG	FG%	3FG%	FT%	APG	RPG	PPG	BLK	STL
1996–97	79	37.2	.402	.378	.825	8.5	2.9	15.3	10	75
Career	314	35.3	.408	.359	.796	7.3	2.8	15.1	34	327

Isaac Austin

Miami
HEAT

Franchise History: Miami joined the league in 1988–89 as a member of the Western Conference. The Heat posted a paltry 15 victories in their inaugural run, five fewer than fellow expansionites Charlotte. After drafting Rony Seikaly, Glen Rice, and Steve Smith, Miami switched conferences, then made its first trip to the playoffs in 1991–92. Two years later, the Heat were postseason participants again, but the franchise smoldered until Pat Riley was hired to clean house in 1995–96.

1996–97 Review: With the personnel-reshuffling process nearly complete, Riley's warriors quickly established that they would be division-title contenders. Tim Hardaway put together a campaign that spurred MVP consideration, and Zo Mourning dominated when healthy. Following a 61-win regular season, Miami slipped by cross-state foe Orlando, 3–2. Next to fall was arch rival New York, in a controversy-riddled seven-game semifinals. After all that, the season ended rather quietly at the hands of the Bulls.

1997–98 Preview: Riley has done a masterful job in a short time, and the team has his stamp all over it. Miami plays the type of defense that makes opposition offenses look inept. On the other hand, there were crucial stretches in both the Knicks and Bulls playoff series when the Heat just couldn't score. They have the look and feel of a club that squeezes every drop from its talent—much as the Knicks did under Riley—but may not be equipped to reach the top of the mountain.

Heat Veteran Roster

No	Player	Pos	Ht	Wt	Exp
35	Willie Anderson	G	6-8	200	9
2	Keith Askins	G/F	6-8	224	7
8	Isaac Austin	C	6-10	270	4
42	P.J. Brown	F	6-11	240	4
11	John Crotty	G	6-1	185	5
23	Gary Grant	G	6-3	185	9
10	Tim Hardaway	G	6-0	195	8
21	Voshon Lenard	G	6-4	205	2
9	Dan Majerle	G/F	6-6	220	9
24	Jamal Mashburn	F	6-8	250	4
33	Alonzo Mourning	C	6-10	261	5
54	Ed Pinckney	F	6-9	240	12
30	Mark Strickland	F	6-9	220	2

Head Coach: Pat Riley

Heat 1997 Draft Picks

Rookie	College	Position
Charles Smith (1-26)	New Mexico	Guard
Mark Sanford (2-31)	Washington	Forward

Smith handles the ball well and can create opportunities for himself and his teammates. He paced the Lobos in scoring in each of the past three seasons, and he departs New Mexico with impressive career numbers, including 1,000 points, 500 boards, and 200 triples. He was first-team All-WAC as a junior and as a senior. Mark Sanford, who specializes in getting to the hole and converting, was an early-entry candidate who also declared in 1996 but changed his mind and returned to school. He was the leading scorer and rebounder for the Huskies last year.

Heat Scouting Report

Guard: In point guard Tim Hardaway, the Heat have an aggressive on-court leader who creates for himself and his teammates. Miami's offense invariably begins or ends with Tim Bug, as evidenced by his team-leading totals of assists and three-point attempts. He has averaged 129 steals in his eight-year career but is vulnerable to post-ups. Voshon Lenard saw vastly increased minutes in his second season, and he responded by shooting .414 from beyond the arc. His emergence as a reliable perimeter threat was huge in the wake of Dan Majerle's back problems. The backcourt subs are John Crotty at the one, plus Majerle and Keith Askins, who will both swing between the two and the one as Riley deems necessary. **Grade: B**

Forward: P.J. Brown turned in a solid campaign at the four, finishing second on the team in rebounding. He is a top defender who can match up at different positions and make his opponents sweat for points. Unfortunately, he'll struggle to score in double figures himself—regardless of who guards him. Small forward Jamal Mashburn can score from any spot on the floor, but his defense and shot selection typically rate equal to Brown's production on offense. He remains a potential All-Star, with "potential" being the operative word. **Grade: C+**

Center: Alonzo Mourning was hampered by a foot injury but wound up second on the team in scoring and tops in rebounding. He brings plenty of intensity and muscle to the interior, and he is tough to stop when fed the ball on the low blocks. Speaking of feeding, Zo's backup at the five is Isaac Austin, who shed about 70 pounds of fat and returned to the NBA after a two-season absence. He still carries 270 pounds on his 6-10 frame but is surprisingly mobile and active in the paint. **Grade: A**

Heat 1996–97 Player Statistics

	G	MIN	FG	FGA	FG%	FT	FTA	FT%	3FG	3FGA
Hardaway	81	3136	575	1384	.415	291	364	.799	203	590
Mourning	66	2320	473	885	.534	363	565	.642	1	9
Lenard	73	2111	314	684	.459	86	105	.819	183	442
Mashburn	69	2164	286	743	.385	160	228	.702	90	277
Majerle	36	1264	141	347	.406	40	59	.678	68	201
Austin	82	1881	321	639	.502	150	226	.664	0	3
Brown	80	2592	300	656	.457	161	220	.732	0	2
Askins	78	1773	138	319	.433	39	58	.672	69	172
Crotty	48	659	79	154	.513	54	64	.844	20	49
Grant	28	365	39	110	.355	18	22	.818	14	46
Anderson	28	303	29	64	.453	17	20	.850	8	19
Pinckney	27	273	23	43	.535	20	25	.800	0	0
Strickland	31	153	25	60	.417	12	21	.571	0	1
Fish	6	8	1	3	.333	0	0	.000	0	0
Scott	8	32	0	8	.000	1	2	.500	0	4
Bowen	1	1	0	0	.000	0	0	.000	0	0

	ORB	REB	AST	STL	TO	BLK	PF	PTS	PPG
Hardaway	49	277	695	151	230	9	165	1644	20.3
Mourning	189	656	104	56	226	189	272	1310	19.8
Lenard	38	217	161	50	109	18	168	897	12.3
Mashburn	69	294	204	78	114	12	186	822	11.9
Majerle	45	162	116	54	50	14	75	390	10.8
Austin	136	470	101	45	161	43	244	792	9.7
Brown	239	670	92	85	113	98	283	761	9.5
Askins	86	271	75	53	59	19	196	384	4.9
Crotty	15	47	102	18	42	0	79	232	4.8
Grant	8	38	45	16	27	0	39	110	3.9
Anderson	15	42	34	14	19	4	36	83	3.0
Pinckney	25	65	6	8	19	9	30	66	2.4
Strickland	16	37	1	4	15	10	17	62	2.0
Fish	1	5	0	0	2	0	2	2	0.3
Scott	1	6	3	2	2	0	5	1	0.1
Bowen	0	0	0	0	0	1	0	0	0.0

Heat 1996–97 Team Statistics

Final Record: 61–21

Home Record: 29–12

Road Record: 32–9

Division Record: 16–8

Conference Record: 40–14

Overtime Record: 3–1

Points Per Game: 94.8

Opponents Points Per Game: 89.3

Field Goal Percentage: .453

Opponents Field Goal Percentage: .432

Turnovers Per Game: 15.9

Opponents Turnovers Per Game: 16.1

Offensive Rebounding Percentage: .292

Defensive Rebounding Percentage: .706

Total Rebounding Percentage: .499

Scored Fewer Than 100 Points: 54

Opponents Scored Fewer Than 100 Points: 71

Heat Clipboard

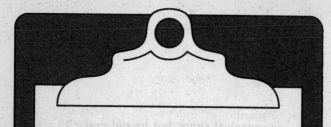

Why the Heat win: It all starts with the defense, which allows Hardaway to get into the open floor, where he can drive and finish or kick the rock out to Lenard. The presence of Zo and P.J. usually gives Miami control of the lane.

Why the Heat lose: Mourning can be a very unsteady shooter beyond 12 feet, and his passing out of double teams doesn't draw raves. As a team, the Heat will turn the ball over when pressured. Zo's emotions and penchant for fouls often cause problems.

1996–97 MVP: Tim Hardaway

Projected MVP: Alonzo Mourning

Fast Fact: At 32–9, Miami was the only team not to post double-figure losses in road games last season.

Keith Askins   *G/F*

Age: 30
Seasons: 7
Height: 6-8
Weight: 224
College: Alabama

Askins wasn't a full-on member of the Miami career-revival show, but he did make 30 starts (double his previous high) while finishing second on the team in three-point accuracy.

	G	MPG	FG%	3FG%	FT%	APG	RPG	PPG	BLK	STL
1996–97	78	22.7	.433	.401	.672	1.0	3.5	4.9	19	53
Career	407	16.9	.411	.367	.725	0.8	3.2	4.1	155	234

Isaac Austin   *C*

Age: 28
Seasons: 4
Height: 6-10
Weight: 270
College: Arizona State

Austin, who went from scarfing down cheeseburgers and playing in the Turkish league to being one of the NBA's best-ever comeback stories, was a huge factor when Mourning was injured.

	G	MPG	FG%	3FG%	FT%	APG	RPG	PPG	BLK	STL
1996–97	82	22.9	.502	.000	.664	1.2	5.8	9.7	43	45
Career	173	14.5	.488	.000	.656	0.7	3.8	6.1	69	60

P.J. Brown F

Age: 28
Seasons: 4
Height: 6-11
Weight: 240
College: Louisiana Tech

Brown is a below-average shooter but a great defender and rebounder. Strong and agile, with long arms and a willingness to mix it up down low, he has a blue-collar work ethic in a millionaire's league.

	G	MPG	FG%	3FG%	FT%	APG	RPG	PPG	BLK	STL
1996–97	80	32.4	.457	.000	.732	1.1	8.4	9.5	98	85
Career	320	31.1	.443	.170	.733	1.5	6.9	8.7	426	304

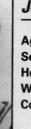

John Crotty G

Age: 28
Seasons: 5
Height: 6-1
Weight: 185
College: Virginia

A journeyman point guard who has bounced around the U.S. (Utah, Cleveland) and Italy, Crotty doesn't attempt many shots but tends to make the ones he does take.

	G	MPG	FG%	3FG%	FT%	APG	RPG	PPG	BLK	STL
1996–97	48	13.7	.513	.408	.844	2.1	1.0	4.8	0	18
Career	271	10.5	.455	.347	.819	2.0	0.9	3.4	13	105

Gary Grant   G

Age: 32
Seasons: 9
Height: 6-3
Weight: 185
College: Michigan

After seven years with the Clippers, Grant signed with the Knicks in 1995–96, then joined the Heat last season. He sat out the bulk of the campaign recovering from back surgery.

	G	MPG	FG%	3FG%	FT%	APG	RPG	PPG	BLK	STL
1996–97	28	13.0	.355	.304	.818	1.6	1.4	3.9	0	16
Career	521	23.4	.450	.272	.775	5.6	2.4	8.1	67	802

Tim Hardaway   G

Age: 31
Seasons: 8
Height: 6-0
Weight: 195
College: Texas–El Paso

Hardaway does everything a point guard should, except shoot for a high percentage. His crossover is a sight to behold, and he gets the ball into the right hands at the right time.

	G	MPG	FG%	3FG%	FT%	APG	RPG	PPG	BLK	STL
1996–97	81	38.7	.415	.344	.799	8.6	3.4	20.3	9	151
Career	531	37.3	.447	.353	.776	9.2	3.6	19.7	87	1030

Voshon Lenard   G

Age: 24
Seasons: 2
Height: 6-4
Weight: 205
College: Minnesota

Lenard gave Miami's offense a lift last season while doing the same for his own career. After averaging just 4.8 minutes in his first 10 games, he ended up seventh in the NBA in three-pointers converted.

	G	MPG	FG%	3FG%	FT%	APG	RPG	PPG	BLK	STL
1996–97	73	28.3	.459	.414	.819	2.2	3.0	12.3	18	50
Career	103	23.6	.445	.403	.811	1.9	2.6	10.4	19	56

Dan Majerle   G/F

Age: 32
Seasons: 9
Height: 6-6
Weight: 220
College: Central Michigan

Majerle shot fairly well in the playoffs after struggling through an injury-spoiled season. He still has incredible range and can contribute good defense at either the two or the three.

	G	MPG	FG%	3FG%	FT%	APG	RPG	PPG	BLK	STL
1996–97	36	35.1	.406	.338	.678	3.2	4.5	10.8	14	54
Career	648	33.7	.441	.362	.740	3.2	4.8	13.9	291	898

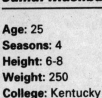

Jamal Mashburn F

Age: 25
Seasons: 4
Height: 6-8
Weight: 250
College: Kentucky

When his shots are falling, Mashburn looks like a rising star, but a quick glance at his field-goal success rate reveals otherwise. He may still be a Maverick at heart, but his defensive skills remain subpar.

	G	MPG	FG%	3FG%	FT%	APG	RPG	PPG	BLK	STL
1996–97	69	31.4	.385	.325	.702	3.0	4.3	11.9	12	78
Career	246	35.4	.411	.316	.719	3.3	4.4	19.0	37	263

Alonzo Mourning C

Age: 27
Seasons: 5
Height: 6-10
Weight: 261
College: Georgetown

Zo is such a great player—one of the five best centers in the NBA—but one wonders if he has the internal makeup to win a championship at this phase of his career. It takes more than intensity; it takes focus.

	G	MPG	FG%	3FG%	FT%	APG	RPG	PPG	BLK	STL
1996–97	66	35.2	.534	.111	.642	1.6	9.9	19.8	189	56
Career	351	35.9	.519	.269	.727	1.5	10.1	21.4	1062	229

Vin Baker

Milwaukee
BUCKS

Franchise History: The Bucks entered the NBA in 1968–69, finished last in their division, won a coin toss with the Suns, and drafted Lew Alcindor. The next year they won 56 games, then added Oscar Robertson in the offseason and brought home an NBA title in 1970–71. After trading Alcindor, who by that time was Kareem Abdul-Jabbar, the franchise rebuilt around Sidney Moncrief and Marques Johnson. Milwaukee won seven straight division titles in the 1980s but never made it back to the Finals.

1996–97 Review: The Bucks added a rookie shooting guard, Ray Allen, to the forward duo of Glenn Robinson and Vin Baker, and the team improved by eight wins over the previous season. Of course, the franchise was still far from upper echelon. Head coach Chris Ford made the most of the mediocre roster assembled by general manager Mike Dunleavy, who was fired at season's end, but only the two-year-old Toronto Raptors kept Milwaukee out of the division cellar.

1997–98 Preview: The Bucks are attempting to address a serious weakness—the lack of an interior enforcer—by putting Ervin Johnson at center. It cost them two veteran bench players and their top draft pick to acquire Johnson, who blocked 227 shots for the awful Nuggets last year. If he delivers as hoped, Baker and Big Dog stay healthy, and Allen makes progress, the Bucks will be set at four spots. With the Cavaliers and Pacers struggling, this could be Milwaukee's year to make the playoffs.

Bucks Veteran Roster

No	Player	Pos	Ht	Wt	Exp
34	Ray Allen	G	6-5	205	1
42	Vin Baker	F	6-11	245	4
20	Sherman Douglas	G	6-1	195	8
55	Acie Earl	F/C	6-10	240	4
10	Armon Gilliam	F	6-9	260	10
—	Ervin Johnson	C	6-11	245	4
28	Andrew Lang	C	6-11	275	9
5	Elliot Perry	G	6-0	160	5
13	Glenn Robinson	F	6-7	235	3

Head Coach: Chris Ford

Bucks 1997 Draft Picks

Rookie	College	Position
Danny Fortson (1-10)	Cincinnati	Forward
Jerald Honeycutt (2-39)	Tulane	Forward

The Bucks delivered Danny Fortson, along with veterans Joe Wolf and Johnny Newman, to Denver on draft day in exchange for center Ervin Johnson. They used the 39th pick to acquire Jerald Honeycutt, a 6-9, 245-pound forward from Tulane. As a senior, he was a first-team all-conference selection for the third year in a row. He amassed over 200 steals and 800 rebounds in his career. His ballhandling skills and midrange shot may be good enough for him to swing between small forward and the four, but if not, he'll be used primarily at power forward. Known more for his raw talent than his intangibles—his attitude and work ethic have often been questioned—he played very well in the Chicago pre-draft camp and could have been selected late in the first round.

Bucks Scouting Report

Guard: Milwaukee could do worse than the two-player rotation of Elliot Perry and Sherman Douglas at the point. They combined to hand out over 650 assists and shoot .490 from the floor last season. Both have paid some dues and survived to see quality NBA minutes, but neither is ever going to be considered an All-Star. One player who many scouts feel is on his way toward elite status is Ray Allen, who went through the typical rookie growing pains but flashed the inside-outside ability that made him 1996's fifth pick overall. **Grade: C**

Forward: The Bucks boasted one of the three 20-ppg duos in the NBA last year, and the only such frontcourt tandem. Glenn Robinson plays the three, and although he is far from perfect, there is no questioning his knack for scoring. His jumper is soft and reliable, his post-up repertoire can be unstoppable, and he can create off the dribble. Knocks about his leadership and defense continue to dog him. In contrast to Big Dog, power forward Vin Baker is often called underrated. Of course, if everyone thinks that a player is underrated, does that not render the perception false by definition? Just asking. In any case, Baker is graceful and intense, with a balanced array of low-post skills. The prime flaw in Milwaukee's frontcourt is turnovers: Robinson and Baker committed an outrageous 500 between them. Backup forward/center Armon Gilliam remains an adept scorer in the twilight of his career. **Grade: B+**

Center: Like so many middle-tier centers, Ervin Johnson is one-dimensional. He bagged better than 900 rebounds for the chicken Nuggets last year, but he scored barely seven points per game. His backup, Andrew Lang, is another prolific defender. He has had one year of double-figure scoring in nine seasons as a pro. **Grade: C**

Bucks 1996–97 Player Statistics

	G	MIN	FG	FGA	FG%	FT	FTA	FT%	3FG	3FGA
Robinson	80	3114	669	1438	.465	288	364	.791	63	180
Baker	78	3159	632	1251	.505	358	521	.687	15	54
Allen	82	2532	390	908	.430	205	249	.823	117	298
Douglas	79	2316	306	610	.502	114	171	.667	38	114
Newman	82	2060	246	547	.450	189	247	.765	34	98
Gilliam	80	2050	246	522	.471	199	259	.768	0	0
Perry	82	1595	217	458	.474	79	106	.745	49	137
Lang	52	1194	115	248	.464	44	61	.721	0	0
Earl	47	500	67	180	.372	54	84	.643	0	5
Brown	70	757	78	154	.506	47	70	.671	1	6
Wolf	56	525	40	89	.449	14	19	.737	1	7
Tower	5	72	3	8	.375	1	8	.152	0	0
Carruth	4	21	2	3	.667	1	1	1.000	0	0
Wood	46	240	20	38	.526	12	18	.667	5	15
Martin	3	13	0	7	.000	0	0	.000	0	2

	ORB	REB	AST	STL	TO	BLK	PF	PTS	PPG
Robinson	130	502	248	103	269	68	225	1689	21.1
Baker	267	804	211	81	245	112	275	1637	21.0
Allen	97	326	210	75	149	10	218	1102	13.4
Douglas	57	193	427	78	153	10	191	764	9.7
Newman	66	186	116	73	115	17	257	715	8.7
Gilliam	136	497	53	61	105	40	206	691	8.6
Perry	24	124	247	98	111	3	117	562	6.9
Lang	94	278	25	26	39	47	140	274	5.3
Earl	35	96	20	15	35	28	61	188	4.0
Brown	41	148	28	9	19	22	100	204	2.9
Wolf	32	112	20	14	14	11	105	95	1.7
Tower	2	9	1	2	2	1	12	7	1.4
Carruth	0	4	0	0	1	2	4	5	1.3
Wood	5	27	13	7	6	6	36	57	1.2
Martin	1	1	1	0	1	0	1	0	0.0

Bucks 1996–97 Team Statistics

Final Record: 33–49

Home Record: 20–21

Road Record: 13–28

Division Record: 10–18

Conference Record: 22–32

Overtime Record: 2–0

Points Per Game: 95.3

Opponents Points Per Game: 97.2

Field Goal Percentage: .471

Opponents Field Goal Percentage: .472

Turnovers Per Game: 15.7

Opponents Turnovers Per Game: 14.6

Offensive Rebounding Percentage: .297

Defensive Rebounding Percentage: .699

Total Rebounding Percentage: .498

Scored Fewer Than 100 Points: 52

Opponents Scored Fewer Than 100 Points: 50

Bucks Clipboard

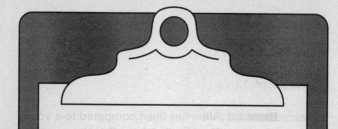

Why the Bucks win: Milwaukee is one of the few non-playoff teams that has three legitimate scorers. Allen, Baker, and Robinson are all capable of pouring in 30. The defense should be bolstered by the presence of Ervin Johnson.

Why the Bucks lose: The Bucks seem to lack the crucial ingredient of winning teams: All-Star veteran leadership. Few opponents fear the Milwaukee point guards. The bench is both shallow and weak.

1996–97 MVP: Vin Baker

Projected MVP: Vin Baker

Fast Fact: Milwaukee's new center, Ervin Johnson, finished fifth in the league in blocks per game and fourth in rebounding last season.

Ray Allen G

Age: 22
Seasons: 1
Height: 6-5
Weight: 205
College: Connecticut

Allen has been compared to a young Jordan (who hasn't?) and called Jerry Stackhouse with a jump shot. Given his age, talent, and the quality of his first-year numbers, it's easy to justify the hype.

	G	MPG	FG%	3FG%	FT%	APG	RPG	PPG	BLK	STL
1996–97	82	30.9	.430	.393	.823	2.6	4.0	13.4	10	75
Career	82	30.9	.430	.393	.823	2.6	4.0	13.4	10	75

Vin Baker F

Age: 26
Seasons: 4
Height: 6-11
Weight: 245
College: Hartford

Baker can score from any spot inside 18 feet, control the boards, and wreak havoc on defense. He has averaged a double-double for three consecutive seasons while averaging 100-plus blocked shots.

	G	MPG	FG%	3FG%	FT%	APG	RPG	PPG	BLK	STL
1996–97	78	40.5	.505	.278	.687	2.7	10.3	21.0	112	81
Career	324	38.3	.494	.252	.634	2.7	9.5	18.3	433	295

Chucky Brown   F

Age: 29
Seasons: 8
Height: 6-8
Weight: 215
College: North Carolina State

Brown, who has played for six NBA franchises, found his way through the CBA-to-Houston pipeline. He isn't a very strong or silky scorer, but he will run the floor and make his layups.

	G	MPG	FG%	3FG%	FT%	APG	RPG	PPG	BLK	STL
1996–97	70	10.8	.506	.167	.671	0.4	2.1	2.9	22	9
Career	462	17.4	.514	.083	.701	0.8	3.3	6.2	154	158

Sherman Douglas   G

Age: 31
Seasons: 8
Height: 6-1
Weight: 195
College: Syracuse

Douglas is not a pure shooter, and he doesn't have the quickness of most starting point guards. Yet he gets to the basket, finishes in traffic, and usually won't embarrass himself on defense.

	G	MPG	FG%	3FG%	FT%	APG	RPG	PPG	BLK	STL
1996–97	79	29.3	.502	.333	.667	5.4	2.4	9.7	10	78
Career	576	29.9	.489	.274	.674	6.8	2.4	12.3	62	650

Armon Gilliam F

Age: 33
Seasons: 10
Height: 6-9
Weight: 260
College: UNLV

The Hammer is slowing down a bit, but he still attacks the hoop with a variety of short shots and his trademark aggressiveness. Last season was the first in which he has failed to score in double figures.

	G	MPG	FG%	3FG%	FT%	APG	RPG	PPG	BLK	STL
1996–97	80	25.6	.471	.000	.768	0.7	6.2	8.6	40	61
Career	763	30.0	.492	.000	.773	1.2	7.4	14.6	542	577

Andrew Lang C

Age: 31
Seasons: 9
Height: 6-11
Weight: 275
College: Arkansas

Lang has a wide body but is agile for his size. He hustles on defense, rejects shots with gusto, and works hard in practice. A touch-and-go scorer, he looks capable in spurts but rarely sees double figures.

	G	MPG	FG%	3FG%	FT%	APG	RPG	PPG	BLK	STL
1996–97	52	23.0	.464	.000	.721	0.5	5.3	5.3	47	26
Career	640	21.9	.479	.263	.746	0.6	5.0	6.5	1054	301

Johnny Newman   G/F

Age: 34
Seasons: 11
Height: 6-7
Weight: 200
College: Richmond

Now playing for Denver, the athletic Newman used to be a scorer who could slash to the rack or knock down the three. These days he is used primarily as a defensive stopper.

	G	MPG	FG%	3FG%	FT%	APG	RPG	PPG	BLK	STL
1996–97	82	25.1	.450	.347	.765	1.4	2.3	8.7	17	73
Career	824	25.2	.471	.324	.804	1.6	2.4	11.5	185	814

Elliot Perry   G

Age: 28
Seasons: 5
Height: 6-0
Weight: 160
College: Memphis State

Perry worked his way out of the CBA and into Phoenix in 1993-94. He made a solid impression in semi-regular duty, then moved on to Milwaukee last season. He's a decent shooter and a pest on defense.

	G	MPG	FG%	3FG%	FT%	APG	RPG	PPG	BLK	STL
1996–97	82	19.5	.474	.358	.745	3.0	1.5	6.9	3	98
Career	322	19.0	.476	.372	.773	3.7	1.5	7.1	16	400

Glenn Robinson   F

Age: 25
Seasons: 3
Height: 6-7
Weight: 235
College: Purdue

Big Dog is an all-around talent, able to light it up from anywhere and against anyone. He led the Bucks in scoring and steals last season, and finished second in total rebounds and assists.

	G	MPG	FG%	3FG%	FT%	APG	RPG	PPG	BLK	STL
1996–97	80	38.9	.465	.350	.791	3.1	6.3	21.1	68	103
Career	242	38.5	.457	.336	.800	3.0	6.3	21.1	132	313

Joe Wolf   F/C

Age: 33
Seasons: 9
Height: 6-11
Weight: 260
College: North Carolina

Wolf, who has been traded to Denver, will be with his eighth NBA team. He isn't a bad player to have around in a pinch, but his skills are just barely pro quality.

	G	MPG	FG%	3FG%	FT%	APG	RPG	PPG	BLK	STL
1996–97	56	9.4	.449	.143	.737	0.4	2.0	1.7	11	14
Career	532	16.9	.428	.160	.780	1.1	3.4	4.5	124	237

Paul Grant

Minnesota
TIMBERWOLVES

Franchise History: The T-wolves entered the league with Orlando in 1989–90; and that has been the only season in which Minnesota has posted a better record than their expansion sister. In fact, it wasn't until 1995–96 that the Timberwolves managed to have a .500 month, much less a winning season. But the prevailing wind has started to change since Kevin McHale took over as GM in 1995–96. The subsequent arrival of Kevin Garnett and Stephon Marbury led to the franchise's first playoff appearance.

1996–97 Review: Minnesota took advantage of a very soft schedule in January and February to go 17–9 during that span. They played roughly .400 ball for the other four months of the campaign, but it was enough to earn them a first taste of postseason action. Garnett, Marbury, and Tom Gugliotta were the mainstays of Minnesota's success, but the team would not have won 40 games without the help of center Dean Garrett, the NBA's oldest rookie at age 30. The T-wolves were swept by Houston in the first round.

1997–98 Preview: Googs, Garnett, Garrett, and Marbury have a mere nine years of NBA experience combined. By comparison, the Houston playoff roster featured seven players with at least 13 seasons of league service apiece. Experience is the one factor that separates championship contenders from the rest of the playoff pack. Minnesota has taken an initial step on the path to excellence and will probably progress further this season, but don't expect postseason advancement just yet.

Timberwolves Veteran Roster

No	Player	Pos	Ht	Wt	Exp
43	Chris Carr	G	6-6	220	2
15	Bill Curley	F	6-9	245	3
21	Kevin Garnett	F	6-11	220	2
22	Dean Garrett	C	6-11	250	1
24	Tom Gugliotta	F	6-10	240	5
3	Stephon Marbury	G	6-2	180	1
42	Sam Mitchell	F	6-7	215	8
44	Cherokee Parks	F/C	6-11	240	2
30	Terry Porter	G	6-3	195	12
—	Stanley Roberts	C	7-0	290	6
26	James Robinson	G	6-2	180	4
5	Doug West	G/F	6-6	220	8
4	Micheal Williams	G	6-2	175	9

Head Coach: Phil "Flip" Saunders

Timberwolves 1997 Draft Picks

Rookie	College	Position
Paul Grant (1-20)	Wisconsin	Center
Gordon Malone (2-44)	West Virginia	Center

Grant put in three unremarkable years at Boston College (4.3 ppg, 3.1 rpg) before transferring to Wisconsin for his senior season. A late bloomer, he topped the Badgers in scoring (12.5 ppg). He has NBA size (7-0, 245) but doesn't have great bulk and isn't a force on the boards. T-wolves fans can expect durability and hustle from Grant. Gordon Malone joins the NBA after playing two seasons at West Virginia; he sat out his freshman year and left following his junior campaign. He is a strong rebounder who can be used at the four or five.

Timberwolves Scouting Report

Guard: After just one season at Georgia Tech, point guard Stephon Marbury arrived in Minnesota and finished as runner-up for Rookie of the Year. He sat out 15 games with minor injuries but still became the first T-wolves rookie to register 1,000 points and 500 assists. His outside shooting was predictably erratic but should improve over time. Terry Porter, who saw action in every contest and made 18 starts at the point, was also unreliable from long range. Doug West, the last of the original T-wolves, was a starter in all but two of his 68 appearances. A true survivor, he is tremendous in the open court but is not an explosive scorer or a threat from three-point range. Chris Carr flashed an improved shooting stroke before an ankle injury put him on a shelf for the final 18 games. **Grade: C**

Forward: Tom Gugliotta emerged as one of the league's most complete forwards last season, pacing the T-wolves in rebounding and scoring, while ranking seventh among NBA forwards in steals. No frontcourt player commits more turnovers, but only an elite few (Mason, Pippen, Hill, Malone) dish out more assists. Kevin Garnett joined Googs on the All-Star squad and is arguably the NBA's hottest property in terms of established value and future potential. He lacks bulk and experience but is otherwise a rare all-around talent who swats shots, collects caroms, and piles up points. **Grade: A**

Center: Dean Garrett, who made his NBA debut after seven seasons in Italy and Greece, stabilized the five spot by averaging ten points on 60-percent shooting, plus nine rebounds, as a starter in the final 44 games of the year. He understands the interior game and rarely gives up the rock. Stanley Roberts, who was picked up (it took ten men) in a trade with the Clippers, is a hefty backup. **Grade: B**

Timberwolves 1996–97 Player Statistics

	G	MIN	FG	FGA	FG%	FT	FTA	FT%	3FG	3FGA
Gugliotta	81	3131	592	1339	.442	464	566	.820	24	93
Garnett	77	2995	549	1100	.499	205	272	.754	6	21
Marbury	67	2324	355	871	.408	245	337	.727	102	288
Mitchell	82	2044	269	603	.446	224	295	.759	4	25
Robinson	69	1309	196	482	.407	78	114	.684	102	267
Garrett	68	1665	223	389	.573	96	138	.696	0	0
West	68	1920	226	484	.467	64	94	.681	15	45
Porter	82	1568	187	449	.416	127	166	.765	67	200
Carr	55	830	125	271	.461	56	73	.767	31	88
Vrankovic	53	766	78	139	.561	25	37	.676	0	0
Parks	76	961	103	202	.510	46	76	.605	0	1
Jordan	19	130	16	26	.615	8	17	.471	0	0
Heal	43	236	26	97	.268	3	5	.600	20	65

	ORB	REB	AST	STL	TO	BLK	PF	PTS	PPG
Gugliotta	187	702	335	130	293	89	237	1672	20.6
Garnett	190	618	236	105	175	163	199	1309	17.0
Marbury	54	184	522	67	210	19	159	1057	15.8
Mitchell	112	326	79	51	93	20	232	766	9.3
Robinson	24	112	126	30	69	8	125	572	8.3
Garrett	149	495	38	40	34	95	158	542	8.0
West	37	148	113	61	66	24	218	531	7.8
Porter	31	176	295	54	128	11	104	568	6.9
Carr	31	113	48	24	37	10	93	337	6.1
Vrankovic	57	168	14	10	52	67	121	181	3.4
Parks	83	195	34	41	32	48	150	252	3.3
Jordan	11	27	12	7	8	3	15	40	2.1
Heal	2	18	33	3	17	3	20	75	1.7

Timberwolves 1996–97 Team Statistics

Final Record: 40–42

Home Record: 25–16

Road Record: 15–26

Division Record: 16–8

Conference Record: 28–24

Overtime Record: 2–1

Points Per Game: 96.1

Opponents Points Per Game: 97.6

Field Goal Percentage: .456

Opponents Field Goal Percentage: .450

Turnovers Per Game: 15.2

Opponents Turnovers Per Game: 15.6

Offensive Rebounding Percentage: .288

Defensive Rebounding Percentage: .683

Total Rebounding Percentage: .486

Scored Fewer Than 100 Points: 52

Opponents Scored Fewer Than 100 Points: 44

Timberwolves Clipboard

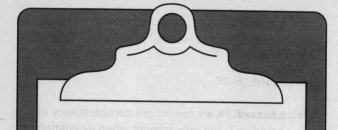

Why the Timberwolves win: When the T-wolves shoot well from the perimeter, which keeps opposition defenses from sagging down, Gugliotta and Garnett can use their mobility to full advantage.

Why the Timberwolves lose: Minnesota gives up some muscle down low and is often beaten on the boards. The lack of a top scorer at the two, which traditionally is a position of high-octane production, was a glaring weakness last season. The T-wolves sometimes struggle to close out opponents, especially on the road.

1996–97 MVP: Tom Gugliotta

Projected MVP: Kevin Garnett

Fast Fact: Flip Saunders won two CBA titles (1990 and 1992) as head coach of the La Crosse Catbirds.

Chris Carr   *G*

Age: 23
Seasons: 2
Height: 6-6
Weight: 220
College: Southern Illinois

Carr turned pro comparatively early, which should be taken into account when evaluating his progress. He improved dramatically in his three years at SIU and may do the same in the NBA if given minutes.

	G	MPG	FG%	3FG%	FT%	APG	RPG	PPG	BLK	STL
1996–97	55	15.1	.461	.352	.767	0.9	2.1	6.1	10	24
Career	115	12.3	.441	.323	.789	0.8	1.9	5.0	15	34

Kevin Garnett   *F*

Age: 21
Seasons: 2
Height: 6-11
Weight: 220
College: None

Just two years removed from Farragut Academy high school, Garnett has already become one of the best all-around frontcourt defenders in the NBA. He finished ninth in the league in blocks last year.

	G	MPG	FG%	3FG%	FT%	APG	RPG	PPG	BLK	STL
1996–97	77	38.9	.499	.286	.754	3.1	8.0	17.0	163	105
Career	157	33.7	.496	.286	.736	2.4	7.1	13.7	294	191

Dean Garrett   C

Age: 31
Seasons: 1
Height: 6-11
Weight: 250
College: Indiana

Garrett honed his skills in Europe for seven years, so his rookie status was strictly technical. He does a nice job of getting position for rebounds and has the mobility to be a defensive stopper.

	G	MPG	FG%	3FG%	FT%	APG	RPG	PPG	BLK	STL
1996-97	68	24.5	.573	.000	.696	0.6	7.3	8.0	95	40
Career	68	24.5	.573	.000	.696	0.6	7.3	8.0	95	40

Tom Gugliotta   F

Age: 28
Seasons: 5
Height: 6-10
Weight: 240
College: North Carolina State

Much of the Minnesota offense is run through Googs because he is so versatile and unselfish, but his ratio of turnovers to assists isn't impressive. Few forwards get fouled more often than Gugliotta does.

	G	MPG	FG%	3FG%	FT%	APG	RPG	PPG	BLK	STL
1996-97	81	38.7	.442	.258	.820	4.1	8.7	20.6	89	130
Career	395	35.8	.449	.290	.740	3.6	8.8	16.3	333	707

Stephon Marbury   *G*

Age: 20
Seasons: 1
Height: 6-2
Weight: 180
College: Georgia Tech

Marbury had an up-and-down, albeit promising, rookie season. He registered two months of sub-.300 three-point accuracy, two others of plus-.440 success, and he spent two stints on the injured list.

	G	MPG	FG%	3FG%	FT%	APG	RPG	PPG	BLK	STL
1996–97	67	34.7	.408	.354	.727	7.8	2.7	15.8	19	67
Career	67	34.7	.408	.354	.727	7.8	2.7	15.8	19	67

Sam Mitchell   *F*

Age: 34
Seasons: 8
Height: 6-7
Weight: 215
College: Mercer

Although he doesn't do any one thing consistently well, Mitchell provides flexibility by offering a little of everything (except three-point range). He had a 28-point, 13-rebound effort versus Houston in December.

	G	MPG	FG%	3FG%	FT%	APG	RPG	PPG	BLK	STL
1996–97	82	24.9	.446	.160	.759	1.0	4.0	9.3	20	51
Career	641	24.6	.451	.109	.776	1.0	4.4	9.5	235	384

Cherokee Parks   F/C

Age: 25
Seasons: 2
Height: 6-11
Weight: 240
College: Duke

Parks, who shot .409 from the field as a rookie for Dallas, saw a slight reduction in minutes with the T-wolves but made a noticeable increase in efficiency on both ends of the court.

	G	MPG	FG%	3FG%	FT%	APG	RPG	PPG	BLK	STL
1996–97	76	12.6	.510	.000	.605	0.4	2.6	3.3	48	41
Career	140	13.1	.454	.259	.630	0.5	2.9	3.6	80	66

Terry Porter   G

Age: 34
Seasons: 12
Height: 6-3
Weight: 195
College: Wisconsin–Stevens Point

A championship-caliber point guard in Portland, Porter is now a serviceable veteran backup for the T-wolves. His career totals include 6,000 assists and 3,000 rebounds.

	G	MPG	FG%	3FG%	FT%	APG	RPG	PPG	BLK	STL
1996–97	82	19.1	.416	.335	.765	3.6	2.1	6.9	11	54
Career	922	30.0	.466	.375	.838	6.6	3.3	13.7	118	1325

James Robinson   G

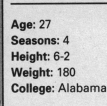

Age: 27
Seasons: 4
Height: 6-2
Weight: 180
College: Alabama

In being a streaky tweener, Robinson exemplifies the two most frustrating characteristics an NBA player can possess. He scored 23 points in a quarter at Cleveland last year, 28 in the season finale at Utah.

	G	MPG	FG%	3FG%	FT%	APG	RPG	PPG	BLK	STL
1996–97	69	19.0	.407	.382	.684	1.8	1.6	8.3	8	30
Career	274	18.8	.399	.358	.650	1.9	1.7	7.8	52	142

Doug West   G/F

Age: 30
Seasons: 8
Height: 6-6
Weight: 220
College: Villanova

West finally experienced postseason play after seven seasons with the T-wolves. His skills and durability have deteriorated, but he still has a knack for the spectacular finish.

	G	MPG	FG%	3FG%	FT%	APG	RPG	PPG	BLK	STL
1996–97	68	28.2	.467	.333	.681	1.7	2.2	7.8	24	61
Career	571	26.1	.488	.200	.803	2.1	2.6	10.6	165	417

Kevin Edwards

New Jersey
NETS

Franchise History: The New Jersey Americans were part of the ABA from its inception in 1967. One year later, they moved to Long Island to become the New York Nets. With sharpshooter Rick Barry at forward, the franchise made it to the ABA Finals in 1971–72, but Barry departed for the NBA. The next Nets star, Julius Erving, took the team to a championship in 1975–76. The Nets joined the NBA for the 1976–77 campaign, went to New Jersey the following year, and have cultivated mediocrity ever since.

1996–97 Review: It was the third straight sub-.500 season for the Nets, but head coach John Calipari was inclined to make changes. New Jersey dove into a nine-player trade with Dallas, acquiring Jim Jackson, Eric Montross, Chris Gatling, and Sam Cassell. The woeful Nets continued to lose, but the deal did set the stage for another blockbuster on draft day. The bright spots of the season were the solid performances turned in by rookie Kerry Kittles and free agent signee Kendall Gill.

1997–98 Preview: The Nets sent two first-round picks, plus Jackson and Montross, to the 76ers for the rights to rookie Keith Van Horn. New Jersey also took on the fat contracts of Don MacLean, Lucious Harris, and Michael Cage. Obviously, it will be the development of Van Horn that determines whether this is just a new look for the same old Nets or a bona fide step toward contention. It will require patience to find out because rookies rarely turn bad teams into good ones overnight.

Nets Veteran Roster

No	Player	Pos	Ht	Wt	Exp
2	David Benoit	F	6-8	220	6
—	Michael Cage	F/C	6-9	248	13
10	Sam Cassell	G	6-3	185	4
33	Yinka Dare	C	7-0	265	3
21	Kevin Edwards	G	6-3	210	9
15	Chris Gatling	F/C	6-10	230	6
13	Kendall Gill	G/F	6-5	216	7
54	Jack Haley	C	6-10	242	9
—	Lucious Harris	G	6-5	205	4
30	Kerry Kittles	G	6-5	179	1
—	Don MacLean	F	6-10	235	5
55	Jayson Williams	F/C	6-10	245	7
7	Reggie Williams	F/G	6-7	195	10

Head Coach: John Calipari

Nets 1997 Draft Picks

Rookie	**College**	**Position**
Tim Thomas (1-7)	Villanova	Forward
Anthony Parker (1-21)	Bradley	Guard

Tim Thomas and Anthony Parker were shipped to the 76ers as part of the trade for Keith Van Horn. The four-year forward from Utah draws a ton of fouls in the post and can hit the mid- to long-range jumper. He appears to be somewhat of a cross between NBAers Detlef Schrempf and Christian Laettner—a face-up type with a soft perimeter touch who can also work in the low post. More rangy and refined than quick and explosive, he'll probably be a solid rebounder when playing the four but may struggle to defend on the outside at small forward.

Nets Scouting Report

Guard: Sam Cassell went from winning back-to-back NBA championships with Houston to playing for three teams in a single season. He is lanky and mobile, able to slink past defenders and finish in traffic, and his outside stroke is pretty reliable. He is more of a scorer and a risk taker than a distributor or a defensive stopper. Kerry Kittles put together a fine first season, scoring in double figures 64 times. He is a very versatile offensive weapon, showing consistent three-point range and the instincts of a slasher. Lucious Harris signed a generous contract in Philadelphia but couldn't deliver the desired production. He has talent and can handle either guard spot but is at his best as an off-the-bench shooter. Streaky shooter Kevin Edwards has played just 80 games in the past three seasons combined because of knee problems. **Grade: C**

Forward: Kendall Gill finally got comfortable and played up to his abilities, leading the Nets in scoring and finishing among the NBA's top 15 in minutes and steals. He swings between the two and the three with a game that is fluid, dynamic, and complete, but his fragile mental makeup is always a concern. Chris Gatling made the All-Star squad last year in the best offensive season of his career. He plays with terrific energy and efficiency. Don MacLean will try to overcome his susceptibility to injuries and regain his reputation as a dangerous off-the-bench shooter. The rookie, Van Horn, will be getting acclimated to life in the NBA but should contribute at both forward spots. **Grade: B+**

Center: The Nets have been getting progressively smaller at the five, and the position may belong to 6-10 bruiser Jayson Williams this season. The team's top rebounder, he is also its most unhappy camper. Veteran banger Michael Cage is an adequate backup. **Grade: C–**

Nets 1996–97 Player Statistics

	G	MIN	FG	FGA	FG%	FT	FTA	FT%	3FG	3FGA
Gill	82	3199	644	1453	.443	427	536	.797	74	220
Gatling	47	1283	327	623	.525	236	329	.717	1	6
Kittles	82	3012	507	1189	.426	175	227	.771	158	419
Jackson	77	2831	444	1029	.431	252	310	.813	86	247
Cassell	61	1714	337	783	.430	212	251	.845	81	231
J. Williams	41	1432	221	540	.409	108	183	.590	0	4
Massenburg	79	1954	219	452	.485	130	206	.631	0	1
Edwards	32	477	69	183	.377	37	43	.860	15	43
R. Williams	13	200	29	76	.382	9	12	.750	9	34
McDaniel	62	1170	138	355	.389	65	89	.730	5	25
Daniels	22	310	36	119	.303	5	6	.833	21	70
Montross	78	1828	159	349	.456	21	62	.339	0	0
Kleine	59	848	69	170	.406	28	38	.737	2	3
Gray	5	42	4	15	.267	4	4	1.000	1	4
Haley	20	74	13	37	.351	14	19	.737	0	0
Werdann	6	31	3	7	.429	3	3	1.000	0	0
Dare	41	313	19	54	.352	19	37	.514	0	0

	ORB	REB	AST	STL	TO	BLK	PF	PTS	PPG
Gill	183	499	326	154	218	46	225	1789	21.8
Gatling	134	370	28	39	120	31	138	891	19.0
Kittles	106	319	249	157	127	35	165	1347	16.4
Jackson	132	411	316	86	208	32	194	1226	15.9
Cassell	47	182	305	77	168	19	200	967	15.9
J. Williams	242	553	51	24	82	36	158	550	13.4
Massenburg	222	517	23	38	91	50	217	568	7.2
Edwards	9	43	57	17	49	4	34	190	5.9
R. Williams	5	31	10	8	12	4	33	76	5.8
McDaniel	124	318	65	36	70	17	144	346	5.6
Daniels	19	43	26	10	14	3	33	98	4.5
Montross	181	518	61	20	77	73	268	339	4.3
Kleine	62	203	35	17	41	18	110	168	2.8
Gray	1	3	2	1	3	0	5	13	2.6
Haley	13	32	5	1	2	1	14	40	2.0
Werdann	3	6	0	2	2	1	10	9	1.5
Dare	35	82	3	4	21	28	51	57	1.4

Nets 1996–97 Team Statistics

Final Record: 26–56

Home Record: 16–25

Road Record: 10–31

Division Record: 11–13

Conference Record: 16–38

Overtime Record: 4–0

Points Per Game: 97.2

Opponents Points Per Game: 101.8

Field Goal Percentage: .422

Opponents Field Goal Percentage: .464

Turnovers Per Game: 15.7

Opponents Turnovers Per Game: 15.3

Offensive Rebounding Percentage: .364

Defensive Rebounding Percentage: .690

Total Rebounding Percentage: .527

Scored Fewer Than 100 Points: 42

Opponents Scored Fewer Than 100 Points: 39

Nets Clipboard

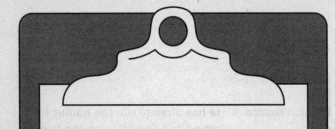

Why the Nets win: The Nets crash the offensive boards and are one of the best all-around rebounding teams in the NBA. Gill and Kittles must go off for 40 points between them.

Why the Nets lose: The franchise has no stability, the team has no chemistry, and those facts cannot be refuted. Until the Nets find a mix of players that they want and who want to be in New Jersey, there will be no reason to expect 40 wins, much less a postseason appearance.

1996–97 MVP: Kendall Gill

Projected MVP: Kendall Gill

Fast Fact: On the last day of November, the Nets and Clippers played to an 81–81 draw in regulation. New Jersey scored 25 points in overtime, an NBA record.

Sam Cassell   G

Age: 28
Seasons: 4
Height: 6-3
Weight: 185
College: Florida State

He has already run the gamut from champion to journeyman, but Cassell is on the bubble between being a catalyst off the bench or a mid-quality starting point guard.

	G	MPG	FG%	3FG%	FT%	APG	RPG	PPG	BLK	STL
1996–97	61	28.1	.430	.351	.845	5.0	3.0	15.9	19	77
Career	270	23.7	.430	.338	.837	4.4	2.6	11.4	44	283

Chris Gatling   F/C

Age: 30
Seasons: 6
Height: 6-10
Weight: 230
College: Old Dominion

Gatling was an All-Star last season despite making only one start. He played most of the campaign in Dallas, then contracted a year-ending ear infection shortly after coming to New Jersey.

	G	MPG	FG%	3FG%	FT%	APG	RPG	PPG	BLK	STL
1996–97	47	27.3	.525	.167	.717	0.6	7.9	19.0	31	39
Career	382	19.2	.570	.053	.667	0.6	5.6	10.7	275	229

Kendall Gill   *G/F*

Age: 29
Seasons: 7
Height: 6-5
Weight: 216
College: Illinois

Although he isn't known for being an emotional rock, Gill put together a season's worth of very consistent all-around play. He became only the fifth player in the '90s to score in double figures 82 times in a year.

	G	MPG	FG%	3FG%	FT%	APG	RPG	PPG	BLK	STL
1996–97	82	39.0	.443	.336	.797	4.0	6.1	21.8	46	154
Career	511	32.7	.453	.327	.778	3.8	4.5	16.2	251	842

Jim Jackson   *G*

Age: 27
Seasons: 5
Height: 6-6
Weight: 220
College: Ohio State

Shipped to Philadelphia on draft day 1997, Jackson will try to get his career back on track. He has triple-double talent, but his numbers and reputation are in sharp decline.

	G	MPG	FG%	3FG%	FT%	APG	RPG	PPG	BLK	STL
1996–97	77	36.8	.431	.348	.813	4.1	5.3	15.9	32	86
Career	320	36.4	.441	.340	.812	3.9	5.0	19.3	102	288

Kerry Kittles G

Age: 23
Seasons: 1
Height: 6-5
Weight: 179
College: Villanova

In a superb debut campaign, Kittles flashed inside-outside scoring skills and a knack for solid defense. He paced the Nets in steals and was the team's only consistent scorer other than Gill.

	G	MPG	FG%	3FG%	FT%	APG	RPG	PPG	BLK	STL
1996–97	82	36.7	.426	.377	.771	3.0	3.9	16.4	35	157
Career	82	36.7	.426	.377	.771	3.0	3.9	16.4	35	157

Joe Kleine C

Age: 35
Seasons: 12
Height: 7-0
Weight: 270
College: Arkansas

Traded twice last season (Lakers and Suns), Kleine is now on a twilight-of-his-career tour of the NBA. He provides a big, tough body in the paint—but that's about it.

	G	MPG	FG%	3FG%	FT%	APG	RPG	PPG	BLK	STL
1996–97	59	14.4	.406	.667	.737	0.6	3.4	2.8	18	17
Career	881	15.8	.456	.283	.794	0.7	4.4	5.1	278	248

Tony Massenburg   F

Age: 30
Seasons: 5
Height: 6-9
Weight: 250
College: Maryland

Massenburg has seen minutes with eight NBA franchises, in addition to spending a couple of years in Spain. He is a valuable complementary player, as evidenced by his 1996–97 numbers.

	G	MPG	FG%	3FG%	FT%	APG	RPG	PPG	BLK	STL
1996–97	79	24.7	.485	.000	.631	0.3	6.5	7.2	50	38
Career	266	21.8	.479	.000	.691	0.5	5.3	7.4	138	119

Xavier McDaniel   F

Age: 34
Seasons: 11
Height: 6-7
Weight: 218
College: Wichita State

McDaniel's scoring average had been dropping for years, from 21.3 in 1989–90, and he wound up toiling in Greece two seasons ago. He isn't good, but he still plays a lot bigger than his listed size.

	G	MPG	FG%	3FG%	FT%	APG	RPG	PPG	BLK	STL
1996–97	62	18.9	.389	.200	.730	1.0	5.1	5.6	17	36
Career	850	29.4	.486	.261	.718	2.1	6.2	16.0	414	788

Eric Montross   C

Age: 26
Seasons: 3
Height: 7-0
Weight: 270
College: North Carolina

Montross will now be tied around Philadelphia's collective neck, as he was shuttled to the 76ers in the Van Horn exchange. He is regressing on the offensive end but will grab the caroms that come his way.

	G	MPG	FG%	3FG%	FT%	APG	RPG	PPG	BLK	STL
1996–97	78	23.4	.456	.000	.339	0.8	6.6	4.3	73	20
Career	217	25.7	.521	.000	.520	0.6	6.6	7.2	163	68

Jayson Williams   F/C

Age: 29
Seasons: 7
Height: 6-10
Weight: 245
College: St. John's

Williams, who took it upon himself to uphold the Derrick Coleman/Chris Morris tradition in New Jersey, played like an All-Star before getting hurt, then started trying to whine his way to another team.

	G	MPG	FG%	3FG%	FT%	APG	RPG	PPG	BLK	STL
1996–97	41	34.9	.409	.000	.590	1.2	13.5	13.4	36	24
Career	380	17.0	.423	.167	.590	0.5	6.2	6.3	192	135

Patrick Ewing

New York
KNICKS

Franchise History: Charter members of the league, the Knickerbockers saw postseason action every season from 1946–47 through 1954–55, including three Finals losses in the early '50s. New York finally won a league title in 1969–70, led by Willis Reed and Walt Frazier. Frazier was later joined in the backcourt by Earl Monroe, and the Knicks were champs again in 1972–73. New York made the Finals on the sturdy shoulders of Patrick Ewing in 1993–94 but fell to Houston.

1996–97 Review: Tired of being conference bridesmaids, the Knicks overhauled their roster. Ewing and Charles Oakley remained the soul of the team, but new to the starting rotation were Chris Childs, Allan Houston, and Larry Johnson at spots one through three. The new-look Knicks followed their 57-win regular season with a 3–0 sweep of Charlotte in the first round. In the semis, New York took a 3–1 lead over Miami, then wound up losing 4–3 in a series marred by brawl-related suspensions.

1997–98 Preview: The Knicks appeared to be the better team in their matchup with Miami, and it can be argued that the staggered, single-game suspensions of Ewing, Houston, and Johnson tipped the series unfairly in favor of the Heat. If the Knicks cut back on turnovers and play more as a unit, they may well be the team to beat in the postseason. The condition of Ewing's aging knees are, as always, a major factor, and this could be the best (and last?) chance for him to earn a championship ring.

Knicks Veteran Roster

No	Player	Pos	Ht	Wt	Exp
4	Scott Brooks	G	5-11	165	9
1	Chris Childs	G	6-3	195	3
33	Patrick Ewing	C	7-0	240	12
20	Allan Houston	G	6-6	200	4
2	Larry Johnson	F	6-7	263	6
5	Dontae' Jones	F	6-8	220	1
40	Walter McCarty	F	6-10	230	1
34	Charles Oakley	F	6-9	245	12
3	John Starks	G	6-5	185	8
44	John Wallace	F	6-9	225	1
21	Charlie Ward	G	6-2	190	3
52	Buck Williams	F	6-8	225	16
32	Herb Williams	C/F	6-11	260	16

Head Coach: Jeff Van Gundy

Knicks 1997 Draft Picks

Rookie	College	Position
John Thomas (1-25)	Minnesota	Forward

Thomas has an NBA body and is not averse to contact. His willingness to bang in the paint has not translated into overwhelming rebound numbers, however. In fact, none of his collegiate statistics say NBA starter, but he was a big hit at the pre-draft camps. Smooth and athletic for a player of his bulk, he doesn't have much range on his shot or depth to his offensive repertoire, but he is a team-first type who does the little things that win games. He'll finish his attempts down low, give help on defense, and stay off the injured list. His personality and work ethic should be a good fit in New York.

Knicks Scouting Report

Guard: After five seasons in the CBA and a battle with alcoholism, Chris Childs made it to the NBA three years ago. His first campaign with the Knicks was marred by injuries, but he still paced the team in assists. New York's backup at the point is Charlie Ward, who made 21 starts when Childs was hurt. Both are tough and unselfish at the point, able to distribute the rock and pester opponents on the perimeter. At the two, Allan Houston rates as one of the game's great shooters. He converts from anywhere on the floor, off the dribble or spotting up. He boasts fine court awareness but is an average defender. John Starks proved to be the league's most valuable sixth man, giving the Knicks a spark with his hard work on defense and his explosiveness on offense. **Grade: B–**

Forward: Larry Johnson shifted from matching up at the four in Charlotte to playing small forward in New York. Back troubles have rendered his game less dynamic than it once was, but he is still an inside-outside threat. Charles Oakley provided his usual interior defense and blue-collar effort under the boards. He has also become dangerous from midrange and at the charity stripe. Off the bench, the frontcourt rotation features 16-year veteran Buck Williams, a warrior in the paint. John Wallace put together a very encouraging debut campaign, shooting .517 from the field in limited action. **Grade: B+**

Center: Patrick Ewing continues to be the center of New York's universe. A remarkable midrange shooter for his size and position, he has averaged better than 180 blocks and 800 rebounds the past two seasons while weathering nagging knee problems. Herb Williams, who amazingly has been in the league since Buck was a rookie, is a fan favorite and a useful backup in the pivot. **Grade: A**

Knicks 1996–97 Player Statistics

	G	MIN	FG	FGA	FG%	FT	FTA	FT%	3FG	3FGA
Ewing	78	2887	655	1342	.488	439	582	.754	2	9
Houston	81	2681	437	1032	.423	175	218	.803	148	384
Starks	77	2042	369	856	.431	173	225	.769	150	407
Johnson	76	2613	376	735	.512	190	274	.693	34	105
Oakley	80	2873	339	694	.488	181	224	.808	5	19
Childs	65	2076	211	510	.414	113	149	.758	70	181
B. Williams	74	1496	175	326	.537	115	179	.642	0	1
Ward	79	1763	133	337	.395	95	125	.760	48	154
Wallace	68	787	122	236	.517	79	110	.718	2	4
Jent	3	10	2	6	.333	0	0	.000	2	3
H. Williams	21	184	18	46	.391	3	4	.750	0	1
McCarty	35	192	26	68	.382	8	14	.571	4	14
Brooks	38	251	19	39	.487	14	15	.933	5	12

	ORB	REB	AST	STL	TO	BLK	PF	PTS	PPG
Ewing	175	834	156	69	269	189	250	1751	22.4
Houston	43	240	179	41	167	18	233	1197	14.8
Starks	36	205	217	90	158	11	196	1061	13.8
Johnson	165	393	174	64	136	36	249	976	12.8
Oakley	246	781	221	111	171	21	305	864	10.8
Childs	22	191	398	78	180	11	213	605	9.3
B. Williams	166	397	53	40	79	38	204	465	6.3
Ward	45	220	326	83	147	15	188	409	5.2
Wallace	51	155	37	21	76	25	102	325	4.8
Jent	1	1	1	0	0	0	2	6	2.0
H. Williams	9	31	5	4	5	5	18	39	1.9
McCarty	8	23	13	7	17	9	38	64	1.8
Brooks	6	18	29	21	17	0	35	57	1.5

Knicks 1996–97 Team Statistics

Final Record: 57–25

Home Record: 31–10

Road Record: 26–15

Division Record: 19–6

Conference Record: 38–16

Overtime Record: 4–2

Points Per Game: 95.4

Opponents Points Per Game: 92.2

Field Goal Percentage: .463

Opponents Field Goal Percentage: .425

Turnovers Per Game: 17.8

Opponents Turnovers Per Game: 16.3

Offensive Rebounding Percentage: .305

Defensive Rebounding Percentage: .734

Total Rebounding Percentage: .519

Scored Fewer Than 100 Points: 55

Opponents Scored Fewer Than 100 Points: 62

Knicks Clipboard

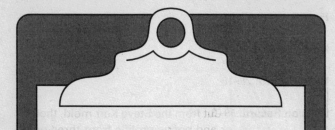

Why the Knicks win: New York is oh so physical on defense, and no team hits the boards harder. Ewing is a go-to option in the post, while Houston and Starks are money from downtown.

Why the Knicks lose: Although not as slow as they once were, New York still isn't the most athletic team in the league. On those occasions when neither Starks nor Houston is connecting, the offense can become all Ewing.

1996–97 MVP: Patrick Ewing

Projected MVP: Patrick Ewing

Fast Fact: The Knicks allowed opponents a paltry .425 field-goal percentage last year, the franchise's best defensive FG% since the league began keeping the stat in 1970–71.

Scott Brooks   *G*

Age: 32
Seasons: 9
Height: 5-11
Weight: 165
College: Cal-Irvine

Cut from the Steve Kerr mold, though four inches shorter and not as prolific from three-point range, Brooks garnered playing time as a backup at the point because of injuries to Chris Childs.

	G	MPG	FG%	3FG%	FT%	APG	RPG	PPG	BLK	STL
1996–97	38	6.6	.487	.417	.933	0.8	0.5	1.5	0	21
Career	637	14.0	.451	.371	.848	2.4	1.0	5.1	27	462

Chris Childs   *G*

Age: 30
Seasons: 3
Height: 6-3
Weight: 195
College: Boise State

Childs took a long, arduous route to the NBA, so he is comparatively old in relation to his years of league service. He works hard but is neither a great scorer nor a superior playmaker.

	G	MPG	FG%	3FG%	FT%	APG	RPG	PPG	BLK	STL
1996–97	65	31.9	.414	.387	.758	6.1	2.9	9.3	11	78
Career	196	28.1	.409	.365	.812	5.9	2.6	9.8	22	231

Patrick Ewing   C

Age: 35
Seasons: 12
Height: 7-0
Weight: 240
College: Georgetown

Ewing's leadership and consistency have made him one of the ten greatest centers ever, but the 11-time All-Star is still waiting to taste championship champagne.

	G	MPG	FG%	3FG%	FT%	APG	RPG	PPG	BLK	STL
1996–97	78	37.0	.488	.222	.754	2.0	10.7	22.4	189	69
Career	913	36.6	.513	.164	.745	2.1	10.4	23.6	2516	979

Allan Houston   G

Age: 26
Seasons: 4
Height: 6-6
Weight: 200
College: Tennessee

A coach's son, Houston understands the game. He also has plenty of natural ability and is unstoppable when in rhythm. He paced the Knicks in games played and was second on the team in scoring.

	G	MPG	FG%	3FG%	FT%	APG	RPG	PPG	BLK	STL
1996–97	81	33.1	.423	.385	.803	2.2	3.0	14.8	18	41
Career	318	29.1	.439	.403	.825	2.2	2.6	14.4	61	197

Larry Johnson F

Age: 28
Seasons: 6
Height: 6-7
Weight: 263
College: UNLV

L.J. is an extreme tweener, but he usually causes more problems for opponents than for his own team. He had a somewhat quiet regular season but scorched his former team in the first round.

	G	MPG	FG%	3FG%	FT%	APG	RPG	PPG	BLK	STL
1996–97	76	34.4	.512	.324	.693	2.3	5.2	12.8	36	64
Career	453	38.1	.498	.343	.762	3.8	8.5	18.5	199	360

Charles Oakley F

Age: 34
Seasons: 12
Height: 6-9
Weight: 245
College: Virginia Union

Oakley knows every trick, dives for all the loose balls, and believes that every rebound is his. He has shot .813 from the charity stripe the past three years after having shot .736 through his first nine seasons.

	G	MPG	FG%	3FG%	FT%	APG	RPG	PPG	BLK	STL
1996–97	80	35.9	.488	.263	.808	2.8	9.8	10.8	21	111
Career	889	32.4	.492	.253	.751	2.4	10.5	11.0	231	942

John Starks   G

Age: 32
Seasons: 8
Height: 6-5
Weight: 185
College: Oklahoma State

Starks made just one start last year but finished third on the team in scoring. He is a streak shooter who can make or break both opponents and his own team.

	G	MPG	FG%	3FG%	FT%	APG	RPG	PPG	BLK	STL
1996–97	77	26.5	.431	.369	.769	2.8	2.7	13.8	11	90
Career	556	27.7	.427	.348	.763	4.0	2.5	13.6	82	656

John Wallace   F

Age: 23
Seasons: 1
Height: 6-9
Weight: 225
College: Syracuse

The 18th pick overall in 1996, Wallace has a nice touch around the basket, is willing to help on defense, and shows good instincts on caroms. Like any rookie, he still has a lot to learn.

	G	MPG	FG%	3FG%	FT%	APG	RPG	PPG	BLK	STL
1996–97	68	11.6	.517	.500	.718	0.5	2.3	4.8	25	21
Career	68	11.6	.517	.500	.718	0.5	2.3	4.8	25	21

Charlie Ward   *G*

Age: 27
Seasons: 3
Height: 6-2
Weight: 190
College: Florida State

Ward has a knack for getting into the lane and converting, and he finished second on the team in steals last year. If he were a more consistent perimeter shooter, he'd be getting a starter's minutes.

	G	MPG	FG%	3FG%	FT%	APG	RPG	PPG	BLK	STL
1996–97	79	22.3	.395	.312	.760	4.1	2.8	5.2	15	83
Career	151	17.2	.390	.312	.735	3.1	2.2	4.4	21	139

Buck Williams   *F*

Age: 37
Seasons: 16
Height: 6-8
Weight: 225
College: Maryland

A playoff-tested veteran, Williams is among the NBA's all-time top 20 in minutes (41,726) and rebounds (12,834). He has never failed to shoot .500 and remains a stellar weakside defender.

	G	MPG	FG%	3FG%	FT%	APG	RPG	PPG	BLK	STL
1996–97	74	20.2	.537	.000	.642	0.7	5.4	6.3	38	40
Career	1266	33.0	.550	.167	.663	1.3	10.1	13.1	1085	1063

Penny Hardaway

Orlando *MAGIC*

Franchise History: From an 18–64 debut in 1989–90, the Magic conjured a trip to the NBA Finals in just six seasons of existence. Having the top pick overall in both 1992 and 1993 provided the crucial ingredients—Shaquille O'Neal and Penny Hardaway—for Orlando's rise. The signing of Horace Grant helped propel the upstart franchise to a 1994–95 Finals matchup with the Rockets, who sent the Magic packing in an 0–4 sweep. Orlando won 60 games in 1995–96 but fell to Chicago in the semifinals.

1996–97 Review: Considering that O'Neal left for L.A. via free agency, Hardaway missed all but five of the first 28 games with a knee injury, and head coach Brian Hill was dumped in midseason, it's a wonder that Orlando posted 45 victories. Rony Seikaly filled in admirably at center, and Penny was terrific when healthy, but injuries to Nick Anderson and Horace Grant kept the team running in place. In the first phase of the playoffs, the Magic bowed to Miami in five games after falling behind 0–2.

1997–98 Preview: Chuck Daly, who won two NBA titles as head coach in Detroit, will try to instill a philosophy of 48-minute defense and mental toughness in a team not known for either. He'll have quality starters, including a budding superstar in Hardaway, and a decent bench. The Magic can be a 55-win team again, but they must avoid the injury bug and get consistent shooting from Anderson at the two and Dennis Scott at the three. It will be a shock if Orlando isn't a better team this year than in 1996–97.

Magic Veteran Roster

No	Player	Pos	Ht	Wt	Exp
25	Nick Anderson	G/F	6-6	228	8
10	Darrell Armstrong	G	6-1	180	3
34	Brian Evans	F	6-8	220	1
54	Horace Grant	F	6-10	245	10
1	Penny Hardaway	G	6-7	215	4
00	Amal McCaskill	F/C	6-11	235	1
24	Dan Schayes	C	6-11	260	16
3	Dennis Scott	F	6-8	235	7
4	Rony Seikaly	C	6-11	253	9
20	Brian Shaw	G	6-6	200	8
33	Derek Strong	F	6-9	240	6
42	David Vaughn	F/C	6-9	240	2

Head Coach: Chuck Daly

Magic 1997 Draft Picks

Rookie	College	Position
Johnny Taylor (1-17)	UT-Chattanooga	Forward
Eric Washington (2-47)	Alabama	Guard

In many respects the opposite of incumbent starter Dennis Scott, Taylor has good quickness and can be a contributor on the offensive glass. His perimeter shooting figures to be inconsistent, but he is a slasher who runs the floor and finishes. He played JUCO ball at Indian Hills C.C. (Iowa), where his team went 31–3 in his sophomore year. He then transferred to UT-Chattanooga and wound up as the tenth 1,000-point scorer in school history. In 62 games with the Mocs, he averaged over 17 points and seven rebounds. Orlando dealt Eric Washington to Denver for center Jason Lawson, who had 105 blocks at Villanova last season.

Magic Scouting Report

Guard: It would be absurd to describe Penny Hardaway as a tweener, but he is more of a hybrid than a pure one or two. He struggles defensively against waterbug point guards, and he isn't the reliable perimeter shooter teams look for at the off-guard spot. Of course, none of that keeps him from being one of the top all-around players in the NBA. Nick Anderson, the only player remaining from Orlando's inaugural season, is a tough matchup on both ends of the court, but his ballhandling and shooting are spotty. Brian Shaw, who has good size for rebounding and defense, and small but explosive Darrell Armstrong offer spark off the bench. **Grade: B+**

Forward: Horace Grant provides the muscle, experience, and blue-collar effort Orlando needs at the four, and he can also knock down the midrange jumper. Derek Strong stepped in when Grant was unavailable due to various injuries. A six-year veteran who has seen duty with five NBA teams, Strong logged career highs in rebounding and scoring. He was the only Orlando player to appear in all 82 contests. Small forward Dennis Scott, one of the most prolific long-range shooters ever, had an injury-marred campaign but still hit 39 percent of 373 attempted triples. Far from being multidimensional, he is a nonfactor on the boards, lacks quickness on defense, and has not been a clutch performer in the playoffs. **Grade: B**

Center: Veteran pivotman Rony Seikaly posted strong numbers in his first year with the Magic, bouncing back after two subpar seasons in Golden State. He runs the floor, moves without the ball, works well with his back to the basket, and sweeps the glass with aplomb. Orlando got maximum output from 16-year veteran Dan Schayes, serving as Seikaly's backup. **Grade: B−**

Magic 1996–97 Player Statistics

	G	MIN	FG	FGA	FG%	FT	FTA	FT%	3FG	3FGA
Hardaway	59	2221	421	941	.447	283	345	.820	85	267
Seikaly	74	2615	460	907	.507	357	500	.714	0	3
Grant	67	2496	358	695	.515	128	179	.715	1	6
Scott	66	2166	298	749	.398	80	101	.792	147	373
Anderson	63	2163	288	725	.397	38	94	.404	143	405
Wilkins	80	2202	323	759	.426	136	190	.716	66	203
Strong	82	2004	262	586	.447	175	218	.803	0	13
Shaw	77	1867	189	516	.366	111	140	.793	63	194
Armstrong	67	1010	132	345	.383	92	106	.868	55	181
Schayes	45	540	47	120	.392	39	52	.750	0	1
Vaughn	35	298	31	72	.431	19	30	.633	0	0
McCaskill	17	109	10	32	.313	8	12	.667	0	2
Evans	14	59	8	22	.364	0	0	.000	4	8
Demps	2	10	0	3	.000	2	2	1.000	0	1

	ORB	REB	AST	STL	TO	BLK	PF	PTS	PPG
Hardaway	82	263	332	93	145	35	123	1210	20.5
Seikaly	274	701	92	49	218	107	275	1277	17.3
Grant	206	600	163	101	99	65	157	845	12.6
Scott	40	203	139	74	81	19	138	823	12.5
Anderson	66	304	182	120	86	32	160	757	12.0
Wilkins	59	173	173	54	123	12	144	848	10.6
Strong	174	519	73	47	102	20	196	699	8.5
Shaw	47	194	319	67	170	26	197	552	7.2
Armstrong	35	76	175	61	99	9	114	411	6.1
Schayes	41	125	14	15	27	16	74	133	3.0
Vaughn	35	95	7	8	29	15	43	81	2.3
McCaskill	4	22	7	3	11	5	7	28	1.6
Evans	1	8	7	1	2	2	6	20	1.4
Demps	0	0	0	1	0	0	1	2	1.0

Magic 1996–97 Team Statistics

Final Record: 45–37

Home Record: 26–15

Road Record: 19–22

Division Record: 13–11

Conference Record: 29–25

Overtime Record: 2–4

Points Per Game: 94.1

Opponents Points Per Game: 94.5

Field Goal Percentage: .437

Opponents Field Goal Percentage: .460

Turnovers Per Game: 15.2

Opponents Turnovers Per Game: 16.0

Offensive Rebounding Percentage: .309

Defensive Rebounding Percentage: .673

Total Rebounding Percentage: .491

Scored Fewer Than 100 Points: 58

Opponents Scored Fewer Than 100 Points: 55

Magic Clipboard

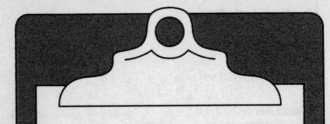

Why the Magic win: When the starting five are healthy and the perimeter shots are falling, the Magic are tough to check. Seikaly and Grant are gritty and versatile in the frontcourt. Scott and Anderson are dangerous from the perimeter. Hardaway does a superb job of creating.

Why the Magic lose: Anderson and Scott are susceptible to ice-cold streaks that can put the Magic offense in a deep freeze. Last year's rash of injuries kept the team out of rhythm.

1996–97 MVP: Rony Seikaly

Projected MVP: Penny Hardaway

Fast Fact: Orlando currently owns the league's longest streak of consecutive games with at least one three-point field goal (313).

Nick Anderson G/F

Age: 29
Seasons: 8
Height: 6-6
Weight: 228
College: Illinois

A solid on-ball defender but a streaky shooter, Anderson had a career-worst year from the field and an atrocious one from the free throw line, but he did lead the Magic in steals last season.

	G	MPG	FG%	3FG%	FT%	APG	RPG	PPG	BLK	STL
1996–97	63	34.3	.397	.353	.404	2.9	4.8	12.0	32	120
Career	587	32.6	.459	.366	.682	2.9	5.3	15.4	300	868

Darrell Armstrong G

Age: 29
Seasons: 3
Height: 6-1
Weight: 180
College: Fayetteville State

Undrafted out of college, Armstrong made his mark in various pro leagues before joining the Magic. He has rare ups and is a scrappy defender, but his shooting stroke is suspect.

	G	MPG	FG%	3FG%	FT%	APG	RPG	PPG	BLK	STL
1996–97	67	15.1	.383	.304	.868	2.6	1.1	6.1	9	61
Career	83	12.8	.392	.317	.875	2.2	1.0	5.6	9	68

Horace Grant F

Age: 32
Seasons: 10
Height: 6-10
Weight: 245
College: Clemson

Grant has not been durable the past two years, and Orlando has struggled without him. He is a warrior in the paint and has a decent touch from 18 feet, but he rarely creates shots for himself or others.

	G	MPG	FG%	3FG%	FT%	APG	RPG	PPG	BLK	STL
1996–97	67	37.3	.515	.167	.715	2.4	9.0	12.6	65	101
Career	750	34.3	.530	.087	.685	2.4	8.8	12.7	806	826

Penny Hardaway G

Age: 26
Seasons: 4
Height: 6-7
Weight: 215
College: Memphis State

Orlando's offensive catalyst, Penny can slash to the hole, stick the midrange jumper, or get the rock to his teammates. The Magic went 7–19 in games he missed last year.

	G	MPG	FG%	3FG%	FT%	APG	RPG	PPG	BLK	STL
1996–97	59	37.6	.447	.318	.820	5.6	4.5	20.5	35	93
Career	300	37.2	.487	.315	.774	6.7	4.6	19.7	153	579

Dan Schayes C

Age: 38
Seasons: 16
Height: 6-11
Weight: 260
College: Syracuse

Schayes is just a warm body at this stage of his career, but don't tell that to the Knicks. He lit them up for 21 points, 11 rebounds, and six steals at the Garden in April.

	G	MPG	FG%	3FG%	FT%	APG	RPG	PPG	BLK	STL
1996–97	45	12.0	.392	.000	.750	0.3	2.8	3.0	16	15
Career	1045	19.7	.485	.133	.806	1.2	5.2	8.0	805	525

Dennis Scott F

Age: 29
Seasons: 7
Height: 6-8
Weight: 235
College: Georgia Tech

Scott has the height and leg strength to get his jumper off from anywhere on the floor, and he has been both prolific and accurate from beyond the arc. He had a career season in 1995–96 but fell off last year.

	G	MPG	FG%	3FG%	FT%	APG	RPG	PPG	BLK	STL
1996–97	66	32.8	.398	.394	.792	2.1	3.1	12.5	19	74
Career	446	30.7	.422	.403	.789	1.0	2.3	14.8	146	429

Rony Seikaly   C

Age: 32
Seasons: 9
Height: 6-11
Weight: 253
College: Syracuse

Seikaly paced the Magic in rebounds and was second in scoring last season. Though not much of a threat facing the basket, he is productive in the post and fantastic in transition.

	G	MPG	FG%	3FG%	FT%	APG	RPG	PPG	BLK	STL
1996–97	74	35.3	.507	.000	.714	1.2	9.5	17.3	107	49
Career	613	32.1	.489	.200	.675	1.3	9.8	15.1	823	421

Brian Shaw   G

Age: 31
Seasons: 8
Height: 6-6
Weight: 200
College: California–Santa Barbara

Shaw isn't particularly quick, and his jumper is unreliable, but few guards are more versatile off the bench. He distributes the ball efficiently and is a quality defender.

	G	MPG	FG%	3FG%	FT%	APG	RPG	PPG	BLK	STL
1996–97	77	24.2	.366	.325	.793	4.1	2.5	7.2	26	67
Career	599	25.9	.413	.296	.791	5.0	3.7	8.4	178	557

Derek Strong   F

Age: 29
Seasons: 6
Height: 6-9
Weight: 240
College: Xavier

Though his game lacks refinement, Strong is aptly named and can be difficult to check in the paint. He averaged 12.9 points and 9.5 rebounds in 21 games as a starter last season.

	G	MPG	FG%	3FG%	FT%	APG	RPG	PPG	BLK	STL
1996–97	82	24.4	.447	.000	.803	0.9	6.3	8.5	20	47
Career	306	18.2	.438	.200	.799	0.7	4.8	6.4	60	138

Gerald Wilkins   G/F

Age: 34
Seasons: 12
Height: 6-6
Weight: 225
College: Tennessee-Chattanooga

Wilkins had played just 28 games the previous two seasons because of a ruptured Achilles, but he came back last year to log 2,000-plus minutes and score in double figures 44 times.

	G	MPG	FG%	3FG%	FT%	APG	RPG	PPG	BLK	STL
1996–97	80	27.5	.426	.325	.716	2.2	2.2	10.6	12	54
Career	825	30.1	.456	.321	.747	3.2	3.1	13.8	202	873

Jerry Stackhouse

Philadelphia
76ERS

Franchise History: As the Syracuse Nationals in the days of Dolph Schayes, the franchise was a losing participant versus Minneapolis in the 1949–50 Finals. The Nats also made the Finals in 1953–54, losing again to the Lakers. The team moved to Philadelphia ten years later and regularly battled the Celtics for league supremacy. With the help of Wilt Chamberlain, the 76ers were NBA champs in 1966–67. In the mid-'70s, Philly imported ABA star Julius Erving, who went to three Finals before winning a title in 1982–83.

1996–97 Review: Johnny Davis was charged with the task of getting the Sixers on track after an 18-win performance in 1995–96. But a 1–12 December and a 2–14 January were enough to put Davis on borrowed time. By year's end, the only points of interest concerned Allen Iverson's chances of winning Rookie of the Year (he did), speculation as to who would take over as head coach (Larry Brown), and anticipation about where Philly would figure in the lottery (second overall).

1997–98 Preview: Larry Brown sports a well-deserved reputation for rebuilding floundering teams quickly, given a modicum of talent with which to work. The Sixers have drafted high and well the past two years, and although it hasn't helped them in the wins column, it does provide Brown some quality raw material. On paper, Philadelphia should be at least a 35-win team, and if anyone can coax the 76ers to use their individual abilities to fulfill team goals, Brown is the man.

76ers Veteran Roster

No	Player	Pos	Ht	Wt	Exp
44	Derrick Coleman	F	6-10	260	7
7	Mark Davis	F	6-7	210	2
14	Mark Hendrickson	F	6-9	220	1
3	Allen Iverson	G	6-0	165	1
—	Jim Jackson	G	6-6	220	5
20	Frankie King	G	6-1	185	2
—	Eric Montross	C	7-0	270	3
9	Doug Overton	G	6-3	190	5
42	Jerry Stackhouse	G/F	6-6	218	2
23	Rex Walters	G	6-4	190	4
55	Scott Williams	C/F	6-10	230	7

Head Coach: Larry Brown

76ers 1997 Draft Picks

Rookie	College	Position
Keith Van Horn (1-2)	Utah	Forward
Marko Milic (2-34)	Slovenia	Guard
Kebu Stewart (2-36)	Cal St.–Bakersfield	Forward
James Collins (2-37)	Florida State	Guard

Van Horn was immediately sent to New Jersey, and the 76ers picked up rookies Tim Thomas and Anthony Parker. Thomas, who joins the pros after just one year of college ball, actually rated ahead of Kobe Bryant coming out of high school. Parker plays tough defense but is unsteady from the perimeter. Marko Milic is a tough European two who led his team in scoring, assists, and rebounding. Kebu Stewart, who began his collegiate career at UNLV, is a monster on the boards. James Collins was delivered to the Clippers for a 1998 second-round selection.

76ers Scouting Report

Guard: Allen Iverson may not be the old school's idea of an NBA hero, but they'd better get used to seeing him on the highlight reels. The ultimate extreme in modern point guards, Iverson shoots first and keeps shooting until the final buzzer. And yet, lest it be said that he can't or won't distribute the rock, his assists total would have paced 18 other teams. At the off-guard spot, Jim Jackson is more of a scorer than a shooter, but he rang up two triple-doubles in ten days at the end of last season. His on-ball defense is top notch. The Sixers use scrappy spot-up shooter Rex Walters as a substitute at the point and an occasional starter at the two. **Grade: B**

Forward: Clarence Weatherspoon, who invariably evokes comparisons to Charles Barkley, has a power forward's mobility but a small forward's height. Fearless in the paint, he has strong post-up moves, the explosiveness to swat shots, and a desire to dominate the boards. Jerry Stackhouse is potentially the complete package, capable of lighting up the scoreboard and shutting down his match-up. Like many young players, he turns the ball over and blows hot and cold from the perimeter. Derrick Coleman has All-Star talent, plenty of confidence, and...you know the rest. He has missed 122 games the past three seasons. Tim Thomas will see action at the four but is probably too raw to push the veterans for minutes. **Grade: B**

Center: His stock continues to plummet as he joins his fourth team in four seasons, but Eric Montross will still be a starter in the NBA because of his size. He can't pass or shoot, but his shotblocking has improved and he isn't bad on the glass. Undersized bruiser Scott Williams was the only regular to shoot over .500 from the field, which says more about the Sixers than it does about Williams. **Grade: C–**

76ers 1996–97 Player Statistics

	G	MIN	FG	FGA	FG%	FT	FTA	FT%	3FG	3FGA
Iverson	76	3045	625	1504	.416	382	544	.702	155	455
Stackhouse	81	3166	533	1308	.407	511	667	.766	102	342
Coleman	57	2102	364	836	.435	272	365	.745	32	119
Weatherspoon	82	2949	398	811	.491	206	279	.738	1	6
MacLean	37	733	163	365	.447	64	97	.660	12	38
Davis	75	1705	251	535	.469	113	168	.673	24	93
Walters	59	1041	148	325	.455	49	62	.790	57	148
Williams	62	1317	162	318	.509	38	55	.691	0	2
Harris	54	813	112	294	.381	33	47	.702	36	99
Overton	61	634	81	190	.426	45	48	.938	10	40
Hendrickson	29	301	32	77	.416	18	26	.692	3	12
King	7	59	7	17	.412	5	5	1.000	1	2
Caldwell	45	569	40	92	.435	21	50	.420	0	2
Cage	82	1247	66	141	.468	19	41	.463	0	0
Bradtke	36	251	25	58	.431	9	13	.692	0	0

	ORB	REB	AST	STL	TO	BLK	PF	PTS	PPG
Iverson	115	312	567	157	337	24	233	1787	23.5
Stackhouse	156	338	253	93	316	63	219	1679	20.7
Coleman	157	573	193	50	184	75	164	1032	18.1
Weatherspoon	219	679	140	74	137	86	187	1003	12.2
MacLean	41	140	37	12	47	10	71	402	10.9
Davis	138	323	135	85	118	31	230	639	8.5
Walters	21	107	113	28	61	3	75	402	6.8
Williams	155	397	41	44	50	41	206	362	5.8
Harris	27	71	50	41	34	3	45	293	5.4
Overton	18	68	101	24	39	0	44	217	3.6
Hendrickson	35	92	3	10	14	4	32	85	2.9
King	4	14	5	4	3	0	7	20	2.9
Caldwell	58	167	12	16	28	8	87	101	2.2
Cage	112	320	43	48	17	42	118	151	1.8
Bradtke	26	68	7	5	9	5	34	59	1.6

Sixers 1996–97 Team Statistics

Final Record: 22–60

Home Record: 11–29

Road Record: 11–31

Division Record: 11–14

Conference Record: 14–40

Overtime Record: 1–3

Points Per Game: 100.2

Opponents Points Per Game: 106.7

Field Goal Percentage: .438

Opponents Field Goal Percentage: .470

Turnovers Per Game: 17.5

Opponents Turnovers Per Game: 15.6

Offensive Rebounding Percentage: .341

Defensive Rebounding Percentage: .665

Total Rebounding Percentage: .503

Scored Fewer Than 100 Points: 35

Opponents Scored Fewer Than 100 Points: 23

76ers Clipboard

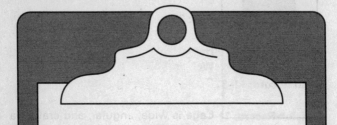

Why the 76ers win: The Sixers win if someone in addition to Stackhouse and Iverson is involved in the offense. It is crucial that the 76ers help each other on defense to make up for the lack of height on the frontline.

Why the 76ers lose: When a point guard takes 22 more shots than Gary Payton and converts 81 fewer, the offense is not going to function efficiently. The 76ers score plenty of points, then allow their opponents too many easy opportunities. Philadelphia's bench has been anemic.

1996–97 MVP: Allen Iverson

Projected MVP: Allen Iverson

Fast Fact: During one stretch in April, Allen Iverson rang up 40-plus points in five straight games. The 76ers lost all five.

Michael Cage F/C

Age: 35
Seasons: 13
Height: 6-9
Weight: 248
College: San Diego State

Cage is wide, angular, and crafty—a veteran of the trenches. He registered the lowest scoring average in the NBA among players appearing in all 82 games last year. He'll be in New Jersey this season.

	G	MPG	FG%	3FG%	FT%	APG	RPG	PPG	BLK	STL
1996–97	82	15.2	.468	.000	.463	0.5	3.9	1.8	42	48
Career	1041	27.2	.515	.000	.665	1.0	7.9	7.8	673	997

Derrick Coleman F

Age: 30
Seasons: 7
Height: 6-10
Weight: 260
College: Syracuse

Over the past three seasons, D.C. has been absent a whopping 122 games and has shot a tepid .428 from the field. He topped the 76ers in rebounds per game last year.

	G	MPG	FG%	3FG%	FT%	APG	RPG	PPG	BLK	STL
1996–97	57	36.9	.435	.269	.745	3.4	10.1	18.1	75	50
Career	416	35.7	.456	.276	.765	3.2	10.4	19.4	644	374

Mark Davis   **F**

Age: 24
Seasons: 2
Height: 6-7
Weight: 210
College: Texas Tech

Drafted 48th overall by Dallas in 1995, Davis signed with the 76ers as a free agent and showed vast improvement in his second season. He topped his rookie shooting percentage by 100 points.

	G	MPG	FG%	3FG%	FT%	APG	RPG	PPG	BLK	STL
1996–97	75	22.7	.469	.258	.673	1.8	4.3	8.5	31	85
Career	132	17.2	.447	.264	.658	1.4	3.4	6.3	53	125

Lucious Harris   **G**

Age: 27
Seasons: 4
Height: 6-5
Weight: 205
College: Long Beach State

Now with the Nets, Harris suffered the worst year of his career and finished the season on the injured list with a broken nose. He is a serviceable reserve at either the one or the two.

	G	MPG	FG%	3FG%	FT%	APG	RPG	PPG	BLK	STL
1996–97	54	15.1	.381	.364	.702	0.9	1.3	5.4	3	41
Career	271	19.3	.437	.363	.766	1.4	2.1	7.2	30	183

Allen Iverson   *G*

Age: 22
Seasons: 1
Height: 6-0
Weight: 165
College: Georgetown

A pest on defense and a nightmare with the rock in his hands, Iverson is stirring up the league with his skills and personality. He can get to the rack at will and is no slouch from the perimeter.

	G	MPG	FG%	3FG%	FT%	APG	RPG	PPG	BLK	STL
1996–97	76	40.1	.416	.341	.702	7.5	4.1	23.5	24	157
Career	76	40.1	.416	.341	.702	7.5	4.1	23.5	24	157

Don MacLean   *F*

Age: 27
Seasons: 5
Height: 6-10
Weight: 235
College: UCLA

MacLean is one of the NBA's purest midrange shooters, the owner of a quick and consistent release. Unable to stay healthy, MacLean has sagged in recent years, but he'll try to prop it up in New Jersey.

	G	MPG	FG%	3FG%	FT%	APG	RPG	PPG	BLK	STL
1996–97	37	19.8	.447	.316	.660	1.0	3.8	10.9	10	12
Career	269	22.5	.461	.273	.778	1.4	4.1	12.0	44	106

Jerry Stackhouse   *G/F*

Age: 23
Seasons: 2
Height: 6-6
Weight: 218
College: North Carolina

Stackhouse is no M.J. (Jordan never shot worse than .480 for a full season), but if he develops into a less wasteful offensive player and a more intense defensive one, he'll be the next best thing.

	G	MPG	FG%	3FG%	FT%	APG	RPG	PPG	BLK	STL
1996–97	81	39.1	.407	.298	.766	3.1	4.2	20.7	63	93
Career	153	38.3	.411	.308	.758	3.5	3.9	20.0	142	169

Rex Walters   *G*

Age: 27
Seasons: 4
Height: 6-4
Weight: 190
College: Kansas

Walters gets by on heart, hustle, and a pretty good jumper. He is competent to run the offense but is at his best when given open space and a green light behind the three-point arc.

	G	MPG	FG%	3FG%	FT%	APG	RPG	PPG	BLK	STL
1996–97	59	17.6	.455	.385	.790	1.9	1.8	6.8	3	28
Career	231	15.0	.449	.374	.795	1.8	1.3	5.5	26	105

Clarence Weatherspoon   F

Age: 27
Seasons: 5
Height: 6-6
Weight: 245
College: Southern Mississippi

Inch for inch, Spoon is arguably the NBA's top shot blocker among non-centers. He has great ups and uncanny timing. Spoon is a steady scorer and tenacious rebounder; few players get more from their abilities.

	G	MPG	FG%	3FG%	FT%	APG	RPG	PPG	BLK	STL
1996–97	82	36.0	.491	.167	.738	1.7	8.3	12.2	86	74
Career	400	37.1	.471	.200	.727	2.1	8.4	16.2	444	486

Scott Williams   F/C

Age: 29
Seasons: 7
Height: 6-10
Weight: 230
College: North Carolina

Williams is still in the league by virtue of his willingness to pound the glass. He has a stunted offensive repertoire (no range, no moves) and is prone to injuries.

	G	MPG	FG%	3FG%	FT%	APG	RPG	PPG	BLK	STL
1996–97	62	21.2	.509	.000	.691	0.7	6.4	5.8	41	44
Career	375	16.9	.485	.071	.690	0.7	5.1	5.2	223	217

Jason Kidd

Phoenix
SUNS

Franchise History: Following a 16-win debut in 1968–69, the Suns lost a coin toss that would have earned them the right to draft Lew Alcindor. That flip set the tone for a franchise that has rarely gotten a break at crux moments. Phoenix made it to the 1975–76 Finals, the high point of which was a triple-overtime fifth game that has been called the greatest ever played, but the Suns lost both that contest and the series. Phoenix also came up short in the 1992–93 Finals, bowing to the Bulls in six.

1996–97 Review: Saying goodbye to Charles Barkley and dropping their first 13 games assured the Suns a sub-.500 record, but trading for Jason Kidd and winning 11 straight in a March-April stretch propelled them into the playoffs. Mirroring head coach Danny Ainge's qualities as a player, the Suns as a team were undersized underdogs who came up big under pressure. Phoenix had division champion Seattle on the run in the first round, but the spirited Suns finally fell in five.

1997–98 Preview: Exciting and innovative is all well and good, but the fact remains that it took a sensational effort for Phoenix to make the playoffs, then still fail to advance in the postseason. If the Suns are to grow from underdogs into top dogs, they must shore up their interior defense. That will require the health of fragile center John "Hot Rod" Williams, plus a level of defensive intensity that few teams deliver on a nightly basis. In any case, the Suns will score a ton of points and be fun to watch.

Suns Veteran Roster

No	Player	Pos	Ht	Wt	Exp
2	Mark Bryant	F/C	6-9	245	9
1	Cedric Ceballos	F	6-7	220	7
3	Rex Chapman	G	6-4	195	9
7	Kevin Johnson	G	6-1	190	10
32	Jason Kidd	G	6-4	212	3
17	Horacio Llamas	C	6-11	285	1
15	Danny Manning	F	6-10	234	9
40	Loren Meyer	F/C	6-10	260	2
13	Steve Nash	G	6-3	195	1
11	Wesley Person	G/F	6-6	195	3
23	Wayman Tisdale	F/C	6-9	260	12
18	John Williams	C/F	6-11	245	11

Head Coach: Danny Ainge

Suns 1997 Draft Picks

Rookie	College	Position
Stephen Jackson (2-43)	None	Guard

The NBA scouts know every player on the planet inside and out, but Jackson is a virtual unknown quantity among even the most ardent basketball fans. He signed a letter of intent to attend Arizona but failed to qualify for the fall semester. He then enrolled at Butler Community College in El Dorado, Kansas, but he didn't play college basketball before entering the NBA draft. He tested well at pre-draft workouts, flashing terrific passing skills and a lot of raw athleticism. At the 1996 McDonalds All-America game, he scored a team-high 21 points, going eight for ten from the field and four for four from the line. He has a pro shooting guard's size and skills but is not yet 20 years old.

Suns Scouting Report

Guard: Liberated from Dallas, point guard Jason Kidd set free the Phoenix offense after spending 21 games on the disabled list. A rare playmaker, he pushes the ball up the court and gets it to the right player at the right time in the right spot. The arrival of Kidd allowed veteran point guard Kevin Johnson to focus on scoring from the two. Still one of the league's most explosive players, K.J. paced the Suns in scoring and assists last year. Wesley Person streak shot his way onto the bench, then emerged as a valuable sixth man who connected at a .413 clip from beyond the arc. Speaking of success from three-point range, perennial underachiever Rex Chapman signed for the NBA minimum and wound up sparking the Phoenix offense in the postseason. **Grade: B+**

Forward: Cedric Ceballos, who returned to Phoenix after a two-year stint with the Lakers, is one of the NBA's best rebounding and scoring small forwards. An extreme lack of consistency has been his primary weakness. Danny Manning's star shines less brightly after ACL operations on both knees, but he continues to show a more complete game than 99 percent of NBA fours. His offensive arsenal features everything except three-point range, and he has twice logged 100-plus blocks and 100-plus steals in his nine-year career. **Grade: B–**

Center: His knees are suspect and he is deteriorating offensively, but Hot Rod Williams is still able to man the pivot and provide 100 swats. Wayman Tisdale still has the bulk to bang in the post, but he is coming off the worst season of his 12-year career. Mark Bryant connects at a high percentage and works hard underneath the glass. Loren Meyer and Horacio Llamas are available as space eaters. **Grade: C–**

Suns 1996–97 Player Statistics

	G	MIN	FG	FGA	FG%	FT	FTA	FT%	3FG	3FGA
Johnson	70	2658	441	890	.496	439	515	.852	89	202
Ceballos	50	1426	282	617	.457	139	186	.747	26	102
Chapman	65	1833	332	749	.443	124	149	.832	110	314
Manning	77	2134	426	795	.536	181	251	.721	7	36
Person	80	2326	409	903	.453	91	114	.798	171	414
Kidd	55	1964	213	529	.403	112	165	.679	61	165
Bryant	41	1018	152	275	.553	76	108	.704	0	0
Williams	68	2137	204	416	.490	133	198	.672	0	2
Tisdale	53	778	158	371	.426	30	48	.625	0	0
Meyer	54	708	108	244	.443	46	64	.719	4	7
Dumas	24	278	33	96	.344	16	25	.640	4	28
Nash	65	684	74	175	2423	42	51	.824	23	55
Brown	6	83	5	12	.417	6	10	.600	0	0
Boney	8	48	6	19	.316	6	8	.750	1	6
Llamas	20	101	15	28	.536	4	8	.500	0	0
Davis	20	98	10	26	.385	9	20	.450	0	0

	ORB	REB	AST	STL	TO	BLK	PF	PTS	PPG
Johnson	54	253	653	102	217	12	141	1410	20.1
Ceballos	102	330	64	33	85	23	113	729	14.6
Chapman	25	181	182	52	96	7	108	898	13.8
Manning	137	469	173	81	161	74	268	1040	13.5
Person	68	292	123	86	76	20	102	1080	13.5
Kidd	64	249	496	124	142	20	114	599	10.9
Bryant	67	212	47	22	46	5	136	380	9.3
Williams	178	562	100	67	66	88	176	541	8.0
Tisdale	35	120	20	8	36	21	111	346	6.5
Meyer	53	145	19	11	62	15	125	266	4.9
Dumas	3	16	25	10	16	2	45	86	3.6
Nash	16	63	138	20	63	0	92	213	3.3
Brown	9	25	5	1	2	1	9	16	2.7
Boney	3	6	0	2	1	1	3	19	2.4
Llamas	4	18	4	10	11	5	25	34	1.7
Davis	12	27	0	4	3	1	16	29	1.5

Suns 1996–97 Team Statistics

Final Record: 40–42

Home Record: 25–16

Road Record: 15–26

Division Record: 13–11

Conference Record: 27–25

Overtime Record: 2–5

Points Per Game: 102.8

Opponents Points Per Game: 102.2

Field Goal Percentage: .469

Opponents Field Goal Percentage: .467

Turnovers Per Game: 14.4

Opponents Turnovers Per Game: 15.8

Offensive Rebounding Percentage: .271

Defensive Rebounding Percentage: .694

Total Rebounding Percentage: .483

Scored Fewer Than 100 Points: 31

Opponents Scored Fewer Than 100 Points: 37

Suns Clipboard

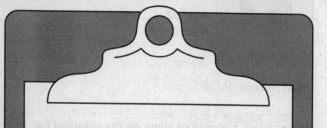

Why the Suns win: When the Suns go with four guards and Hot Rod protects the middle, they can turn up the heat and get into the open floor. Phoenix is prolific and dangerous from beyond the three-point arc. The Suns have a trio of great passers in Kidd, K.J., and Manning.

Why the Suns lose: No other playoff team gave up 100-plus points per game last year; in fact, the Suns were the only such club to win more than 30 games. They lack inside muscle.

1996–97 MVP: Kevin Johnson

Projected MVP: Jason Kidd

Fast Fact: Kevin Johnson and Jason Kidd both rank among the NBA's all-time top 20 in career triple-doubles. They had two apiece last season.

Mark Bryant   F/C

Age: 32
Seasons: 9
Height: 6-9
Weight: 245
College: Seton Hall

Playing his first season with the Suns, Bryant spent a couple of stints on the disabled list. He's an efficient but limited scorer who is known for playing rugged interior defense.

	G	MPG	FG%	3FG%	FT%	APG	RPG	PPG	BLK	STL
1996–97	41	24.8	.553	.000	.704	1.1	5.2	9.3	5	22
Career	543	16.7	.506	.100	.684	0.6	3.8	5.7	128	220

Cedric Ceballos   F

Age: 28
Seasons: 7
Height: 6-7
Weight: 220
College: Fullerton State

A super athlete and a great finisher, Ceballos is at his best when working near the basket. He has shot just .269 in 286 attempts from beyond the arc over the past two seasons.

	G	MPG	FG%	3FG%	FT%	APG	RPG	PPG	BLK	STL
1996–97	50	28.5	.457	.255	.747	1.3	6.6	14.6	23	33
Career	440	24.4	.517	.301	.740	1.2	5.4	15.0	132	338

Rex Chapman   G

Age: 30
Seasons: 9
Height: 6-4
Weight: 195
College: Kentucky

Never a great defender at the two, Chapman was overmatched at the three in Phoenix's four-guard set. Still, he is a deadly streak shooter from long distance.

	G	MPG	FG%	3FG%	FT%	APG	RPG	PPG	BLK	STL
1996–97	65	28.2	.443	.350	.832	2.8	2.8	13.8	7	52
Career	507	29.9	.437	.344	.802	2.8	2.5	15.5	105	465

Kevin Johnson   G

Age: 31
Seasons: 10
Height: 6-1
Weight: 190
College: California

K.J. was injured for the first 11 games, talked about retirement, then had his best season since 1993–94. He ranks fourth all-time in career assists per game, behind Stockton, Magic, and the Big O.

	G	MPG	FG%	3FG%	FT%	APG	RPG	PPG	BLK	STL
1996–97	70	38.0	.496	.441	.852	9.3	3.6	20.1	12	102
Career	679	34.8	.494	.312	.839	9.5	3.3	18.6	168	1053

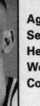

Jason Kidd   **G**

Age: 24
Seasons: 3
Height: 6-4
Weight: 212
College: California

Kidd is a phenomenal drive-and-dish point guard who also crashes the boards harder than any other player in the league at his position. His shooting is inconsistent but improving.

	G	MPG	FG%	3FG%	FT%	APG	RPG	PPG	BLK	STL
1996–97	55	35.7	.403	.370	.679	9.0	4.5	10.9	20	124
Career	215	35.7	.387	.323	.691	8.8	5.7	13.3	70	450

Danny Manning   **F**

Age: 31
Seasons: 9
Height: 6-10
Weight: 234
College: Kansas

Bad knees have kept him from being a perennial All-Star, but Manning is a brilliant all-around player when healthy. He has the court sense of a one, the moves of a swingman, and the height of a four.

	G	MPG	FG%	3FG%	FT%	APG	RPG	PPG	BLK	STL
1996–97	77	27.7	.536	.194	.721	2.3	6.1	13.5	74	81
Career	555	32.6	.517	.206	.731	2.9	6.2	17.7	586	754

Loren Meyer   F/C

Age: 25
Seasons: 2
Height: 6-10
Weight: 260
College: Iowa State

A throw-in from Dallas as part of the deal for Jason Kidd, Meyer has just enough size and skill to garner minor minutes for center-starved teams like the Mavericks and Suns.

	G	MPG	FG%	3FG%	FT%	APG	RPG	PPG	BLK	STL
1996–97	54	13.1	.443	.571	.719	0.4	2.7	4.9	15	11
Career	126	15.7	.441	.389	.699	0.6	3.7	5.0	47	31

Wesley Person   G/F

Age: 26
Seasons: 3
Height: 6-6
Weight: 195
College: Auburn

Person lacks both the muscle and the quickness to be an above-average NBA defender, but he is a perimeter sharpshooter who can deliver big numbers off the bench.

	G	MPG	FG%	3FG%	FT%	APG	RPG	PPG	BLK	STL
1996–97	80	29.1	.453	.413	.798	1.5	3.6	13.5	20	86
Career	240	28.1	.458	.407	.784	1.5	3.4	12.2	65	189

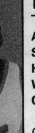

Wayman Tisdale *F/C*

Age: 33
Seasons: 12
Height: 6-9
Weight: 260
College: Oklahoma

Once a formidable low-post threat, Tisdale's game is in rapid decline. He contributes next to nothing on defense and has been injury prone the past couple of years.

	G	MPG	FG%	3FG%	FT%	APG	RPG	PPG	BLK	STL
1996–97	53	14.7	.426	.000	.625	0.4	2.3	6.5	8	21
Career	840	28.4	.505	.000	.760	1.3	6.1	15.3	500	464

John Williams *C/F*

Age: 35
Seasons: 11
Height: 6-11
Weight: 245
College: Tulane

He can't drive left, but Williams has a decent face-up game, plus the extension and instincts of a player who has averaged 125 blocked shots per year over the course of his career.

	G	MPG	FG%	3FG%	FT%	APG	RPG	PPG	BLK	STL
1996–97	68	31.4	.490	.000	.672	1.5	8.3	8.0	88	67
Career	791	31.1	.481	.105	.727	1.9	7.1	12.0	1378	700

Kenny Anderson

Portland
TRAIL BLAZERS

Franchise History: Portland entered the NBA in 1970–71 and, after a few years of growing pains, became a team to be feared in the latter half of the '70s. Blazermania took hold with Bill Walton at center and Jack Ramsey as head coach, and Portland won its only league title in 1976–77, winning four straight games after falling behind 2–0 to the favored Sixers. The Blazers made two unsuccessful trips to the Finals in the early '90s, and they have been to the playoffs for each of the past 15 seasons.

1996–97 Review: Inconsistent chemistry may have made the Blazers less than the sum of their individual talents, but on a position-by-position basis, they matched up well with just about every team in the league. Under head coach P.J. Carlesimo, Portland won 20 of its final 25 games prior to the postseason. Despite having taken the season series with first-round opponent Los Angeles (only a one-point defeat in OT prevented a 4–0 season sweep), the Lakers ousted Portland with comparative ease when it counted.

1997–98 Preview: After exiting the playoffs in the first round for the fifth consecutive season, Portland dumped Carlesimo and hired Mike Dunleavy, who is coming off a rather unimpressive stint in Milwaukee. The Blazers are loaded with firepower at spots one through four and are huge at the five, but they also have more than their share of free spirits. Great teams have veteran All-Stars and a team-first mentality. At this stage of their development, the up-and-coming Blazers have neither.

Trail Blazers Veteran Roster

No	Player	Pos	Ht	Wt	Exp
7	Kenny Anderson	G	6-1	168	6
2	Stacey Augmon	G/F	6-8	205	6
24	Chris Dudley	C	6-11	240	10
5	Jermaine O'Neal	F	6-11	226	1
34	Isaiah Rider	G	6-5	215	4
3	Clifford Robinson	F/C	6-10	225	8
21	Rumeal Robinson	G	6-2	195	6
11	Arvydas Sabonis	C	7-3	292	2
33	Gary Trent	F	6-8	250	2
30	Rasheed Wallace	F	6-10	225	2
10	Dontonio Wingfield	F	6-8	256	3

Head Coach: Mike Dunleavy

Trail Blazers 1997 Draft Picks

Rookie	College	Position
Chris Anstey (1-18)	Australia	Center
Alvin Williams (2-48)	Villanova	Guard

The Blazers traded Chris Anstey to Dallas on draft day in exchange for Iowa State center Kelvin Cato, the 15th pick overall. He's a very athletic 6-11, 255-pounder who was an intimidating shot blocker in college. His ability to score versus NBA pivots is a question mark, and he reminds some scouts of a cross between Rodney Rogers and Carlos Rogers. Alvin Williams has a nice all-around game and was a 1,000-point scorer despite not being a fulltime starter until his junior season. As a senior, he set career highs in points, assists, steals, and rebounds, then scored 31 points and hauled down eight caroms in a second-round NCAA tournament loss.

Trail Blazers Scouting Report

Guard: Point guard Kenny Anderson paced Portland in assists, steals, and scoring last year. He misses too many shots and he has yet to lead a team beyond the first round of the playoffs, but there is no denying his ability to spark an offense. At the two, Isaiah Rider can really fill it up when motivated. He is strong and athletic, able to get his shot from anywhere on the floor, but his commitment to defense and teamwork doesn't equal his offensive prowess. After five solid years in Atlanta, Stacey Augmon was withering in Detroit through the early part of last season. A trade to Portland and a regular role coming off the bench were just what Plastic Man needed to get back on track. **Grade: B–**

Forward: Clifford Robinson is another borderline star who can do everything his position requires—although not with consistency. A natural small forward, he has a vast offensive arsenal but iffy shot selection, especially in the playoffs. Rasheed Wallace, who was acquired in the deal that sent Rod Strickland to Washington, flashed All-Star potential in his second NBA campaign. He ranked third in the league in shooting, third on the team in scoring, swats, and rebounding. Gary Trent saw action in all 82 contests and finished tenth in the league in field-goal percentage. He lacks range and is slightly undersized for the four. The Blazers surprised NBA insiders by taking 6-11 prep star Jermaine O'Neal in the first round of the 1996 draft. He did flash some potential but remains a project. **Grade: B–**

Center: Massive pivotman Arvydas Sabonis is unique among NBA fives in his ability to make creative passes, connect from three-point territory, and dominate the boards. Chris Dudley is a solid backup with an Ivy League brain and a blue-collar heart. **Grade: B–**

Trail Blazers 1996–97 Player Statistics

	G	MIN	FG	FGA	FG%	FT	FTA	FT%	3FG	3FGA
Anderson	82	3081	485	1137	.427	334	435	.768	132	366
Rider	76	2563	456	983	.464	212	261	.812	99	257
Wallace	62	1892	380	681	.558	169	265	.638	9	33
C. Robinson	81	3077	444	1043	.426	215	309	.696	121	350
Sabonis	69	1762	328	658	.498	223	287	.777	49	132
Trent	82	1918	361	674	.536	160	229	.699	0	11
Augmon	60	942	105	220	.477	69	97	.711	0	0
Wingfield	47	569	79	193	.409	27	40	.675	26	77
O'Neal	45	458	69	153	.451	47	78	.603	0	1
Nembhard	10	113	16	37	.432	8	10	.800	0	6
Dudley	81	1840	126	293	.430	65	137	.474	0	0
Brown	21	184	28	70	.400	13	19	.684	13	32
R. Robinson	54	508	66	164	.402	26	35	.743	18	56
Djordjevic	8	61	8	16	.500	4	5	.800	5	7
Butler	49	465	52	125	.416	32	50	.640	12	39
Whatley	3	22	2	4	.500	0	0	.000	0	0

	ORB	REB	AST	STL	TO	BLK	PF	PTS	PPG
Anderson	91	363	584	162	193	15	222	1436	17.5
Rider	94	304	198	45	212	19	199	1223	16.1
Wallace	122	419	74	48	114	59	198	938	15.1
C. Robinson	90	321	261	99	172	66	251	1224	15.1
Sabonis	114	547	146	63	151	84	203	928	13.4
Trent	156	428	87	48	129	35	186	882	10.8
Augmon	47	138	56	42	64	17	87	279	4.7
Wingfield	63	137	45	14	49	6	101	211	4.5
O'Neal	39	124	8	2	27	26	46	185	4.1
Nembhard	3	8	17	9	8	0	12	40	4.0
Dudley	204	593	41	39	80	96	247	317	3.9
Brown	4	15	20	8	13	2	26	82	3.9
R. Robinson	6	47	73	24	43	2	60	176	3.3
Djordjevic	1	5	5	0	5	0	3	25	3.1
Butler	19	53	30	13	27	2	55	148	3.0
Whatley	0	3	3	0	1	0	5	4	1.3

Trail Blazers 1996–97 Team Statistics

Final Record: 49–33

Home Record: 29–12

Road Record: 20–21

Division Record: 14–9

Conference Record: 36–16

Overtime Record: 2–5

Points Per Game: 99.0

Opponents Points Per Game: 94.8

Field Goal Percentage: .464

Opponents Field Goal Percentage: .436

Turnovers Per Game: 16.5

Opponents Turnovers Per Game: 15.1

Offensive Rebounding Percentage: .325

Defensive Rebounding Percentage: .724

Total Rebounding Percentage: .524

Scored Fewer Than 100 Points: 42

Opponents Scored Fewer Than 100 Points: 56

Trail Blazers Clipboard

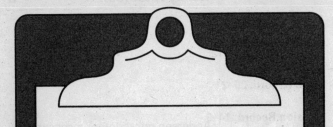

Why the Trail Blazers win: Portland has tremendous size up front and exceptional explosiveness in the backcourt. The young Blazers can get by on sheer athleticism on both ends of the court. Few teams control the boards better than Portland.

Why the Trail Blazers lose: The Blazers have too many individualists and not enough on-court leadership. They take the wrong shots at the wrong times and often fail to play "good help" defense.

1996–97 MVP: Kenny Anderson

Projected MVP: Rasheed Wallace

Fast Fact: Portland is the NBA's sixth-smallest market, yet the Blazers were the third-highest home draw in the league last year on a per-game basis, behind the Hornets and Bulls.

Kenny Anderson   *G*

Age: 27
Seasons: 6
Height: 6-1
Weight: 168
College: Georgia Tech

Anderson put together a season very similar to his All-Star campaign of 1993–94 (albeit with 200 fewer assists). He's an erratic perimeter shooter but not a shy one.

	G	MPG	FG%	3FG%	FT%	APG	RPG	PPG	BLK	STL
1996–97	82	37.6	.427	.361	.768	7.1	4.4	17.5	15	162
Career	424	33.8	.416	.342	.794	7.7	3.5	15.7	78	697

Stacey Augmon   *G/F*

Age: 29
Seasons: 6
Height: 6-8
Weight: 205
College: UNLV

Before being shipped from Atlanta to Detroit, Plastic Man had averaged 114 steals in five NBA seasons. It's too bad that his offensive repertoire isn't as expansive as his wingspan.

	G	MPG	FG%	3FG%	FT%	APG	RPG	PPG	BLK	STL
1996–97	60	15.7	.477	.000	.711	0.9	2.3	4.7	17	42
Career	450	28.5	.488	.213	.738	2.1	4.2	12.5	185	612

Chris Dudley C

Age: 32
Seasons: 10
Height: 6-11
Weight: 240
College: Yale

Dudley made just 13 starts last year but wound up second on the team in blocks and boards per contest. He works his tail off but is one of the worst shooters in the league.

	G	MPG	FG%	3FG%	FT%	APG	RPG	PPG	BLK	STL
1996–97	81	22.7	.430	.000	.474	0.5	7.3	3.9	96	39
Career	643	20.8	.413	.000	.462	0.5	7.1	4.7	873	284

Jermaine O'Neal F

Age: 19
Seasons: 1
Height: 6-11
Weight: 226
College: None

The youngest player in league annals, O'Neal made the move from prep star to first-round pick. Among his season highlights, he scored 20 points in 25 minutes at Seattle.

	G	MPG	FG%	3FG%	FT%	APG	RPG	PPG	BLK	STL
1996–97	45	10.2	.451	.000	.603	0.2	2.8	4.1	26	2
Career	45	10.2	.451	.000	.603	0.2	2.8	4.1	26	2

Isaiah Rider G

Age: 26
Seasons: 4
Height: 6-5
Weight: 215
College: UNLV

Rider is one of the strongest twos in the NBA, and he is tough to check when his jumper is falling. He is not an above-average all-around defender or an exceptional ball handler.

	G	MPG	FG%	3FG%	FT%	APG	RPG	PPG	BLK	STL
1996–97	76	33.7	.464	.385	.812	2.6	4.0	16.1	19	45
Career	305	33.5	.460	.365	.820	2.8	3.9	18.2	93	216

Clifford Robinson F/C

Age: 31
Seasons: 8
Height: 6-10
Weight: 225
College: Connecticut

Robinson hasn't exactly developed a reputation for clutch play or leadership, but his offensive skills speak for themselves. He is ultra-versatile and very durable.

	G	MPG	FG%	3FG%	FT%	APG	RPG	PPG	BLK	STL
1996–97	81	38.0	.426	.346	.696	3.2	4.0	15.1	66	99
Career	644	30.8	.446	.349	.679	2.1	5.2	16.2	724	696

Arvydas Sabonis   *C*

Age: 33
Seasons: 2
Height: 7-3
Weight: 292
College: None

Like most European big men, Sabonis is an adept interior passer with a nice feel for the finesse aspects of the game. Of course, he is also a behemoth under the boards.

	G	MPG	FG%	3FG%	FT%	APG	RPG	PPG	BLK	STL
1996–97	69	25.5	.498	.371	.777	2.1	7.9	13.4	84	63
Career	142	24.6	.523	.373	.767	1.9	8.0	14.0	162	127

Gary Trent   *F*

Age: 23
Seasons: 2
Height: 6-8
Weight: 250
College: Ohio

Once dubbed the Shaq of the MAC, Trent is a tweener who lacks the height for his position but not the desire. He made solid progress in his second pro season.

	G	MPG	FG%	3FG%	FT%	APG	RPG	PPG	BLK	STL
1996–97	82	23.4	.536	.000	.699	1.1	5.2	10.8	35	48
Career	151	20.8	.527	.000	.643	0.9	4.4	9.3	73	137

Rasheed Wallace   F

Age: 23
Seasons: 2
Height: 6-10
Weight: 225
College: North Carolina

Wallace hasn't been durable in his two NBA seasons, but he played like a future All-Star when not nursing a broken thumb last year. He is smooth and dynamic, with confidence to spare.

	G	MPG	FG%	3FG%	FT%	APG	RPG	PPG	BLK	STL
1996–97	62	30.5	.558	.273	.638	1.2	6.8	15.1	59	48
Career	127	29.0	.526	.313	.642	1.3	5.7	12.5	113	90

Dontonio Wingfield   F

Age: 23
Seasons: 3
Height: 6-8
Weight: 256
College: Cincinnati

Wingfield, who played just one year of college ball, entered the NBA as the league's youngest player in 1994–95. He has made incremental progress but is still a long way from being a quality pro.

	G	MPG	FG%	3FG%	FT%	APG	RPG	PPG	BLK	STL
1996–97	47	12.1	.409	.338	.675	1.0	2.9	4.5	6	14
Career	111	10.2	.392	.309	.726	0.7	2.4	3.8	15	39

Michael Smith

Sacramento
KINGS

Franchise History: The franchise has traveled from New York to California, but its only NBA title came in 1950–51 as the Rochester Royals. The team moved to Cincinnati in 1957–58, adding Oscar Robertson in 1960, but as the losing seasons mounted, the Royals shifted to Kansas City and Omaha to become the Kings in 1972–73. Tiny Archibald posted big numbers, and the franchise enjoyed occasional but limited success before setting out for Sacramento in 1985–86.

1996–97 Review: Despite expectations elevated by the previous season's playoff showing, Sacramento won just eight of its first 25 games last year to fall into a deep hole. Mitch Richmond, who finished fourth in the NBA in scoring (25.9), carried the Kings back toward contention (20–15 over the next 35 contests), but they collapsed from there, losing 13 of 14 to cost head coach Garry St. Jean his job. The club righted itself under Eddie Jordan down the stretch, but it was too little too late.

1997–98 Preview: The Kings haven't had a winning year since their arrival in Sacramento, so it probably wouldn't be prudent to expect one now. Still, with Richmond at the top of his game and a bruising young frontcourt hitting the boards, the Kings are capable of winning 40-plus and sneaking back into the playoffs. If that's going to happen, Sacramento will need to get consistent scoring from two highly erratic but talented players, Mahmoud Abdul-Rauf and Billy Owens.

Kings Veteran Roster

No	Player	Pos	Ht	Wt	Exp
3	Mahmoud Abdul-Rauf	G	6-1	162	7
40	Kevin Gamble	F/G	6-6	225	10
33	Brian Grant	F	6-9	254	3
7	Bobby Hurley	G	6-0	165	4
30	Billy Owens	F/G	6-9	225	6
0	Olden Polynice	C/F	7-0	250	10
2	Mitch Richmond	G	6-5	215	9
22	Lionel Simmons	F	6-7	210	7
34	Michael Smith	F	6-8	230	3
4	Corliss Williamson	F	6-7	245	2

Head Coach: Eddie Jordan

Kings 1997 Draft Picks

Rookie	College	Position
Olivier Saint-Jean (1-11)	San Jose State	Forward
Anthony Johnson (2-40)	Coll. of Charleston	Guard

Saint-Jean, a French subject, is a swingman who began his collegiate tenure at Michigan. He blew out a knee, then transferred to the Bay Area, where his stock really took off. He explodes off the floor, is very versatile, and has a quick release on the jumper. His raw tools rate with any small forward or shooting guard in the draft, and he paced the WAC in scoring last season. Anthony Johnson is a point guard who thinks pass first but can also score. He dished out over seven assists per contest as a senior, and topped his team in scoring seven times. Charleston went 101–17 in his four seasons. Both players bring plenty of energy and enthusiasm to the game, qualities which the Kings could certainly use.

Kings Scouting Report

Guard: As goes Mitch Richmond, so goes the Sacramento offense. He leads all NBA guards in total points over the past four seasons, and last year was perhaps the finest of his career. He not only topped the Kings in scoring, he paced them in steals and assists. Of course, the latter stat is in part a function of the team's weakness at the one, and Richmond's acute moping about his contract, combined with his lack of leadership, reduces his value. Mahmoud Abdul-Rauf has a quick release and unlimited range, but he lacks the size of a two or the passing skills of a one. Bobby Hurley has made a comeback from injuries suffered in a 1993 auto accident, but poor shooting has kept a lid on his career. **Grade: B–**

Forward: Billy Owens saw his scoring average decline for the fourth straight year while playing fewer than 70 games for the second. A swingman with super all-around skills, he rarely seems to fulfill his perceived potential. Kevin Gamble came off the bench and hit 48 percent of his shots from three-point range. At power forward, Michael Smith snagged 769 rebounds, shot .539 from the field, and chipped in his usual tenacious defense. Corliss Williamson posted solid numbers in his second year as a pro, scoring in double figures 52 times, but he has a tweener's mix of size and skills. Sacramento really missed the more complete game provided by Brian Grant, who missed most of the 1996–97 campaign after shoulder surgery. He is a deluxe interior scorer and rebounder. **Grade: C–**

Center: Since joining the Kings midway through 1993–94, Olden Polynice has started 272 of 275 games, missing three games due to league suspensions for fighting. He is half a rebound per game shy of averaging a double-double in that span. **Grade: C–**

Kings 1996–97 Player Statistics

	G	MIN	FG	FGA	FG%	FT	FTA	FT%	3FG	3FGA
Richmond	81	3125	717	1578	.454	457	531	.861	204	477
Abdul-Rauf	75	2131	411	924	.445	115	136	.846	94	246
Polynice	82	2893	442	967	.457	141	251	.562	0	6
Williamson	79	1992	371	745	.498	173	251	.689	0	3
Owens	66	1995	299	640	.467	101	145	.697	25	72
Grant	24	607	91	207	.440	70	90	.778	0	0
Edney	70	1376	150	391	.384	177	215	.823	8	42
Smith	81	2526	202	375	.539	128	258	.496	0	0
Gamble	62	953	123	286	.430	7	10	.700	54	112
Grayer	25	316	38	83	.458	11	20	.550	4	11
Simmons	41	521	45	136	.331	42	48	.875	7	30
Hurley	49	632	46	125	.368	37	53	.698	14	45
Causwell	46	581	48	94	.511	20	37	.541	2	3
Salvadori	23	154	12	33	.364	13	18	.722	0	0

	ORB	REB	AST	STL	TO	BLK	PF	PTS	PPG
Richmond	59	319	338	118	237	24	211	2095	25.9
Abdul-Rauf	16	122	189	56	119	6	174	1031	13.7
Polynice	272	772	178	46	166	80	298	1025	12.5
Williamson	139	326	124	60	157	49	263	915	11.6
Owens	134	392	187	62	133	25	187	724	11.0
Grant	49	142	28	19	44	25	75	252	10.5
Edney	34	113	226	60	112	2	98	485	6.9
Smith	257	769	191	82	130	60	251	532	6.6
Gamble	13	107	77	21	27	17	76	307	5.0
Grayer	21	38	25	8	15	7	42	91	3.6
Simmons	30	104	57	8	34	13	63	139	3.4
Hurley	9	38	146	27	55	3	53	143	2.9
Causwell	57	127	20	15	34	38	131	118	2.6
Salvadori	6	25	10	2	12	13	17	37	1.6

Kings 1996–97 Team Statistics

Final Record: 34–48

Home Record: 22–19

Road Record: 12–29

Division Record: 8–16

Conference Record: 23–29

Overtime Record: 4–2

Points Per Game: 96.4

Opponents Points Per Game: 99.8

Field Goal Percentage: .454

Opponents Field Goal Percentage: .462

Turnovers Per Game: 16.2

Opponents Turnovers Per Game: 15.3

Offensive Rebounding Percentage: .320

Defensive Rebounding Percentage: .685

Total Rebounding Percentage: .502

Scored Fewer Than 100 Points: 51

Opponents Scored Fewer Than 100 Points: 39

Kings Clipboard

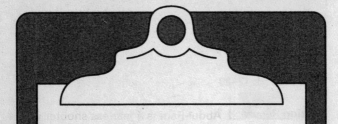

Why the Kings win: The Kings are tough in the paint and aggressive on the glass. Mitch Richmond is an explosive scorer who can carry an offense.

Why the Kings lose: Too many tweeners and too many one-dimensional players make the Kings unsteady from game to game. Sacramento lacks a third scoring option and could use a more reliable and potent second option.

1996–97 MVP: Mitch Richmond

Projected MVP: Mitch Richmond

Fast Fact: Mitch Richmond is the sixth player in league history to average 21.0 or more points in each of his first nine seasons as a pro, joining Abdul-Jabbar, Bird, Chamberlain, Jordan, and Oscar Robertson.

Mahmoud Abdul-Rauf G

Age: 28
Seasons: 7
Height: 6-1
Weight: 162
College: Louisiana State

Abdul-Rauf is a fearless shooter who can torch the nets with his quick-release jumper. Not a natural point guard and too small for the two, he may be best utilized to provide offense off the bench.

	G	MPG	FG%	3FG%	FT%	APG	RPG	PPG	BLK	STL
1996–97	75	28.4	.445	.382	.846	2.5	1.6	13.7	6	56
Career	514	28.4	.443	.359	.908	3.8	2.0	15.7	44	462

Tyus Edney G

Age: 24
Seasons: 2
Height: 5-10
Weight: 152
College: UCLA

A waterbug point guard, Edney can cause opponents problems when he uses his quickness and ballhandling to penetrate and distribute. His outside shooting is spotty and his size is a defensive liability.

	G	MPG	FG%	3FG%	FT%	APG	RPG	PPG	BLK	STL
1996–97	70	19.7	.384	.190	.823	3.2	1.6	6.9	2	60
Career	150	25.7	.402	.328	.801	4.8	2.1	9.0	5	149

Kevin Gamble   G/F

Age: 32
Seasons: 10
Height: 6-6
Weight: 225
College: Iowa

Gamble's playing time has steadily dropped since his days with Boston in the early '90s. He was on track to lead the NBA in three-point accuracy last year but fell 28 attempts short of qualifying.

	G	MPG	FG%	3FG%	FT%	APG	RPG	PPG	BLK	STL
1996–97	62	15.4	.430	.482	.700	1.2	1.8	5.0	17	21
Career	649	22.4	.502	.359	.810	2.0	2.2	9.5	176	470

Brian Grant   F

Age: 25
Seasons: 3
Height: 6-9
Weight: 254
College: Xavier

A shoulder injury rendered Grant a virtual nonfactor last year, but he is a promising young talent at power forward. His defense is strong and his offensive arsenal is developing.

	G	MPG	FG%	3FG%	FT%	APG	RPG	PPG	BLK	STL
1996–97	24	25.3	.440	.000	.778	1.2	5.9	10.5	25	19
Career	182	29.1	.501	.238	.694	1.4	7.1	13.4	244	108

Bobby Hurley   G

Age: 26
Seasons: 4
Height: 6-0
Weight: 165
College: Duke

Having faced extraordinary obstacles off the court, Hurley may now be looking at professional extinction. His perimeter shooting and on-ball defense have drastically limited his playing time.

	G	MPG	FG%	3FG%	FT%	APG	RPG	PPG	BLK	STL
1996–97	49	12.9	.368	.311	.698	3.0	0.8	2.9	3	27
Career	208	15.8	.341	.277	.766	3.4	1.0	3.8	7	97

Billy Owens   G/F

Age: 28
Seasons: 6
Height: 6-9
Weight: 225
College: Syracuse

Owens is versatile and athletic, able to crash the boards, defend at either the two or three, and score in transition. On the downside, his jumper comes and goes, and he hasn't stayed healthy in recent years.

	G	MPG	FG%	3FG%	FT%	APG	RPG	PPG	BLK	STL
1996–97	66	30.2	.467	.347	.697	2.8	5.9	11.0	25	62
Career	394	30.2	.497	.252	.637	3.3	7.2	13.9	246	399

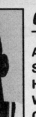

Olden Polynice   *C/F*

Age: 33
Seasons: 10
Height: 7-0
Weight: 250
College: Virginia

Polynice doesn't have star quality, but he gets the job done. Despite post moves that are rote, he usually scores in low double figures, and few pivots work harder on defense.

	G	MPG	FG%	3FG%	FT%	APG	RPG	PPG	BLK	STL
1996–97	82	35.3	.457	.000	.562	2.2	9.4	12.5	80	46
Career	775	23.9	.513	.143	.574	0.7	7.0	8.4	415	401

Mitch Richmond   *G*

Age: 32
Seasons: 9
Height: 6-5
Weight: 215
College: Kansas State

In addition to ranking fifth in the NBA in three-point accuracy, Rock recorded a league-record six four-point plays last year. He's a pure scorer who also chips in plenty of steals and assists.

	G	MPG	FG%	3FG%	FT%	APG	RPG	PPG	BLK	STL
1996–97	81	38.6	.454	.428	.861	4.2	3.9	25.9	24	118
Career	681	37.5	.465	.400	.843	3.9	4.4	23.1	203	888

Michael Smith   F

Age: 25
Seasons: 3
Height: 6-8
Weight: 230
College: Providence

Smith topped the Kings in caroms (RPG) and field-goal percentage last season. His offensive moments are generally limited to putbacks, and he is an incredibly poor shooter from the charity stripe.

	G	MPG	FG%	3FG%	FT%	APG	RPG	PPG	BLK	STL
1996–97	81	31.2	.539	.000	.496	2.4	9.5	6.6	60	82
Career	228	24.8	.555	.333	.463	1.6	7.2	6.4	155	190

Corliss Williamson   F

Age: 24
Seasons: 2
Height: 6-7
Weight: 245
College: Arkansas

Williamson has soft hands, a nose for the basket, and muscle to spare. A man without a position, his height isn't conducive to matching up at the four, and his mobility isn't adequate for checking NBA threes.

	G	MPG	FG%	3FG%	FT%	APG	RPG	PPG	BLK	STL
1996–97	79	25.2	.498	.000	.689	1.6	4.1	11.6	49	60
Career	132	19.7	.490	.000	.657	1.1	3.3	9.2	58	71

Sean Elliott

San Antonio
SPURS

Franchise History: The franchise was a charter member of the ABA, first as the Dallas Chaparrals (1967–1972), then as the San Antonio Spurs. After joining the NBA for the 1976–77 campaign, the team won five of seven division titles, and George Gervin won four scoring titles. Despite the regular season success, the Spurs never made it to the NBA Finals. David Robinson came to San Antonio for the 1989–90 campaign, and the Spurs have been contenders, but never champions, ever since.

1996–97 Review: Robinson missed the first 18 games of the season with a back injury. The Spurs were 3–15 by the time he returned, and head coach Bob Hill was replaced by general manager Gregg Popovich. When the Admiral came back, he lasted six games before a broken foot put him out for the remainder of the year. Adding insult to injury, Sean Elliott sat out 43 games with a bad quad. Dominique Wilkins stepped in as the team's top scorer, but the Spurs wound up 44 games behind Utah in the standings.

1997–98 Preview: From the worst record in team history to the first pick in the draft, the Spurs are on top of the NBA roller coaster. Tim Duncan is expected to form a sort of Twin Towers II with Robinson. If the rookie adapts quickly, and if Elliott and the Admiral are 100 percent, San Antonio will have formidable firepower in the frontcourt. On the cautionary side, the Spurs have a history of playoff underachievement, but they'll be expected to put an end to that sometime in the next three seasons.

Spurs Veteran Roster

No	Player	Pos	Ht	Wt	Exp
1	Cory Alexander	G	6-1	190	2
15	Vinny Del Negro	G	6-4	200	7
32	Sean Elliott	F	6-8	220	8
7	Carl Herrera	F	6-9	225	6
6	Avery Johnson	G	5-11	180	9
11	Vernon Maxwell	G	6-4	190	9
41	Will Perdue	C	7-0	250	9
45	Chuck Person	F	6-8	235	11
50	David Robinson	C	7-1	250	8
54	Charles Smith	F	6-10	245	9
3	Monty Williams	F	6-8	225	3

Head Coach: Gregg Popovich

Spurs 1997 Draft Picks

Rookie	College	Position
Tim Duncan (1-1)	Wake Forest	Center

Duncan needs no introduction to basketball fans of either stripe, college or pro. Oddly enough, the best center to enter the draft since Shaq figures to be used extensively at power forward, due to the presence of the Admiral. He is not likely to have trouble acclimating, as his face-up moves are as polished as his post-up repertoire. He scores from all over the court, makes gorgeous passes, helps on defense, and handles the ball like a guard. In his four seasons at Wake Forest, he amassed 2,000 points and 1,000 caroms. Only nine other players in NCAA Division I history have accomplished that feat. He was a consensus Player of the Year as a senior. As for potential flaws, his style is more finesse than power, and his free throw shooting is erratic.

Spurs Scouting Report

Guard: Avery Johnson got a new contract this offseason and will be back at the point. A pure point guard, he is quick off the dribble and always thinking pass first. His shooting range is limited to about 18 feet, but he usually connects at a high percentage. Cory Alexander, who is more or less a poor man's A.J., has more range but less overall accuracy from the field. Shooting guard Vinny Del Negro plays just well enough to keep the Spurs from upgrading their weakest position. Although fundamentally sound and quite versatile, he is neither a prolific scorer nor a strong defender. In fact, his game is downright tame compared to most starting twos. **Grade: C+**

Forward: A healthy Sean Elliott, which the Spurs did not have last year, is essential to the team's offensive scheme. He is San Antonio's most explosive dribble-drive weapon. His game is strictly finesse—he doesn't have the size to bang in the paint—but few small forwards can match his inside-outside scoring skills. At the four, rookie Duncan is slated to log a starter's minutes. The complete package, he should combine with Elliott and the Admiral to form the league's most athletic frontcourt. The Spurs hope Charles Smith can bounce back from a knee injury that cut 59 straight games out of his 1996–97 campaign. Injuries and inconsistency have derailed his career. **Grade: B**

Center: It is anticipated that David Robinson's foot will be fully healed for the coming season, but his back problems remain a concern. If he is in peak condition, he'll reassume his place among the top tier of NBA centers. A typical year in Mr. Robinson's neighborhood includes 25 to 30 points per game, 200 to 300 blocked shots, and 800 to 1,000 boards. The Admiral's backup is Will Perdue, who is effective near the basket on both ends of the floor. **Grade: A+**

Spurs 1996–97 Player Statistics

	G	MIN	FG	FGA	FG%	FT	FTA	FT%	3FG	3FGA
Wilkins	63	1945	397	953	.417	281	350	.803	70	239
Robinson	6	147	36	72	.500	34	52	.654	0	0
Elliott	39	1393	196	464	.422	148	196	.755	42	126
Maxwell	72	2068	340	906	.375	134	180	.744	115	372
Del Negro	72	2243	365	781	.467	112	129	.868	44	140
Johnson	76	2472	327	685	.477	140	203	.690	6	26
Williams	65	1345	234	460	.509	120	186	.645	0	1
Perdue	65	1918	233	410	.568	99	171	.579	0	0
Herrera	75	1837	257	593	.433	81	118	.686	2	6
Alexander	80	1454	194	490	.396	95	129	.736	94	252
Smith	19	329	34	84	.405	20	26	.769	0	1
Anderson	82	1659	130	262	.496	62	93	.667	0	1
Feick	41	624	56	157	.357	34	67	.507	5	14
Gray	6	49	8	26	.308	2	5	.400	0	0
Courtney	9	100	11	30	.367	3	5	.600	0	0
Kempton	10	59	1	5	.200	2	2	1.000	0	0

	ORB	REB	AST	STL	TO	BLK	PF	PTS	PPG
Wilkins	169	402	119	39	135	31	100	1145	18.2
Robinson	19	51	8	6	8	6	9	106	17.7
Elliott	48	190	124	24	89	24	105	582	14.9
Maxwell	27	159	153	87	121	19	168	929	12.9
Del Negro	39	210	231	59	92	7	131	886	12.3
Johnson	32	147	513	96	146	15	158	800	10.5
Williams	98	206	91	55	116	52	161	588	9.0
Perdue	251	638	38	32	87	102	184	565	8.7
Herrera	118	340	50	62	95	53	217	597	8.0
Alexander	29	123	254	82	146	16	148	577	7.2
Smith	18	65	14	13	22	22	44	88	4.6
Anderson	157	448	34	63	73	67	225	322	3.9
Feick	82	214	26	16	31	14	78	151	3.7
Gray	6	14	2	4	5	0	11	18	3.0
Courtney	9	16	0	0	3	0	14	25	2.8
Kempton	3	8	2	1	7	1	4	4	0.4

Spurs 1996–97 Team Statistics

Final Record: 20–62

Home Record: 12–29

Road Record: 8–33

Division Record: 8–15

Conference Record: 12–40

Overtime Record: 0–2

Points Per Game: 90.5

Opponents Points Per Game: 98.3

Field Goal Percentage: .442

Opponents Field Goal Percentage: .471

Turnovers Per Game: 15.2

Opponents Turnovers Per Game: 14.4

Offensive Rebounding Percentage: .324

Defensive Rebounding Percentage: .670

Total Rebounding Percentage: .497

Scored Fewer Than 100 Points: 64

Opponents Scored Fewer Than 100 Points: 48

Spurs Clipboard

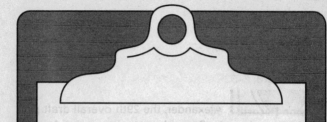

Why the Spurs win: Forget last season. San Antonio will create insurmountable match-up problems for most teams, with two incredibly athletic big men and a small forward capable of going off for 30 on a given night.

Why the Spurs lose: The Spurs call it psychobabble, but that doesn't alter the impression that there is something soft about this team. Also, the San Antonio backcourt does not rate with the NBA's upper echelon.

1996–97 MVP: Dominique Wilkins

Projected MVP: David Robinson

Fast Fact: The Spurs hold the records for best single-season improvement (+35 in 1989–90) and worst one-year collapse (–39 in 1996–97).

Cory Alexander G

Age: 24
Seasons: 2
Height: 6-1
Weight: 190
College: Virginia

Alexander, the 29th overall draft pick in 1995, has given the Spurs decent minutes as a backup point guard. In his six starts last season, he averaged 20.3 points and 9.3 assists.

	G	MPG	FG%	3FG%	FT%	APG	RPG	PPG	BLK	STL
1996–97	80	18.2	.396	.373	.736	3.2	1.5	7.2	16	82
Career	140	14.4	.398	.377	.721	2.7	1.2	5.3	18	109

Greg Anderson F/C

Age: 33
Seasons: 9
Height: 6-10
Weight: 250
College: Houston

Which is more definitive of a 60-loss season: being led in scoring by 'Nique or being paced in appearances by Cadillac? Anderson hasn't played more than a season for any one team since 1988–89.

	G	MPG	FG%	3FG%	FT%	APG	RPG	PPG	BLK	STL
1996–97	82	20.2	.496	.000	.667	0.4	5.5	3.9	67	63
Career	630	21.7	.493	.111	.561	0.6	6.6	7.7	581	461

Vinny Del Negro   G

Age: 31
Seasons: 7
Height: 6-4
Weight: 200
College: North Carolina State

Del Negro, who lacks both quickness and strength, may be more affected than most by the new "no forearms" defensive rule. As always, he'll have to get by with savvy and shot selection.

	G	MPG	FG%	3FG%	FT%	APG	RPG	PPG	BLK	STL
1996–97	72	31.2	.467	.314	.868	3.2	2.9	12.3	7	59
Career	535	26.7	.483	.357	.839	3.4	2.6	10.5	53	442

Sean Elliott   F

Age: 29
Seasons: 8
Height: 6-8
Weight: 220
College: Arizona

What he lacks in power, Elliott makes up in first-step explosiveness and a sweet shooting stroke. He missed the final 38 games last year after undergoing surgery for quadriceps tendinitis.

	G	MPG	FG%	3FG%	FT%	APG	RPG	PPG	BLK	STL
1996–97	39	35.7	.422	.333	.755	3.2	4.9	14.9	24	24
Career	585	34.8	.474	.374	.808	2.8	4.5	15.6	226	491

Carl Herrera F

Age: 31
Seasons: 6
Height: 6-9
Weight: 225
College: Houston

Herrera broke his nose twice and was hampered by sore knees, but he still made 58 starts due to injuries to other players. He's a fantastic leaper but an unreliable shooter.

	G	MPG	FG%	3FG%	FT%	APG	RPG	PPG	BLK	STL
1996–97	75	24.5	.433	.333	.686	0.7	4.5	8.0	53	62
Career	379	19.0	.483	.167	.664	0.6	4.1	5.9	184	206

Avery Johnson G

Age: 32
Seasons: 9
Height: 5-11
Weight: 180
College: Southern

In a good year, Johnson is one of the best drive-and-dish point guards in the league. He ranked just 17th in assists last year, but he was third in 1995–96 (9.6) and seventh in 1994–95 (8.2).

	G	MPG	FG%	3FG%	FT%	APG	RPG	PPG	BLK	STL
1996–97	76	32.5	.477	.231	.690	6.8	1.9	10.5	15	96
Career	630	25.4	.488	.162	.706	5.9	1.8	8.6	90	682

Will Perdue C

Age: 32
Seasons: 9
Height: 7-0
Weight: 250
College: Vanderbilt

Logging a career high in minutes and making 34 starts in place of the injured Admiral, Perdue posted single-season bests in almost every category. He is a very solid backup pivot.

	G	MPG	FG%	3FG%	FT%	APG	RPG	PPG	BLK	STL
1996–97	65	29.5	.568	.000	.579	0.6	9.8	8.7	102	32
Career	596	15.7	.519	.071	.596	0.8	5.0	5.2	422	178

David Robinson C

Age: 32
Seasons: 8
Height: 7-1
Weight: 250
College: Navy

It was a lost season for Robinson, and the Spurs went straight into the tank without him. For his career, no player in history has blocked more shots per game (3.57).

	G	MPG	FG%	3FG%	FT%	APG	RPG	PPG	BLK	STL
1996–97	6	24.5	.500	.000	.654	1.3	8.5	17.7	6	6
Career	563	37.9	.525	.261	.746	3.1	11.7	25.5	2012	940

Dominique Wilkins F

Age: 37
Seasons: 14
Height: 6-8
Weight: 230
College: Georgia

How many players could leave the NBA for a full season, then come back to lead a team in scoring, albeit a very bad team, at the age of 36? Wilkins is one of eight players in history to score 26,000 points.

	G	MPG	FG%	3FG%	FT%	APG	RPG	PPG	BLK	STL
1996–97	63	30.9	.417	.293	.803	1.9	6.4	18.2	31	39
Career	1047	36.2	.462	.319	.812	2.5	6.8	25.3	641	1374

Monty Williams F

Age: 26
Seasons: 3
Height: 6-8
Weight: 225
College: Notre Dame

He was never given starter's minutes in New York, but Williams flashed double-figure scoring ability for the Spurs last season, registering 14.4 points per game in 26 starts.

	G	MPG	FG%	3FG%	FT%	APG	RPG	PPG	BLK	STL
1996–97	65	20.7	.509	.000	.645	1.4	3.2	9.0	52	55
Career	137	14.8	.486	.000	.619	1.1	2.5	5.8	58	81

Detlef Schrempf

Seattle
SUPERSONICS

Franchise History: Seattle joined the league in 1967. The early years were predictably flat, but the franchise poured championship bubbly in 1978–79, taking the trophy from the Bullets, who had beaten Seattle in the 1977–78 Finals. Paul Silas, Gus Johnson, Fred Brown, Dennis Johnson, and Jack Sikma were starters on the title squad. Mediocrity reigned through the '80s, but the Sonics have made noise in this decade, including a 1995–96 Finals appearance that resulted in a 4–2 loss to Chicago.

1996–97 Review: Coming off a 64-win season, the Sonics defended their division title and became the only NBA team to post at least 55 victories in each of the past five years. Shawn Kemp, Gary Payton, and Detlef Schrempf were again an All-Star trio, but only Payton put together a consistent campaign. The Sonics seemed ripe for an upset entering the playoffs, and scrappy Phoenix nearly pulled a shocker in the first round. Seattle escaped the Suns, only to succumb to Houston in the conference semifinals.

1997–98 Preview: Head coach George Karl has designed an innovative system that perfectly suits his personnel, but Seattle's mental makeup is utterly unstable under postseason pressure. What other team is as likely to either choke in the first round or cruise into the Finals? Payton and Kemp are in their prime, and both are on the verge of being the best in the business at their respective positions, but the supporting cast is getting long in the tooth. It may be now or never for the Sonics as currently configured.

SuperSonics Veteran Roster

No	Player	Pos	Ht	Wt	Exp
34	Terry Cummings	F	6-9	250	15
3	Craig Ehlo	G/F	6-7	205	14
21	Greg Graham	G	6-4	182	4
33	Hersey Hawkins	G	6-3	190	9
40	Shawn Kemp	F	6-10	256	8
22	Jim McIlvaine	C	7-1	260	3
10	Nate McMillan	G/F	6-5	200	11
20	Gary Payton	G	6-4	190	7
14	Sam Perkins	F/C	6-9	255	13
55	Steve Scheffler	C	6-9	250	7
11	Detlef Schrempf	F	6-10	235	12
13	Eric Snow	G	6-3	200	2
23	Larry Stewart	F	6-8	230	5
25	David Wingate	G/F	6-5	185	11

Head Coach: George Karl

SuperSonics 1997 Draft Picks

Rookie	College	Position
Bobby Jackson (1-23)	Minnesota	Guard
Eddie Elisma (2-41)	Georgia Tech	Forward
Mark Blount (2-55)	Pittsburgh	Center

Seattle dealt the rights to Jackson to Denver for guard James Cotton (33rd overall) and a 1998 second-round pick. Cotton scored 23.5 ppg in four years at Long Beach State. Eddie Elisma improved steadily throughout his college career and flashed intriguing athleticism at the pre-draft camps. He blocks shots, runs the floor, and works on the offensive boards. Mark Blount joins the pro ranks after a sophomore season that included 78 blocked shots.

SuperSonics Scouting Report

Guard: The top stopper among NBA point guards, Gary Payton is aptly nicknamed The Glove. He makes steals, forces turnovers, and generally drives opponents crazy. On the offensive end, he's a money shooter who can take defenders off the dribble or post them up at will. At the two, Hersey Hawkins is a durable veteran who has made at least 120 steals in each of his nine seasons and is one of the best from beyond the arc and at the free throw line. More complementary than creative, he has nevertheless been crucial to Seattle's recent success. Veteran defensive specialists Nate McMillan and David Wingate serve as the primary substitutes, but neither was 100 percent healthy last season. **Grade: A–**

Forward: Power forward Shawn Kemp is a force of nature. Dynamic and graceful, he dunks with absolute authority and has become a dangerous midrange shooter as well. Alas, there is a dark side. He is prone to fouls, turnovers, and erratic behavior. Detlef Schrempf creates matchup headaches with his all-around skills. Comfortable in the paint or outside the arc, he is a deft passer, a consistent scorer, and a strong rebounder. No longer a youngster, his inability to stay healthy the past couple of seasons is cause for concern. Terry Cummings made a solid contribution in his 15th NBA season, filling in for the injured Schrempf, then providing depth and muscle in the playoffs. **Grade: A**

Center: The millions of dollars paid to Jim McIlvaine were good for about four points and four boards per contest, equaling the expectations of most league insiders. Sam Perkins, whose sleepy style belies an effective game, uses ultra-long arms and a veteran's savvy to help defend the interior. Big Smooth can score in the post but is better known for drilling triples. **Grade: C**

SuperSonics 1996–97 Player Statistics

	G	MIN	FG	FGA	FG%	FT	FTA	FT%	3FG	3FGA
Payton	82	3213	706	1482	.476	254	355	.715	119	380
Kemp	81	2750	526	1032	.510	452	609	.742	12	33
Schrempf	61	2192	356	724	.492	253	316	.801	57	161
Hawkins	82	2755	369	795	.464	258	295	.875	143	355
Perkins	81	1976	290	661	.439	187	229	.817	122	309
Cummings	45	828	155	319	.486	57	82	.695	3	5
McMillan	37	798	61	149	.409	19	29	.655	25	84
Stewart	70	982	112	252	.444	67	93	.720	9	37
McIlvaine	82	1477	130	276	.471	53	107	.495	1	7
Wingate	65	929	89	214	.416	33	40	.825	25	71
Ehlo	62	848	87	248	.351	13	26	.500	27	95
Graham	28	197	29	80	.363	26	40	.650	9	31
Snow	67	775	74	164	.451	47	66	.712	4	15
Harvey	6	26	5	11	.455	5	6	.833	0	0
Scheffler	7	29	6	7	.857	1	2	.500	0	0
Spencer	1	5	0	1	.000	0	0	.000	0	0

	ORB	REB	AST	STL	TO	BLK	PF	PTS	PPG
Payton	106	378	583	197	215	13	208	1785	21.8
Kemp	275	807	156	125	280	81	320	1516	18.7
Schrempf	87	394	266	63	150	16	151	1022	16.8
Hawkins	92	320	250	159	130	12	146	1139	13.9
Perkins	74	300	103	69	77	49	134	889	11.0
Cummings	70	183	39	33	45	7	113	370	8.2
McMillan	15	118	140	58	32	6	78	169	4.6
Stewart	75	171	52	31	63	23	108	300	4.3
McIlvaine	132	330	23	39	62	164	247	314	3.8
Wingate	23	74	80	44	37	5	108	236	3.6
Ehlo	39	110	68	36	45	4	71	214	3.5
Graham	2	13	11	12	10	1	12	93	3.3
Snow	17	70	159	37	48	3	94	199	3.0
Harvey	2	10	1	0	1	4	8	15	2.5
Scheffler	1	3	0	0	5	0	5	13	1.9
Spencer	0	0	0	1	1	0	0	0	0.0

SuperSonics 1996–97 Team Statistics

Final Record: 57–25

Home Record: 31–10

Road Record: 26–15

Division Record: 16–8

Conference Record: 37–15

Overtime Record: 2–1

Points Per Game: 100.9

Opponents Points Per Game: 93.2

Field Goal Percentage: .467

Opponents Field Goal Percentage: .441

Turnovers Per Game: 15.0

Opponents Turnovers Per Game: 18.7

Offensive Rebounding Percentage: .309

Defensive Rebounding Percentage: .691

Total Rebounding Percentage: .500

Scored Fewer Than 100 Points: 37

Opponents Scored Fewer Than 100 Points: 62

SuperSonics Clipboard

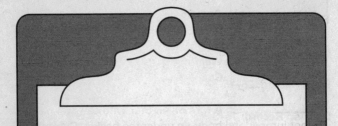

Why the SuperSonics win: Having the Glove at the point allows the Sonics to terrorize most teams with defensive traps and transition baskets. The Sonics feature three All-Stars who can carry the scoring load.

Why the SuperSonics lose: Seattle gets beaten when Kemp gets into foul trouble or Schrempf isn't involved in the offense. The bench is markedly weaker than it was two years ago, and the Sonics can be very temperamental under stress.

1996–97 MVP: Gary Payton

Projected MVP: Shawn Kemp

Fast Fact: Seattle has paced the NBA in steals for five straight seasons. No other team in history has led the league for more than three years in a row.

Terry Cummings F

Age: 36
Seasons: 15
Height: 6-9
Weight: 250
College: DePaul

A former All-Star who can still hit the 15-foot jumper and body-up under the basket, Cummings contributed quality minutes in his first season with the Sonics. He now ranks 39th on the all-time points list.

	G	MPG	FG%	3FG%	FT%	APG	RPG	PPG	BLK	STL
1996–97	45	18.4	.486	.600	.695	0.9	4.1	8.2	7	33
Career	1037	30.2	.486	.293	.705	2.0	7.7	17.7	622	1158

Hersey Hawkins G

Age: 31
Seasons: 9
Height: 6-3
Weight: 190
College: Bradley

Hawkins hasn't missed a start in four seasons, dating back to his tenure in Charlotte. He's one of the league's most consistent shooters from the field and at the charity stripe.

	G	MPG	FG%	3FG%	FT%	APG	RPG	PPG	BLK	STL
1996–97	82	33.6	.464	.403	.875	3.0	3.9	13.9	12	159
Career	731	34.9	.466	.399	.868	3.2	3.8	17.0	243	1287

Shawn Kemp   F

Age: 28
Seasons: 8
Height: 6-10
Weight: 256
College: None

Despite a second-half slump that saw his scoring average decline steadily through the final four months of the season, Kemp still finished with All-Star numbers.

	G	MPG	FG%	3FG%	FT%	APG	RPG	PPG	BLK	STL
1996–97	81	34.0	.510	.364	.742	1.9	10.0	18.7	81	125
Career	625	29.8	.521	.276	.730	1.8	9.6	16.2	959	775

Jim McIlvaine   C

Age: 25
Seasons: 3
Height: 7-1
Weight: 260
College: Marquette

Sort of a destitute man's Mutombo, McIlvaine has the extension and instincts of a premier shot blocker, but he doesn't offer the Sonics anything on offense.

	G	MPG	FG%	3FG%	FT%	APG	RPG	PPG	BLK	STL
1996–97	82	18.0	.471	.143	.495	0.3	4.0	3.8	164	39
Career	217	14.8	.459	.143	.549	0.2	3.1	2.7	390	70

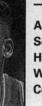

Nate McMillan   G/F

Age: 33
Seasons: 11
Height: 6-5
Weight: 200
College: North Carolina State

A versatile sixth man and designated defensive stopper when healthy, McMillan was limited to just 55 games in 1995–96 and fewer than 800 minutes last season due to leg injuries.

	G	MPG	FG%	3FG%	FT%	APG	RPG	PPG	BLK	STL
1996–97	37	21.6	.409	.333	.655	3.8	3.2	4.6	6	58
Career	778	25.9	.445	.339	.650	6.2	4.1	6.0	351	1530

Gary Payton   G

Age: 29
Seasons: 7
Height: 6-4
Weight: 190
College: Oregon State

Payton is pro basketball's best on-ball defender, and no point guard alive has better all-around offensive skills. He paced the Sonics in steals, assists, and scoring last season.

	G	MPG	FG%	3FG%	FT%	APG	RPG	PPG	BLK	STL
1996–97	82	39.2	.476	.313	.715	7.1	4.6	21.8	13	197
Career	572	34.3	.486	.302	.704	6.5	3.6	15.5	121	1309

Sam Perkins   F/C

Age: 36
Seasons: 13
Height: 6-9
Weight: 255
College: North Carolina

Still causing matchup problems with his reach and range, Big Smooth remains one of the NBA's most unique players. No longer a starter, he fell short of 2,000 minutes last year for the first time in his career.

	G	MPG	FG%	3FG%	FT%	APG	RPG	PPG	BLK	STL
1996–97	81	24.4	.439	.395	.817	1.3	3.7	11.0	49	69
Career	1012	31.1	.465	.351	.812	1.7	6.7	13.6	839	964

Detlef Schrempf   F

Age: 34
Seasons: 12
Height: 6-10
Weight: 235
College: Washington

Schrempf is no longer in his athletic prime—and he wasn't blessed with great quicks or hops to begin with—but he works hard, understands the game, and can score from any spot on the floor.

	G	MPG	FG%	3FG%	FT%	APG	RPG	PPG	BLK	STL
1996–97	61	35.9	.492	.354	.801	4.4	6.5	16.8	16	63
Career	905	29.9	.496	.378	.798	3.4	6.3	14.5	247	711

Larry Stewart F

Age: 29
Seasons: 5
Height: 6-8
Weight: 230
College: Coppin State

Back in 1991–92, Stewart became the first undrafted player ever to make the All-Rookie team. He came to Seattle last season after a year in Spain, making 21 starts for the Sonics.

	G	MPG	FG%	3FG%	FT%	APG	RPG	PPG	BLK	STL
1996–97	70	14.0	.444	.243	.720	0.7	2.4	4.3	23	31
Career	270	20.1	.509	.205	.753	1.3	4.0	7.4	106	147

David Wingate G/F

Age: 34
Seasons: 11
Height: 6-5
Weight: 185
College: Georgetown

Wingate will still put the defensive clamps on opposition twos or threes, but his knees aren't what they once were and his offensive game is as erratic as ever.

	G	MPG	FG%	3FG%	FT%	APG	RPG	PPG	BLK	STL
1996–97	65	14.3	.416	.352	.825	1.2	1.1	3.6	5	44
Career	654	19.2	.444	.269	.745	2.0	2.0	6.1	117	571

Damon Stoudamire

Toronto
RAPTORS

Franchise History: Preparing for their 1995–96 franchise debut, the Raptors chose Isiah Thomas to make all the basketball-related decisions. His wise selection of Damon Stoudamire with 1995's seventh pick overall secured Toronto a future All-Star point guard. Head coach Brendan Malone was able to coax 21 wins, including victories over NBA Finals participants Chicago and Seattle, from 28 different starting lineups, but that didn't keep him from being replaced by Darrell Walker at season's end.

1996–97 Review: The second number-one pick in Toronto history, Marcus Camby, helped the franchise improve by nine wins over its inaugural campaign. The Raptors were again paced in scoring and assists by Stoudamire. He was joined in the backcourt by journeyman Doug Christie, who finished second in the NBA in steals. Camby missed 19 contests because of injuries, and the team struggled when he was absent. Toronto finished the year at 30–52, ahead of seven NBA teams.

1997–98 Preview: Although not expected to be in playoff contention for at least two more years, the Raptors will again be an annoying opponent for the league's elite. Toronto was one of only four clubs (Knicks, Hawks, and Lakers) to defeat the teams with the three best records (Bulls, Jazz, and Heat) last season. Toiling in the NBA's toughest division, the Raptors are growing up fast. They need more height and scoring punch in the frontcourt, but look for the young franchise to continue making progress.

Raptors Veteran Roster

No	Player	Pos	Ht	Wt	Exp
21	Marcus Camby	C/F	6-11	220	1
13	Doug Christie	G/F	6-6	205	5
54	Popeye Jones	F	6-8	250	4
31	Shawn Respert	G	6-2	195	1
34	Carlos Rogers	F/C	6-11	220	3
20	Damon Stoudamire	G	5-10	171	2
3	Zan Tabak	C	7-0	245	3
42	Walt Williams	F/G	6-8	230	5
4	Sharone Wright	F/C	6-11	260	3

Head Coach: Darrell Walker

Raptors 1997 Draft Picks

Rookie	College	Position
Tracy McGrady (1-9)	None	Forward

The Raptors had only one selection, the ninth overall, in this year's draft, and they spent it on the youngest player available: Tracy McGrady, who hails from North Carolina by way of Florida. Only 18 years old, he employs the same agent as Kobe Bryant and Jermaine O'Neal, two other prep ballers to recently turn pro. He attacks the basket, can jump to the sky, and has shown three-point range—albeit only in workouts and exhibition games. A bit frail at 6-8 and 210, he may not be ready for the NBA grind, but playing for the expansion Raptors should give him time to put on muscle while gaining experience. Like those neophytes who have come before him in recent seasons—Kevin Garnett, Bryant, and O'Neal—McGrady has vast upward potential and the talent to make an immediate contribution.

Raptors Scouting Report

Guard: Damon Stoudamire was one of only four guards (Jordan, Sprewell, and Kevin Johnson) to rank among the NBA leaders in five categories last year. On the other hand, the combined field-goal percentage of the All-Star trio was .476, while Mighty Mouse shot .401 in over 1,400 attempts. He is a talented young point guard—quick, confident, and creative—but his iffy shot selection and 288 turnovers are indications that he still has a lot of developing to do. The Raptors received more than could have been anticipated from Doug Christie. Often traded and rarely appreciated, he reached career highs in every area and finished second in the voting for Most Improved Player. He was one of four players (Jordan, Pippen, and Blaylock) to register 400 boards, 300 assists, 100 steals, and 100 triples. **Grade: C+**

Forward: Marcus Camby's lanky frame didn't hold up well under the NBA grind, but he topped last year's rookie crop in shooting percentage and blocks per game. Walt Williams made 73 starts and put together his best season as a pro, finishing second on the team in scoring. One of the NBA's most versatile swingmen, he has been re-signed. Popeye Jones was his usual rebounding-machine self at the four, especially on the offensive glass. Carlos Rogers had an efficient year, despite playing only 56 games. He shot a team-high .525 from the floor, including a surprising .379 from beyond the arc. He is still raw but is beginning to refine his talents into basketball skills. **Grade: C**

Center: Sharone Wright has good size and athleticism, but he is an abysmal shooter who may not have the mettle to be an NBA five. Zan Tabak will try to come back from a heel injury that held him to just 13 games last year. He has a decent hook shot but no range, and he picked up more fouls than defensive boards in 1995–96. **Grade: D–**

Raptors 1996–97 Player Statistics

	G	MIN	FG	FGA	FG%	FT	FTA	FT%	3FG	3FGA
Stoudamire	81	3311	564	1407	.401	330	401	.823	176	496
Williams	73	2647	419	982	.427	186	243	.765	175	437
Camby	63	1897	375	778	.482	183	264	.693	2	14
Christie	81	3127	396	949	.417	237	306	.775	147	383
Rogers	56	1397	212	404	.525	102	170	.600	25	66
Slater	26	406	82	149	.550	39	75	.520	0	2
Jones	79	2421	258	537	.480	99	121	.818	1	13
Wright	60	1009	161	403	.400	68	133	.511	0	1
Tabak	13	218	32	71	.451	20	29	.690	0	0
Davis	36	623	74	184	.402	17	23	.739	16	70
Miller	61	1152	123	238	.517	48	79	.608	0	2
Rozier	42	737	79	174	.454	31	61	.508	0	2
Respert	41	495	59	139	.424	34	39	.872	20	57
Long	32	370	46	117	.393	25	28	.893	12	34
Whiteside	27	259	18	55	.327	11	15	.733	12	36
Lewis	9	150	6	14	.429	1	2	.500	1	3

	ORB	REB	AST	STL	TO	BLK	PF	PTS	PPG
Stoudamire	86	330	709	123	288	13	162	1634	20.2
Williams	103	367	197	97	174	62	282	1199	16.4
Camby	131	394	97	66	134	130	214	935	14.8
Christie	85	432	315	201	200	45	245	1176	14.5
Rogers	120	304	37	42	53	69	140	551	9.8
Slater	40	95	21	9	29	6	34	203	7.8
Jones	270	680	84	58	116	39	269	616	7.8
Wright	79	186	28	15	93	50	146	390	6.5
Tabak	20	49	14	6	21	11	35	84	6.5
Davis	11	40	34	11	21	2	40	181	5.0
Miller	105	306	87	47	90	63	181	294	4.8
Rozier	102	234	31	24	29	44	97	189	4.5
Respert	14	39	40	20	30	2	40	172	4.2
Long	6	40	21	9	24	2	28	129	4.0
Whiteside	2	12	36	11	17	0	23	59	2.2
Lewis	4	6	4	1	1	2	8	14	1.6

Note: Not all players are shown.

Raptors 1996–97 Team Statistics

Final Record: 30–52

Home Record: 19–23

Road Record: 11–29

Division Record: 6–22

Conference Record: 16–38

Overtime Record: 1–3

Points Per Game: 95.5

Opponents Points Per Game: 98.6

Field Goal Percentage: .437

Opponents Field Goal Percentage: .465

Turnovers Per Game: 16.4

Opponents Turnovers Per Game: 16.3

Offensive Rebounding Percentage: .325

Defensive Rebounding Percentage: .686

Total Rebounding Percentage: .506

Scored Fewer Than 100 Points: 55

Opponents Scored Fewer Than 100 Points: 46

Raptors Clipboard

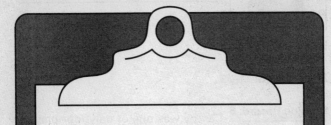

Why the Raptors win: Camby's health and Stoudamire's shooting accuracy are the keys. The Raptors have to play great team defense to make up for the lack of interior presence, and they have to hit their perimeter shots for the same reason.

Why the Raptors lose: In a nutshell, not enough top talent. No matter what the hype mavens imply, youth doesn't win in the NBA. Stoudamire, Camby, etc. may eventually be great players by league standards, but they are not there yet. The support cast is deep but mediocre.

1996–97 MVP: Damon Stoudamire

Projected MVP: Marcus Camby

Fast Fact: The Raptors were 11–2 when they shot at least 50 percent from the field, 3–18 when they shot under 40 percent.

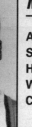

Marcus Camby *C/F*

Age: 23
Seasons: 1
Height: 6-11
Weight: 220
College: Massachusetts

Camby was one of only four players in NCAA history to log 300 career blocked shots, and he brought that ability to the pro ranks. A bit skinny, he had trouble staying healthy in his debut campaign.

	G	MPG	FG%	3FG%	FT%	APG	RPG	PPG	BLK	STL
1996–97	63	30.1	.482	.143	.693	1.5	6.3	14.8	130	66
Career	63	30.1	.482	.143	.693	1.5	6.3	14.8	130	66

Doug Christie *G/F*

Age: 27
Seasons: 5
Height: 6-6
Weight: 205
College: Pepperdine

Christie finally got the chance to play starter's minutes, and he responded by ranking among the league's top 30 in minutes per game and three-point accuracy.

	G	MPG	FG%	3FG%	FT%	APG	RPG	PPG	BLK	STL
1996–97	81	38.6	.417	.384	.775	3.9	5.3	14.5	45	201
Career	236	25.8	.425	.375	.745	2.7	3.8	10.3	98	384

Hubert Davis G

Age: 27
Seasons: 5
Height: 6-5
Weight: 183
College: North Carolina

Davis earned a reputation as a fine spot-up shooter in New York, but he saw far fewer open looks with the Raptors. After hitting 61 percent of his trey tries in preseason, he washed out during the real grind.

	G	MPG	FG%	3FG%	FT%	APG	RPG	PPG	BLK	STL
1996–97	36	17.3	.402	.229	.739	0.9	1.1	5.0	2	11
Career	298	20.9	.468	.429	.825	1.8	1.3	9.0	29	139

Popeye Jones F

Age: 27
Seasons: 4
Height: 6-8
Weight: 250
College: Murray State

Jones uses a wide body and superior instincts to post carom numbers that rate with the best in the business. His 207 offensive boards were good for seventh in the league last season.

	G	MPG	FG%	3FG%	FT%	APG	RPG	PPG	BLK	STL
1996–97	79	30.6	.480	.077	.818	1.1	8.6	7.8	39	58
Career	308	28.9	.458	.246	.740	1.6	9.3	8.7	124	208

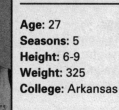

Oliver Miller F/C

Age: 27
Seasons: 5
Height: 6-9
Weight: 325
College: Arkansas

Miller has super court sense and a soft touch from point blank, not to mention the long arms and timing of a shot blocker. His problems have come in the weight and motivation departments.

	G	MPG	FG%	3FG%	FT%	APG	RPG	PPG	BLK	STL
1996–97	61	18.9	.517	.000	.608	1.4	5.0	4.8	63	47
Career	326	24.8	.542	.132	.640	2.3	6.4	8.5	578	336

Carlos Rogers F/C

Age: 26
Seasons: 3
Height: 6-11
Weight: 220
College: Northwestern

Rogers has the type of raw physical ability that makes coaches drool, but he is still learning to parlay his strength and hops into steady production. He missed 16 games due to an upper respiratory infection.

	G	MPG	FG%	3FG%	FT%	APG	RPG	PPG	BLK	STL
1996–97	56	24.9	.525	.379	.600	0.7	5.4	9.8	69	42
Career	161	21.5	.524	.297	.558	0.7	4.7	8.8	169	89

Clifford Rozier   F

Age: 25
Seasons: 3
Height: 6-11
Weight: 255
College: Louisville

Rozier was taken in the first round by Golden State, later traded to Orlando, and then waived. He has plenty of body for setting picks and crashing the boards but is not a skilled offensive player.

	G	MPG	FG%	3FG%	FT%	APG	RPG	PPG	BLK	STL
1996–97	42	17.5	.454	.000	.508	0.7	5.6	4.5	44	24
Career	167	17.7	.496	.182	.466	0.6	5.3	4.9	113	78

Damon Stoudamire   G

Age: 24
Seasons: 2
Height: 5-10
Weight: 171
College: Arizona

With a slick crossover and a knack for finishing in traffic, Stoudamire can score on any point guard in the league. He registered 10 or more points in a quarter 36 times.

	G	MPG	FG%	3FG%	FT%	APG	RPG	PPG	BLK	STL
1996–97	81	40.9	.401	.355	.823	8.8	4.1	20.2	13	123
Career	151	40.9	.412	.371	.812	9.0	4.0	19.6	32	221

Walt Williams F/G

Age: 27
Seasons: 5
Height: 6-8
Weight: 230
College: Maryland

Williams is a swingman or a tweener, depending on how well he's playing, and he has a nice repertoire of scoring weapons. He ranked among the top 40 in both steals and blocked shots.

	G	MPG	FG%	3FG%	FT%	APG	RPG	PPG	BLK	STL
1996–97	73	36.3	.427	.400	.765	2.7	5.0	16.4	62	97
Career	339	31.2	.431	.364	.718	3.1	4.5	15.0	235	423

Sharone Wright F/C

Age: 24
Seasons: 3
Height: 6-11
Weight: 260
College: Clemson

The sixth pick overall in 1994 (76ers), Wright shot .473 in his first two seasons of action but was inept from the field last year. He made 28 starts for the Raptors before injuring his back.

	G	MPG	FG%	3FG%	FT%	APG	RPG	PPG	BLK	STL
1996–97	60	16.8	.400	.000	.511	0.5	3.1	6.5	50	15
Career	196	22.9	.455	.083	.619	0.6	5.2	10.0	203	82

John Stockton

Utah
JAZZ

Franchise History: The franchise that began in jazzy New Orleans in 1974–75 and now resides in Salt Lake City had never been to the NBA Finals before last season. The Jazz didn't post a .500 record in any of their five campaigns in the Crescent City, but Pete Maravich regularly lit up the scoreboard. After arriving in Utah, the team continued to lose until the mid-'80s, when the Jazz wisely drafted John Stockton and Karl Malone. Recent years have produced a string of fine regular seasons and playoff disappointments.

1996–97 Review: The Jazz beat Seattle in their season opener, setting the pace for a campaign that would prove to be the most successful in franchise history. Stockton and Malone were their usual Hall of Fame selves, and the supporting cast chipped in more than expected, with Greg Ostertag bolstering the interior defense and Bryon Russell giving the offense a legit three-point threat. Utah beat both L.A. franchises and Houston en route to the Finals, where they fell to the Bulls in six.

1997–98 Preview: Utah's success reflects the ethic of head coach Jerry Sloan and the team's veteran All-Stars, Malone and Stockton. The Jazz are incredibly efficient on offense, utterly intense on defense, and completely focused on winning. Age is going to become a problem at some point: Stockton is 35, Malone and Jeff Hornacek are 34. But last year's performance rendered such concerns seemingly irrelevant for now, and it remains possible that Malone and Stockton can get a ring before they're done.

Jazz Veteran Roster

No	Player	Pos	Ht	Wt	Exp
40	Shandon Anderson	F	6-6	208	1
55	Antoine Carr	F	6-9	275	13
10	Howard Eisley	G	6-2	177	3
44	Greg Foster	C	6-11	250	7
14	Jeff Hornacek	G	6-4	190	11
31	Adam Keefe	F	6-9	241	5
32	Karl Malone	F	6-9	256	12
34	Chris Morris	F	6-8	220	9
00	Greg Ostertag	C	7-2	280	2
3	Bryon Russell	F	6-7	225	4
12	John Stockton	G	6-1	175	13

Head Coach: Jerry Sloan

Jazz 1997 Draft Picks

Rookie	College	Position
Jacques Vaughn (1-27)	Kansas	Guard
Nate Erdmann (2-57)	Oklahoma	Guard

Jacques Vaughn could be a perfect fit in Utah. As a backup for Stockton, he won't be expected to handle high-pressure minutes as a rookie. His unselfishness and intelligence are made to order for the Jazz, and it's possible that he can develop into a clutch shooter. The knock on Vaughn is the absence of an outstanding non-intangible characteristic, i.e. freaky height, quickness, or strength for his position. His offensive game is better than his college-career numbers (9.6 ppg, 6.4 apg) indicate, and he projects as a solid on-ball defender. Nate Erdmann has the potential to contribute as a designated shooter off the bench, and he is a fundamentally sound (but athletically mediocre) defender.

Jazz Scouting Report

Guard: John Stockton is the greatest of the pure point guards: an absolutely unselfish and highly creative passer, a quiet leader who speaks volumes by example, a master of tempo, a fierce defender who takes his opponents out of rhythm, a balanced and consistent scorer who can go to the basket or hit from outside, and the consummate decision maker. Jeff Hornacek is a perfect complement at the two, rarely turning the ball over or taking a bad shot. He is perhaps the least athletic starter in the NBA at his position (Vinny Del Negro is close), but nobody plays with more savvy and hustle. **Grade: A**

Forward: Karl Malone not only affirmed that he is still the best power forward in the business but also laid claim to his first MVP trophy. If anything, he is getting better with age. He dished out a career-best 4.5 assists last season while becoming the fifth player ever to log 25,000 points and 10,000 rebounds. Small forward Bryon Russell enjoyed a breakout campaign, seeing virtually the same number of minutes he'd received in his first three seasons combined. His blood is icewater, especially from beyond the arc. Adam Keefe hustles and works on defense and will hit the few shots he takes. Antoine Carr is a veteran four with a rugged streak and a reliable turnaround jumper. Shandon Anderson was solid for a second-round draftee but is too tentative to finish consistently near the basket. **Grade: A**

Center: Greg Ostertag has rare size and can be an interior force simply by eating space. He rejects almost two shots per game and snags about 15 caroms per 48 minutes. Of course, he can't shoot straight and is prone to fouls. Greg Foster moves pretty well and has a decent jumper, but his tough-guy demeanor, all sound and fury, belies a baby-soft game that scares nobody. **Grade: C**

Jazz 1996-97 Player Statistics

	G	MIN	FG	FGA	FG%	FT	FTA	FT%	3FG	3FGA
Malone	82	2998	864	1571	.550	521	690	.755	0	13
Hornacek	82	2592	413	856	.482	293	326	.899	72	195
Stockton	82	2896	416	759	.548	275	325	.846	76	180
Russell	81	2525	297	620	.479	171	244	.701	108	264
Carr	82	1460	252	522	.483	99	127	.780	0	3
Ostertag	77	1818	210	408	.515	139	205	.678	0	4
Anderson	65	1066	147	318	.462	68	99	.687	24	47
Eisley	82	1083	139	308	.451	70	89	.787	20	72
Morris	73	977	122	299	.408	39	54	.722	31	113
Keefe	62	915	82	160	.513	71	103	.689	0	1
Howard	49	418	62	108	.574	52	81	.642	0	0
Foster	79	920	111	245	.453	54	65	.831	2	3

	ORB	REB	AST	STL	TO	BLK	PF	PTS	PPG
Malone	193	809	368	113	233	48	217	2249	27.4
Hornacek	60	241	361	124	134	26	188	1191	14.5
Stockton	45	228	860	166	248	15	194	1183	14.4
Russell	79	331	123	129	94	27	237	873	10.8
Carr	60	195	74	24	75	63	214	603	7.4
Ostertag	180	565	27	24	74	152	233	559	7.3
Anderson	52	179	49	27	73	8	113	386	5.9
Eisley	20	84	198	44	110	10	141	368	4.5
Morris	37	162	43	29	45	24	121	314	4.3
Keefe	75	216	32	30	45	13	97	235	3.8
Howard	29	85	11	19	25	12	62	176	3.6
Foster	56	187	31	10	54	20	145	278	3.5

Jazz 1996–97 Team Statistics

Final Record: 64–18

Home Record: 38–3

Road Record: 26–15

Division Record: 19–5

Conference Record: 41–11

Overtime Record: 4–2

Points Per Game: 103.1

Opponents Points Per Game: 94.3

Field Goal Percentage: .504

Opponents Field Goal Percentage: .438

Turnovers Per Game: 15.4

Opponents Turnovers Per Game: 16.2

Offensive Rebounding Percentage: .297

Defensive Rebounding Percentage: .716

Total Rebounding Percentage: .507

Scored Fewer Than 100 Points: 31

Opponents Scored Fewer Than 100 Points: 55

Jazz Clipboard

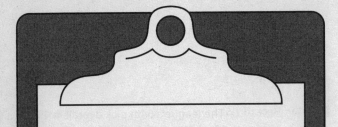

Why the Jazz win: Stockton and Malone run the pick-and-roll to perfection, and the Jazz get bushels of easy buckets with backdoor cuts. The players mirror the characteristics of their coach—unselfish and scrappy. Utah has a knack for making superb second-round draft picks.

Why the Jazz lose: The Jazz are terrific at finding each other for open shots, but they could use a player who can create on his own. The bench is deep but not exceptionally explosive. Team speed is nonexistent in Utah.

1996–97 MVP: Malone and Stockton

Projected MVP: Stockton and Malone

Fast Fact: The Jazz topped the league in shooting percentage (.504) for the third straight season.

Shandon Anderson F

Age: 24
Seasons: 1
Height: 6-6
Weight: 208
College: Georgia

The league's 54th pick overall in 1996, Anderson missed 15 games with a foot injury but still made a substantial contribution. He appears to be more comfortable on the perimeter than at point blank.

	G	MPG	FG%	3FG%	FT%	APG	RPG	PPG	BLK	STL
1996–97	65	16.4	.462	.511	.687	0.8	2.8	5.9	8	27
Career	65	16.4	.462	.511	.687	0.8	2.8	5.9	8	27

Antoine Carr F

Age: 36
Seasons: 13
Height: 6-9
Weight: 275
College: Wichita State

Carr throws his big body around and is a real defensive asset in the paint, but he has never been a dominant rebounder. He paced the Jazz in bench scoring last season.

	G	MPG	FG%	3FG%	FT%	APG	RPG	PPG	BLK	STL
1996–97	82	17.8	.483	.000	.780	0.9	2.4	7.4	63	24
Career	882	20.8	.506	.133	.780	1.2	3.6	9.9	856	346

Howard Eisley   **G**

Age: 25
Seasons: 3
Height: 6-2
Weight: 177
College: Boston College

Eisley handles the ball well enough and knows how to run the Utah offense, which has made him an acceptable backup for Stockton. He played in 147 straight games for Utah over the past two seasons.

	G	MPG	FG%	3FG%	FT%	APG	RPG	PPG	BLK	STL
1996–97	82	13.2	.451	.278	.787	2.4	1.0	4.5	10	44
Career	196	13.2	.421	.251	.806	2.2	1.1	4.0	19	91

Greg Foster   **C**

Age: 29
Seasons: 7
Height: 6-11
Weight: 250
College: Texas–El Paso

Foster's frame doesn't lend itself to holding position in the post against NBA pivots, but he can compensate by leading them away from the basket and popping midrange jumpers.

	G	MPG	FG%	3FG%	FT%	APG	RPG	PPG	BLK	STL
1996–97	79	11.6	.453	.667	.831	0.4	2.4	3.5	20	10
Career	379	11.4	.458	.227	.753	0.5	2.7	4.0	119	53

Jeff Hornacek   G

Age: 34
Seasons: 11
Height: 6-4
Weight: 190
College: Iowa State

Hornacek is a superb catch-and-shoot scorer who can handle duty at the one in a pinch. He is not quick or strong enough to be a great on-ball defender, but he fills the passing lanes and is very crafty.

	G	MPG	FG%	3FG%	FT%	APG	RPG	PPG	BLK	STL
1996–97	82	31.6	.482	.369	.899	4.4	2.9	14.5	26	124
Career	872	32.2	.502	.393	.870	5.2	3.5	14.9	181	1309

Karl Malone   F

Age: 34
Seasons: 12
Height: 6-9
Weight: 256
College: Louisiana State

The Mailman didn't deliver an NBA title, but that shouldn't detract from the MVP effort that helped earn Utah the home court advantage throughout the conference playoffs.

	G	MPG	FG%	3FG%	FT%	APG	RPG	PPG	BLK	STL
1996–97	82	36.6	.550	.000	.755	4.5	9.9	27.4	48	113
Career	979	37.6	.527	.268	.724	3.2	10.8	26.1	804	1417

Chris Morris   F

Age: 31
Seasons: 9
Height: 6-8
Weight: 220
College: Auburn

A monumental draft bust (fourth pick overall in 1988), Morris has always had more athleticism than shot selection. True to form, his field-goal accuracy last year was 96 percentage points off the team average.

	G	MPG	FG%	3FG%	FT%	APG	RPG	PPG	BLK	STL
1996–97	73	13.4	.408	.274	.722	0.6	2.2	4.3	.24	29
Career	649	27.2	.442	.307	.736	1.7	5.1	12.0	512	876

Greg Ostertag   C

Age: 24
Seasons: 2
Height: 7-2
Weight: 280
College: Kansas

Ostertag generally plays within his limits and uses his size to clog the middle. The Jazz have done a nice job of getting him in NBA shape and not putting him in situations that expose his weaknesses.

	G	MPG	FG%	3FG%	FT%	APG	RPG	PPG	BLK	STL
1996–97	77	23.6	.515	.000	.678	0.4	7.3	7.3	152	24
Career	134	18.5	.502	.000	.676	0.2	5.5	5.7	215	29

Bryon Russell   F

Age: 27
Seasons: 4
Height: 6-7
Weight: 225
College: Long Beach State

Russell's minutes and scoring average were decreasing rapidly after three seasons with the Jazz, but he finally found a steady stroke to go with his tough perimeter defense.

	G	MPG	FG%	3FG%	FT%	APG	RPG	PPG	BLK	STL
1996–97	81	31.2	.479	.409	.701	1.5	4.1	10.8	27	129
Career	270	18.8	.463	.370	.679	0.9	2.8	6.2	65	274

John Stockton   G

Age: 35
Seasons: 13
Height: 6-1
Weight: 175
College: Gonzaga

Stockton has averaged 195 steals per year through his career, and few NBA point guards work harder on defense. His knack for clutch play was on full display in the playoffs.

	G	MPG	FG%	3FG%	FT%	APG	RPG	PPG	BLK	STL
1996–97	82	35.3	.548	.422	.846	10.5	2.8	14.4	15	166
Career	1062	32.8	.520	.383	.823	11.5	2.7	13.6	216	2531

Bryant Reeves

Vancouver
GRIZZLIES

Franchise History: Vancouver's 1995–96 opener, the first game in franchise history, was a shocking success, as the Grizzlies beat the Trail Blazers in Portland. Head coach Brian Winters utilized expansion draftees Greg Anthony at the one and Blue Edwards at the two. The team's first rookie, Bryant Reeves, became a fan favorite at center. Vancouver endured a pair of protracted losing streaks en route to a 15-win season, then selected forward Shareef Abdur-Rahim as 1996's third pick overall.

1996–97 Review: Winning one game fewer than they had in their inaugural campaign, the Grizzlies wound up with the worst two-season percentage (.177) in NBA history. Abdur-Rahim shook off a sluggish start to become the only unanimous entry to the All-Rookie squad, while Big Country Reeves upped his scoring and rebounding over the latter half of the campaign. Stu Jackson replaced Brian Winters as head coach, but the outmanned Grizzlies won just six of their final 39 contests.

1997–98 Preview: Vancouver has already been lapped by Toronto in the expansion-wins race, but new head coach Brian Hill will have to be content to keep adding young talent while waiting patiently for Abdur-Rahim and Big Country to develop. Casting one's fate with other team's castoffs—Anthony Peeler, Blue Edwards, George Lynch, Lee Mayberry, etc.—is a great way to pace the NBA in losses. There is nothing for Hill and Vancouver to do but keep fishing the lottery and looking to the future.

Grizzlies Veteran Roster

No	Player	Pos	Ht	Wt	Exp
3	Shareef Abdur-Rahim	F	6-9	225	1
30	Blue Edwards	G/F	6-4	229	8
34	George Lynch	F	6-8	223	4
11	Lee Mayberry	G	6-1	172	5
52	Eric Mobley	C	6-11	257	3
7	Anthony Peeler	G	6-4	212	5
50	Bryant Reeves	C	7-0	275	2
5	Chris Robinson	G	6-5	205	1
44	Roy Rogers	F	6-10	235	1
50	Otis Thorpe	F	6-10	246	13

Head Coach: Brian Hill

Grizzlies 1997 Draft Picks

Rookie	College	Position
Antonio Daniels (1-4)	Bowling Green	Guard
C.J. Bruton (2-53)	Indian Hills C.C.	Guard

Daniels swung between the one and two at Bowling Green but, at roughly 6-3, he'll probably be a point guard in the NBA. His playmaking ability is unclear—no one doubts that he can create for himself—yet he dished out almost seven assists per game as a senior to rank tenth in the nation. Although he has been compared to Lindsey Hunter of the Pistons, the sharpshooting Daniels figures to be a more consistent scorer. Players from small schools tend to be underrated (Pippen, Malone, Majerle, Mason, etc.), but Daniels just might be the exception. Late in the second round, the Grizzlies selected JUCO standout C.J. Bruton, a native of Australia, who projects as a backup at the one. Bruton's team at Indian Hills (Iowa) went 38–1 last season.

Grizzlies Scouting Report

Guard: Lee Mayberry works hard, is a willing leader, and plays better defense than his numbers indicate. He can shoot the rock from outside, but his playmaking isn't up to par for a starting point guard. Look for rookie Antonio Daniels to see significant minutes at the one. The Grizzlies had hoped that Anthony Peeler, arguably one of the ten or fifteen most athletic players in the NBA, would elevate his scoring average and give them some punch at the two. Unfortunately, he kept up the pattern of underachievement he began with the Lakers. **Grade: D**

Forward: The highest-drafted freshman in the history of the league, Shareef Abdur-Rahim made a quick transition to life as an NBA small forward. After a spotty first month of acclimation, he blossomed into perhaps the league's most promising rookie. A smooth shooter who chips in on the boards, he figures to be a 20 ppg scorer for years to come. Backup three George Lynch has a restricted arsenal on offense, but he offers solid defense and will scrap for rebounds. At the four, rookie Roy Rogers converted half of his limited shot attempts and posted an impressive 163 rejections, more than twice the amount swatted by any other Grizzly. Otis Thorpe provides an interior presence with his strength and savvy at the four. He became just the 19th player in league history to log 15,000 career points and 9,000 boards. **Grade: B−**

Center: Bryant Reeves closed his sophomore campaign with a 39-point effort versus size-poor Phoenix, capping the finest month of his pro career. He is huge and agile, with a soft touch around the basket, but his star potential is limited. Eric Mobley also flashes some athleticism for his size, but he is susceptible to injuries and has little to offer on offense. **Grade: C+**

Grizzlies 1996–97 Player Statistics

	G	MIN	FG	FGA	FG%	FT	FTA	FT%	3FG	3FGA
Abdur-Rahim	80	2802	550	1214	.453	387	519	.746	7	27
Reeves	75	2777	498	1025	.486	216	307	.704	1	11
Peeler	72	2291	402	1011	.398	109	133	.820	128	343
Anthony	65	1863	199	507	.393	130	178	.730	88	238
Lynch	41	1059	137	291	.471	60	97	.619	8	31
Edwards	61	1439	182	458	.397	89	109	.817	25	89
Moten	67	1214	171	441	.388	64	99	.646	41	141
Rogers	82	1848	244	483	.505	54	94	.574	1	1
Williams	33	563	85	148	.574	33	49	.673	0	1
Mayberry	80	1952	149	370	.403	29	46	.630	83	221
Robinson	41	681	69	182	.379	16	26	.615	34	89
Chilcutt	54	662	72	165	.436	13	22	.591	25	69
Mobley	28	307	28	63	.444	16	30	.533	0	0
Leckner	20	126	14	33	.424	6	12	.500	0	0
Norris	8	89	4	22	.182	2	5	.400	2	10

	ORB	REB	AST	STL	TO	BLK	PF	PTS	PPG
Abdur-Rahim	216	555	175	79	225	79	199	1494	18.7
Reeves	174	610	160	29	175	67	270	1213	16.2
Peeler	54	247	256	105	157	17	168	1041	14.5
Anthony	25	184	407	129	129	4	122	616	9.5
Lynch	98	261	76	63	64	17	97	342	8.3
Edwards	49	189	114	38	81	20	135	478	7.8
Moten	43	119	129	48	81	24	83	447	6.7
Rogers	139	386	46	21	86	163	214	543	6.6
Williams	62	143	15	16	32	29	72	203	6.2
Mayberry	29	134	329	60	90	8	159	410	5.1
Robinson	23	71	65	28	34	9	85	188	4.6
Chilcutt	67	156	47	26	28	17	52	182	3.4
Mobley	30	58	14	5	29	10	44	72	2.6
Leckner	5	36	5	3	10	2	35	34	1.7
Norris	3	12	23	4	5	0	5	12	1.5

Grizzlies 1996–97 Team Statistics

Final Record: 14–68

Home Record: 8–33

Road Record: 6–35

Division Record: 6–18

Conference Record: 9–43

Overtime Record: 0–3

Points Per Game: 89.2

Opponents Points Per Game: 99.4

Field Goal Percentage: .437

Opponents Field Goal Percentage: .472

Turnovers Per Game: 15.9

Opponents Turnovers Per Game: 15.3

Offensive Rebounding Percentage: .297

Defensive Rebounding Percentage: .641

Total Rebounding Percentage: .469

Scored Fewer Than 100 Points: 70

Opponents Scored Fewer Than 100 Points: 38

Grizzlies Clipboard

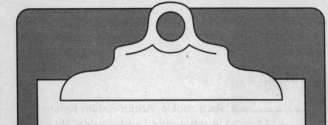

Why the Grizzlies win: It all depends on the matchup. If the Grizzlies catch a slumping team that lacks interior muscle and is streaky from the perimeter (such as the Spurs or Celtics last season), they can steal a victory by playing efficient defense and feeding Abdur-Rahim.

Why the Grizzlies lose: They are simply too young and not talented enough to put fear into quality NBA teams. Most of Vancouver's starters would be coming off the bench for a contender.

1996–97 MVP: Shareef Abdur-Rahim

Projected MVP: Shareef Abdur-Rahim

Fast Fact: The Grizzlies wound up an amazing 50 games behind the first-place Utah Jazz in the Midwest Division last season.

Shareef Abdur-Rahim F

Age: 21
Seasons: 1
Height: 6-9
Weight: 225
College: California

As a rookie, Abdur-Rahim finished in the league's top 30 in rebounding and scoring. He is still green but has unlimited potential and may turn out to be the prototype forward of the future.

	G	MPG	FG%	3FG%	FT%	APG	RPG	PPG	BLK	STL
1996–97	80	35.0	.453	.259	.746	2.2	6.9	18.7	79	79
Career	80	35.0	.453	.259	.746	2.2	6.9	18.7	79	79

Greg Anthony G

Age: 30
Seasons: 6
Height: 6-1
Weight: 176
College: UNLV

Anthony defends with confidence and has never failed to register at least 100 steals when used as a starter. His ballhandling and shooting skills are not exceptional.

	G	MPG	FG%	3FG%	FT%	APG	RPG	PPG	BLK	STL
1996–97	65	28.7	.393	.370	.730	6.3	2.8	9.5	4	129
Career	427	23.7	.403	.323	.746	5.0	2.1	8.2	56	581

Pete Chilcutt   F/C

Age: 29
Seasons: 6
Height: 6-11
Weight: 235
College: North Carolina

Chilcutt moves well for his size and will work hard on the little things, but he just doesn't have the power, quickness, or skill to be an impact player in the post.

	G	MPG	FG%	3FG%	FT%	APG	RPG	PPG	BLK	STL
1996–97	54	12.3	.436	.362	.591	0.9	2.9	3.4	17	26
Career	400	14.2	.452	.378	.686	0.8	3.5	4.5	151	177

Blue Edwards   G/F

Age: 32
Seasons: 8
Height: 6-4
Weight: 229
College: East Carolina

The type of player who does a little of everything but nothing with consistency, Edwards had an off year shooting the rock last season. His athleticism usually outweighs his production.

	G	MPG	FG%	3FG%	FT%	APG	RPG	PPG	BLK	STL
1996–97	61	23.6	.397	.281	.817	1.9	3.1	7.8	20	38
Career	599	27.0	.480	.334	.771	2.0	3.5	11.1	265	625

George Lynch F

Age: 27
Seasons: 4
Height: 6-8
Weight: 223
College: North Carolina

In three years with the Lakers, Lynch built a reputation for crashing the offensive boards. He posted Vancouver's single-game high in that category last season, with eight versus his old team.

	G	MPG	FG%	3FG%	FT%	APG	RPG	PPG	BLK	STL
1996–97	41	25.8	.471	.258	.619	1.9	6.4	8.3	17	63
Career	244	19.6	.477	.214	.639	1.2	4.4	6.8	64	263

Lee Mayberry G

Age: 27
Seasons: 5
Height: 6-1
Weight: 172
College: Arkansas

Mayberry is reliable and workmanlike at the point, but he doesn't create and is not much of a scoring threat. As a defender, he is far more effective than his numbers show.

	G	MPG	FG%	3FG%	FT%	APG	RPG	PPG	BLK	STL
1996–97	80	24.4	.403	.376	.630	4.1	1.7	5.1	8	60
Career	408	20.5	.423	.385	.645	3.4	1.3	5.3	34	280

Lawrence Moten   **G**

Age: 25
Seasons: 2
Height: 6-5
Weight: 186
College: Syracuse

Moten is another one of those players who found ways to score against collegiate competition but doesn't have a physical advantage that he can use to exploit NBA defenders.

	G	MPG	FG%	3FG%	FT%	APG	RPG	PPG	BLK	STL
1996–97	67	18.1	.388	.291	.646	1.9	1.8	6.7	24	48
Career	111	16.1	.411	.301	.649	1.6	1.6	6.6	32	77

Anthony Peeler   **G**

Age: 28
Seasons: 5
Height: 6-4
Weight: 212
College: Missouri

In his first year away from the hype of L.A., Peeler proved to be mediocrity incarnate as a starter. He has rare physical ability but barely average focus and skills.

	G	MPG	FG%	3FG%	FT%	APG	RPG	PPG	BLK	STL
1996–97	72	31.8	.398	.373	.820	3.6	3.4	14.5	17	105
Career	325	24.7	.432	.379	.787	2.3	2.6	11.5	62	319

Bryant Reeves   **C**

Age: 24
Seasons: 2
Height: 7-0
Weight: 275
College: Oklahoma State

Reeves has the size, mobility, and shooting touch to be a very good pro pivot. He needs to put together a full season's worth of consistent offensive production and work on his defensive footwork.

	G	MPG	FG%	3FG%	FT%	APG	RPG	PPG	BLK	STL
1996–97	75	37.0	.486	.091	.704	2.1	8.1	16.2	67	29
Career	152	34.5	.473	.071	.718	1.8	7.8	14.7	122	72

Roy Rogers   **F**

Age: 24
Seasons: 1
Height: 6-10
Weight: 235
College: Alabama

Like his 'Bama predecessors (McKey, Horry, McDyess), Rogers is a superior shot blocker. His scoring and rebounding must improve if he is ever going to garner a starter's minutes on a quality team.

	G	MPG	FG%	3FG%	FT%	APG	RPG	PPG	BLK	STL
1996–97	82	22.5	.505	1.000	.574	0.6	4.7	6.6	163	21
Career	82	22.5	.505	1.000	.574	0.6	4.7	6.6	163	21

Chris Webber

Washington
WIZARDS

Franchise History: This is not the first time that the newly renamed Washington Wizards have undergone a change of identity. The franchise spent two seasons as the Chicago Packers, arrived in Baltimore in 1963–64 to become the Bullets, then moved to the nation's capital ten years later. Hall of Fame center Walt Bellamy brought the franchise to respectability in its first decade of existence. Wes Unseld and Elvin Hayes ruled the paint and carried the team to four Finals appearances and one NBA title in the '70s.

1996–97 Review: For a franchise that hadn't been to a playoff game in the 1990s, the Bullets were facing fairly high expectations entering last season. Young forwards Chris Webber and Juwan Howard didn't disappoint, while the trade for veteran point guard Rod Strickland solidified the backcourt. A difficult victory at Cleveland in the final game of the regular season earned Washington the dubious reward of a first-round matchup with the Bulls, who dispatched the scrappy Bullets in three games.

1997–98 Preview: With a new arena and a new name, it is time for Washington to leave recent history behind. The nucleus is strong—Webber and Howard are a talented frontcourt duo, and Strickland is an ideal drive-and-dish distributor—but the Wizards still need to locate a reliable perimeter shooter. Consistency during the regular season will be crucial, both as an indicator of growth and in the effort to avoid facing one of the top two or three seeds in the first round of the playoffs.

Wizards Veteran Roster

No	Player	Pos	Ht	Wt	Exp
40	Calbert Cheaney	G/F	6-7	215	4
5	Juwan Howard	F	6-9	250	3
23	Tim Legler	G	6-4	200	7
77	Gheorge Muresan	C	7-7	303	4
35	Tracy Murray	F	6-7	228	5
1	Rod Strickland	G	6-3	185	9
4	Chris Webber	F/C	6-10	245	4
43	Lorenzo Williams	C	6-9	230	5

Head Coach: Bernie Bickerstaff

Wizards 1997 Draft Picks

Rookie	College	Position
God Shammgod (2-46)	Providence	Guard
Predrag Drobnjak (2-49)	Yugoslavia	Center

God Shammgod, who enters the league after two years at Providence, is a penetrating point guard who distributes and defends. He elevated his level of play during the NCAA tournament, especially in a second-round upset victory over Duke. There are questions about his ability to finish shots and connect from long range, but he has shown impressive on-court judgment, plus a knack for handling and passing the rock. Predrag Drobnjak rates as perhaps the best of the European big men available in this year's draft. He has decent face-up skills, an attacking style, and a pro pivot's size. As is often the case with such late-round selections of overseas players, there is a good chance that he will never play a game in the States. The Wizards gave up their first-round pick as part of the price for re-signing Juwan Howard last year.

Wizards Scouting Report

Guard: Rod Strickland is a terrific ball handler who can get to the basket at will and finish with consistency. Though not a threat from three-point range, he racks up plenty of steals and assists. On the wings, Calbert Cheaney is a fluid athlete and a good midrange shooter. He can match up at either the two or the three, but his on-ball defense is a bit soft at either spot. Cheaney and Strickland connected on only 17 triples in 107 combined attempts. Tim Legler, the league's most accurate three-point gunner in 1995–96, sat out most of last year with an injury. He has a fast, perfect release and should be even more invaluable now that the three-point line has been moved back. **Grade: B**

Forward: With an ideal blend of size and agility, Chris Webber is a force both in the open floor and under the boards. Few power forwards defend, rebound, dish the rock, or shoot triples better than Webber. The problem is that he has missed more games than he has played (183 to 145) since being selected as the number-one pick overall four seasons ago. Juwan Howard, who swings from the three to the four when Webber is at center, has rare court sense and superb post-up skills. He works hard and is an instinctive defender, but he is not a shot blocker. Tracy Murray provides a good stroke off the bench, but he chips in little defensively or on the glass. **Grade: A–**

Center: Gheorge Muresan is a gigantic presence in the paint, swatting shots and showing an unexpectedly soft shooting touch, but an absence of mobility makes him a liability in transition. Undersized overachiever Lo Williams is trying to return from a quadriceps injury that cost him 57 games. One of the league's hardest workers, he often matches up at center despite being no bigger than 6-9, 230. He made 20 of his 31 (.645) shots last season. **Grade: C+**

Wizards 1996–97 Player Statistics

	G	MIN	FG	FGA	FG%	FT	FTA	FT%	3FG	3FGA
Webber	72	2806	604	1167	.518	177	313	.565	60	151
Howard	82	3324	638	1313	.486	294	389	.756	0	2
Strickland	82	2997	515	1105	.466	367	497	.738	13	77
Muresan	73	1849	327	541	.604	123	199	.618	0	0
Cheaney	79	2411	369	730	.505	95	137	.693	4	30
Murray	82	1814	288	678	.425	135	161	.839	106	300
Whitney	82	1117	139	330	.421	94	113	.832	58	163
Jackson	75	1133	134	329	.407	53	69	.768	53	158
Grant	78	1604	129	314	.411	30	39	.769	28	89
Nickerson	4	42	4	12	.333	7	7	1.000	0	2
Legler	15	182	15	48	.313	6	7	.857	8	29
Williams	19	264	20	31	.645	5	7	.714	0	0
Amaya	31	144	12	40	.300	15	28	.536	1	1
Wallace	34	197	16	46	.348	6	20	.300	0	0

	ORB	REB	AST	STL	TO	BLK	PF	PTS	PPG
Webber	238	743	331	122	230	137	258	1445	20.1
Howard	202	652	311	93	246	23	259	1570	19.1
Strickland	95	335	727	143	270	14	166	1410	17.2
Muresan	141	481	29	43	117	96	230	777	10.6
Cheaney	70	268	114	77	94	18	226	837	10.6
Murray	84	253	78	69	86	19	150	817	10.0
Whitney	13	104	182	49	68	4	100	430	5.2
Jackson	31	132	65	45	60	16	131	374	5.0
Grant	63	256	68	46	30	48	167	316	4.1
Nickerson	1	5	1	1	1	1	1	15	3.8
Legler	0	21	7	3	9	5	21	44	2.9
Williams	28	69	4	6	18	8	49	45	2.4
Amaya	19	52	3	7	10	3	29	40	1.3
Wallace	25	58	2	8	18	11	27	38	1.1

Wizards 1996–97 Team Statistics

Final Record: 44–38

Home Record: 25–16

Road Record: 19–22

Division Record: 14–10

Conference Record: 28–26

Overtime Record: 1–5

Points Per Game: 99.4

Opponents Points Per Game: 97.7

Field Goal Percentage: .480

Opponents Field Goal Percentage: .454

Turnovers Per Game: 15.7

Opponents Turnovers Per Game: 16.5

Offensive Rebounding Percentage: .302

Defensive Rebounding Percentage: .703

Total Rebounding Percentage: .502

Scored Fewer Than 100 Points: 41

Opponents Scored Fewer Than 100 Points: 48

Wizards Clipboard

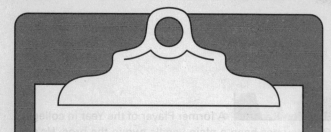

Why the Wizards win: For the Wizards to win consistently, Webber and Howard must be active in the paint while leaving most of the ballhandling to Strickland. The backcourt needs to create open space by hitting from outside, and the team as a whole must play "good help" defense.

Why the Wizards lose: The Wizards are still a bit erratic defensively. Neither of the team's starting guards is a reliable shooter from beyond the arc. The bench is limited, and Webber's injuries have been devastating.

1996–97 MVP: Rod Strickland

Projected MVP: Chris Webber

Fast Fact: Washington hasn't won a playoff game since 1987–88 or a playoff series since 1981–82.

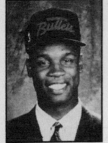

Calbert Cheaney G/F

Age: 26
Seasons: 4
Height: 6-7
Weight: 215
College: Indiana

A former Player of the Year in college, Cheaney has been a plain-vanilla two in the pros. He's a pure shooter from 18 feet in, but he makes few trips to the charity stripe and is a nonfactor from beyond the arc.

	G	MPG	FG%	3FG%	FT%	APG	RPG	PPG	BLK	STL
1996–97	79	30.5	.505	.133	.693	1.4	3.4	10.6	18	77
Career	292	30.8	.475	.312	.749	2.0	3.5	13.6	67	287

Harvey Grant F

Age: 32
Seasons: 9
Height: 6-9
Weight: 225
College: Oklahoma

Neither the banger nor the scorer that his identical twin (Horace) is, Harvey relies on versatility and unselfishness to keep his NBA career afloat. He can be utilized defensively at any of spots two through five.

	G	MPG	FG%	3FG%	FT%	APG	RPG	PPG	BLK	STL
1996–97	78	20.6	.411	.315	.769	0.9	3.3	4.1	48	46
Career	671	28.0	.474	.273	.710	1.7	4.7	11.1	397	556

Juwan Howard   F

Age: 24
Seasons: 3
Height: 6-9
Weight: 250
College: Michigan

Howard inked a deal with Miami prior to the 1996–97 opener, then stayed in Washington when the contract was voided by the league. He led the team in minutes and finished second in scoring.

	G	MPG	FG%	3FG%	FT%	APG	RPG	PPG	BLK	STL
1996–97	82	40.5	.486	.000	.756	3.8	8.0	19.1	23	93
Career	228	39.3	.488	.182	.729	3.7	8.1	19.6	77	212

Jaren Jackson   G

Age: 30
Seasons: 7
Height: 6-6
Weight: 210
College: Georgetown

The ultimate basketball journeyman, Jackson has played for seven NBA teams and four CBA clubs in seven seasons as a pro. He saw by far the most action of his career last year.

	G	MPG	FG%	3FG%	FT%	APG	RPG	PPG	BLK	STL
1996–97	75	15.1	.407	.335	.768	0.9	1.8	5.0	16	45
Career	196	11.1	.396	.307	.778	0.8	1.4	3.9	29	93

Tim Legler G

Age: 31
Seasons: 7
Height: 6-4
Weight: 200
College: LaSalle

A veteran of four CBA All-Star games who has played for seven NBA teams, Legler missed 65 games last year due to a torn ACL. A sweet shooter, he paced the NBA in three-point accuracy two seasons ago.

	G	MPG	FG%	3FG%	FT%	APG	RPG	PPG	BLK	STL
1996–97	15	12.1	.313	.276	.857	0.5	1.4	2.9	5	3
Career	249	18.1	.455	.442	.848	1.4	1.7	7.9	37	140

Gheorge Muresan C

Age: 26
Seasons: 4
Height: 7-7
Weight: 303
College: Cluj

The tallest person ever to play in an NBA game, Muresan has a surprisingly soft shooting touch. He topped the league in field goal percentage last year despite being hampered by back problems.

	G	MPG	FG%	3FG%	FT%	APG	RPG	PPG	BLK	STL
1996–97	73	25.3	.604	.000	.618	0.4	6.6	10.6	96	43
Career	276	23.4	.579	.000	.646	0.5	6.8	10.6	443	171

Tracy Murray   F

Age: 26
Seasons: 5
Height: 6-7
Weight: 228
College: UCLA

Murray is a valuable, one-dimensional player, a deadly perimeter shooter whose contribution is negligible in other areas. He paced Washington in bench scoring 51 times last season.

	G	MPG	FG%	3FG%	FT%	APG	RPG	PPG	BLK	STL
1996–97	82	22.1	.425	.353	.839	1.0	3.1	10.0	19	69
Career	332	18.4	.441	.393	.815	0.8	2.6	9.4	88	199

Rod Strickland   G

Age: 31
Seasons: 9
Height: 6-3
Weight: 185
College: DePaul

Strickland rates with the league's best as a drive-and-dish point guard. He can get to the rack at will and is a terrific finisher. As a shooter, he lacks range and consistency.

	G	MPG	FG%	3FG%	FT%	APG	RPG	PPG	BLK	STL
1996–97	82	36.5	.466	.169	.738	8.9	4.1	17.2	14	143
Career	651	31.9	.469	.299	.714	7.6	3.9	14.6	132	1101

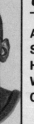

Chris Webber F/C

Age: 24
Seasons: 4
Height: 6-10
Weight: 245
College: Michigan

A former number-one overall draft pick, Webber has cost his teams and coaches a lot while delivering a lot less. He ranked among the top 30 in assists, steals, blocks, rebounding, and scoring last year.

	G	MPG	FG%	3FG%	FT%	APG	RPG	PPG	BLK	STL
1996–97	72	39.0	.518	.397	.565	4.6	10.3	20.1	137	122
Career	217	36.3	.524	.334	.540	4.3	9.5	19.4	395	325

Chris Whitney G

Age: 26
Seasons: 4
Height: 6-0
Weight: 170
College: Clemson

Whitney, who began his career in San Antonio and wound up in the CBA, saw action in every game last season and logged 1,000-plus minutes for the first time in his career.

	G	MPG	FG%	3FG%	FT%	APG	RPG	PPG	BLK	STL
1996–97	82	13.6	.421	.356	.832	2.2	1.3	5.2	4	49
Career	168	11.7	.400	.352	.863	1.9	1.1	4.1	6	82

Tommy Heinsohn

All-Time NBA Final Standings

BAA 1946–47

Eastern Division	Won	Lost	Pct.
Washington	49	11	.817
Philadelphia	35	25	.583
New York	33	27	.550
Providence	28	32	.467
Toronto	22	38	.367
Boston	22	38	.367

Western Division	Won	Lost	Pct.
Chicago	39	22	.639
St. Louis	38	23	.623
Cleveland	30	30	.500
Detroit	20	40	.333
Pittsburgh	15	45	.250

Quarterfinals: Philadelphia 2, St. Louis 1; New York 2, Cleveland 1

Semifinals: Chicago 4, Washington 2; Philadelphia 2, New York 0

BAA Finals: Philadelphia 4, Chicago 1

BAA 1947–48

Eastern Division	Won	Lost	Pct.
Philadelphia	27	21	.563
New York	26	22	.542
Boston	20	28	.417
Providence	6	42	.125

Western Division	Won	Lost	Pct.
St. Louis	29	19	.604
Baltimore	28	20	.583

1947–48 (continued)

Chicago	28	20	.583
Washington	28	20	.583

Quarterfinals: Baltimore 2, New York 1; Chicago 2, Boston 1

Semifinals: Philadelphia 4, St. Louis 3; Baltimore 2, Chicago 0

BAA Finals: Baltimore 4, Philadelphia 2

BAA 1948–49

Eastern Division	Won	Lost	Pct.
Washington	38	22	.633
New York	32	28	.533
Baltimore	29	31	.483
Philadelphia	28	32	.467
Boston	25	35	.417
Providence	12	48	.200

Division Semifinals: Washington 2, Philadelphia 0; New York 2, Baltimore 1

Division Finals: Washington 2, New York 1

Western Division	Won	Lost	Pct.
Rochester	45	15	.750
Minneapolis	44	16	.733
Chicago	38	22	.633
St. Louis	29	31	.483
Fort Wayne	22	38	.367
Indianapolis	18	42	.300

Division Semifinals: Rochester 2, St. Louis 0; Minneapolis 2, Chicago 0

Division Finals: Minneapolis 2, Rochester 0

BAA Finals: Minneapolis 4, Washington 2

NBA 1949–50

Eastern Division	Won	Lost	Pct.
Syracuse	51	13	.797
New York	40	28	.588
Washington	32	36	.471
Philadelphia	26	42	.382
Baltimore	25	43	.368
Boston	22	46	.324

Division Semifinals: Syracuse 2, Philadelphia 0; New York 2, Washington 1

Division Finals: Syracuse 2, New York 1

Central Division	Won	Lost	Pct.
Minneapolis	51	17	.750
Rochester	51	17	.750
Fort Wayne	40	28	.588
Chicago	40	28	.588
St. Louis	26	42	.382

Division Tiebreakers: Minneapolis 78, Rochester 76; Fort Wayne 86, Chicago 69

Division Semifinals: Minneapolis 2, Chicago 0; Fort Wayne 2, Rochester 0

Division Finals: Minneapolis 2, Fort Wayne 0

Western Division	Won	Lost	.Pct.
Indianapolis	39	25	.609
Anderson	37	27	.578
Tri-Cities	29	35	.453
Sheboygan	22	40	.355
Waterloo	19	43	.306
Denver	11	51	.177

1949–50 (continued)

Division Semifinals: Anderson 2, Tri-Cities 1; Indianapolis 2, Sheboygan 1

Division Finals: Anderson 2, Indianapolis 1

NBA Semifinals: Minneapolis 2, Anderson 0
NBA Finals: Minneapolis 4, Syracuse 2

NBA 1950–51

Eastern Division	Won	Lost	Pct.
Philadelphia	40	26	.606
Boston	39	30	.565
New York	36	30	.545
Syracuse	32	34	.485
Baltimore	24	42	.364
Washington	10	25	.286

Division Semifinals: New York 2, Boston 0; Syracuse 2, Philadelphia 0

Division Finals: New York 3, Syracuse 2

Western Division	Won	Lost	Pct.
Minneapolis	44	24	.606
Rochester	41	27	.603
Fort Wayne	32	36	.471
Indianapolis	31	37	.456
Tri-Cities	25	43	.368

Division Semifinals: Rochester 2, Fort Wayne 1; Minneapolis 2, Indianapolis 1

Division Finals: Rochester 3, Minneapolis 1

NBA Finals: Rochester 4, New York 3

NBA 1951–52

Eastern Division	Won	Lost	Pct.
Syracuse	40	26	.606
Boston	39	27	.591
New York	37	29	.561
Philadelphia	33	33	.500
Baltimore	20	46	.303

Division Semifinals: New York 2, Boston 1; Syracuse 2, Philadelphia 1

Division Finals: New York 3, Syracuse 1

Western Division	Won	Lost	Pct.
Rochester	41	25	.621
Minneapolis	40	26	.606
Indianapolis	34	32	.515
Fort Wayne	29	37	.439
Milwaukee	17	49	.258

Division Semifinals: Rochester 2, Fort Wayne 0; Minneapolis 2, Indianapolis 0

Division Finals: Minneapolis 3, Rochester 1

NBA Finals: Minneapolis 4, New York 3

NBA 1952–53

Eastern Division	Won	Lost	Pct.
New York	47	23	.671
Syracuse	47	24	.662
Boston	46	25	.648
Baltimore	16	54	.229
Philadelphia	12	57	.174

Jerry West

1952–53 (continued)

Division Semifinals: New York 2, Baltimore 0; Boston 2, Syracuse 0

Division Finals: New York 3, Boston 1

Western Division	Won	Lost	Pct.
Minneapolis	48	22	.686
Rochester	44	26	.629
Fort Wayne	36	33	.522
Indianapolis	28	43	.394
Milwaukee	27	44	.380

Division Semifinals: Fort Wayne 2, Rochester 1; Minneapolis 2, Indianapolis 1

Division Finals: Minneapolis 3, Fort Wayne 2

NBA Finals: Minneapolis 4, New York 1

NBA 1953–54

Eastern Division	Won	Lost	Pct.
New York	44	28	.611
Boston	42	30	.583
Syracuse	42	30	.583
Philadelphia	29	43	.403
Baltimore	16	56	.222

Division Round Robin: Boston 93, New York 71; Syracuse 96, Boston 95 (OT); Syracuse 75 New York 68; Boston 79, New York 78; Syracuse 103, New York 99; Syracuse 98, Boston 85

Division Finals: Syracuse 2, Boston 0

Western Division	Won	Lost	Pct.
Minneapolis	46	26	.639
Rochester	44	28	.611

1953–54 (continued)

Fort Wayne	40	32	.556
Milwaukee	21	51	.292

Division Round Robin: Rochester 82, Fort Wayne 75; Minneapolis 109, Rochester 88; Minneapolis 90, Fort Wayne 85; Minneapolis 78, Fort Wayne 73; Rochester 89, Fort Wayne 71; Minneapolis at Rochester (cancelled)

Division Finals: Minneapolis 2, Rochester 1

NBA Finals: Minneapolis 4, Syracuse 3

NBA 1954–55

Eastern Division	Won	Lost	Pct.
Syracuse	43	29	.597
New York	38	34	.528
Boston	36	36	.500
Philadelphia	33	39	.458
Baltimore	3	11	.214

Division Semifinals: Boston 2, New York 1
Division Finals: Syracuse 3, Boston 1

Western Division	Won	Lost	Pct.
Fort Wayne	43	29	.597
Minneapolis	40	32	.556
Rochester	29	43	.403
Milwaukee	26	46	.361

Division Semifinals: Minneapolis 2, Rochester 1
Division Finals: Fort Wayne 3, Minneapolis 1

NBA Finals: Syracuse 4, Fort Wayne 3

NBA 1955–56

Eastern Division	Won	Lost	Pct.
Philadelphia	45	27	.625
Boston	39	33	.542
Syracuse	35	37	.486
New York	35	37	.486

Division Tiebreaker: Syracuse 82, New York 77
Division Semifinals: Syracuse 2, Boston 1
Division Finals: Philadelphia 3, Syracuse 2

Western Division	Won	Lost	Pct.
Fort Wayne	37	35	.514
Minneapolis	33	39	.458
St. Louis	33	39	.458
Rochester	31	41	.431

Division Tiebreaker: Minneapolis 103, St. Louis 97
Division Semifinals: St. Louis 2, Minneapolis 1
Division Finals: Fort Wayne 3, St. Louis 2

NBA Finals: Philadelphia 4, Fort Wayne 1

NBA 1956–57

Eastern Division	Won	Lost	Pct.
Boston	44	28	.611
Syracuse	38	34	.528
Philadelphia	37	35	.514
New York	36	36	.500

Division Semifinals: Syracuse 2, Philadelphia 0
Division Finals: Boston 3, Syracuse 0

1956–57 (continued)

Western Division	Won	Lost	Pct.
St. Louis	34	38	.472
Minneapolis	34	38	.472
Fort Wayne	34	38	.472
Rochester	31	41	.431

Division Tiebreakers: St. Louis 115, Fort Wayne 103; St. Louis 114, Minneapolis 111

Division Semifinals: Minneapolis 2, Fort Wayne 0

Division Finals: St. Louis 3, Minneapolis 0

NBA Finals: Boston 4, St. Louis 3

NBA 1957–58

Eastern Division	Won	Lost	Pct.
Boston	49	23	.681
Syracuse	41	31	.569
Philadelphia	37	35	.514
New York	35	37	.486

Division Semifinals: Philadelphia 2, Syracuse 1

Division Finals: Boston 4, Philadelphia 1

Western Division	Won	Lost	Pct.
St. Louis	41	31	.569
Detroit	33	39	.458
Cincinnati	33	39	.458
Minneapolis	19	53	.264

Division Semifinals: Detroit 2, Cincinnati 0

Division Finals: St. Louis 4, Detroit 1

NBA Finals: St. Louis 4, Boston 2

NBA 1958–59

Eastern Division	Won	Lost	Pct.
Boston	52	20	.722
New York	40	32	.556
Syracuse	35	37	.486
Philadelphia	32	40	.444

Division Semifinals: Syracuse 2, New York 0
Division Finals: Boston 4, Syracuse 3

Western Division	Won	Lost	Pct.
St. Louis	49	23	.681
Minneapolis	33	39	.458
Detroit	28	44	.389
Cincinnati	19	53	.264

Division Semifinals: Minneapolis 2, Detroit 1
Division Finals: Minneapolis 4, St. Louis 2

NBA Finals: Boston 4, Minneapolis 0

NBA 1959–60

Eastern Division	Won	Lost	Pct.
Boston	59	16	.787
Philadelphia	49	26	.653
Syracuse	45	30	.600
New York	27	48	.360

Division Semifinals: Philadelphia 2, Syracuse 1
Division Finals: Boston 4, Philadelphia 2

1959–60 (continued)

Western Division	Won	Lost	Pct.
St. Louis	46	29	.613
Detroit	30	45	.400
Minneapolis	25	50	.333
Cincinnati	19	56	.253

Division Semifinals: Minneapolis 2, Detroit 0
Division Finals: St. Louis 4, Minneapolis 3

NBA Finals: Boston 4, St. Louis 3

NBA 1960–61

Eastern Division	Won	Lost	Pct.
Boston	57	22	.722
Philadelphia	46	33	.582
Syracuse	38	41	.481
New York	21	58	.266

Division Semifinals: Syracuse 3, Philadelphia 0
Division Finals: Boston 4, Syracuse 1

Western Division	Won	Lost	Pct.
St. Louis	51	28	.646
Los Angeles	36	43	.456
Detroit	34	45	.430
Cincinnati	33	46	.418

Division Semifinals: Los Angeles 3, Detroit 2
Division Finals: St. Louis 4, Los Angeles 3

NBA Finals: Boston 4, St. Louis 1

NBA 1961–62

Eastern Division	Won	Lost	Pct.
Boston	60	20	.750
Philadelphia	49	31	.613
Syracuse	41	39	.513
New York	29	51	.363

Division Semifinals: Philadelphia 3, Syracuse 2
Division Finals: Boston 4, Philadelphia 3

Western Division	Won	Lost	Pct.
Los Angeles	54	26	.675
Cincinnati	43	37	.538
Detroit	37	43	.463
St. Louis	29	51	.363
Chicago	18	62	.225

Division Semifinals: Detroit 3, Cincinnati 1
Division Finals: Los Angeles 4, Detroit 2

NBA Finals: Boston 4, Los Angeles 3

NBA 1962–63

Eastern Division	Won	Lost	Pct.
Boston	58	22	.725
Syracuse	48	32	.600
Cincinnati	42	38	.525
New York	21	59	.263

Division Semifinals: Cincinnati 3, Syracuse 2
Division Finals: Boston 4, Cincinnati 3

John Havlicek

1962–63 (continued)

Western Division	Won	Lost	Pct.
Los Angeles	53	27	.663
St. Louis	48	32	.600
Detroit	34	46	.425
San Francisco	31	49	.388
Chicago	25	55	.313

Division Semifinals: St. Louis 3, Detroit 1
Division Finals: Los Angeles 4, St. Louis 3

NBA Finals: Boston 4, Los Angeles 2

NBA 1963–64

Eastern Division	Won	Lost	Pct.
Boston	59	21	.738
Cincinnati	55	25	.688
Philadelphia	34	46	.425
New York	22	58	.275

Division Semifinals: Cincinnati 3, Philadelphia 2
Division Finals: Boston 4, Cincinnati 1

Western Division	Won	Lost	Pct.
San Francisco	48	32	.600
St. Louis	46	34	.575
Los Angeles	42	38	.525
Baltimore	31	49	.388
Detroit	23	57	.288

Division Semifinals: St. Louis 3, Los Angeles 2
Division Finals: San Francisco 4, St. Louis 3

NBA Finals: Boston 4, San Francisco 1

NBA 1964–65

Eastern Division	Won	Lost	Pct.
Boston	62	18	.775
Cincinnati	48	32	.600
Philadelphia	40	40	.500
New York	31	49	.388

Division Semifinals: Philadelphia 3, Cincinnati 1
Division Finals: Boston 4, Philadelphia 3

Western Division	Won	Lost	Pct.
Los Angeles	49	31	.613
St. Louis	45	35	.563
Baltimore	37	43	.463
Detroit	31	49	.388
San Francisco	17	63	.213

Division Semifinals: Baltimore 3, St. Louis 1
Division Finals: Los Angeles 4, Baltimore 2

NBA Finals: Boston 4, Los Angeles 1

NBA 1965–66

Eastern Division	Won	Lost	Pct.
Philadelphia	55	25	.688
Boston	54	26	.675
Cincinnati	45	35	.563
New York	30	50	.375

Division Semifinals: Boston 3, Cincinnati 2
Division Finals: Boston 4, Philadelphia 1

Western Division	Won	Lost	Pct.
Los Angeles	45	35	.563
Baltimore	38	42	.475
St. Louis	36	44	.450
San Francisco	35	45	.438
Detroit	22	58	.275

Division Semifinals: St. Louis 3, Baltimore 0
Division Finals: Los Angeles 4, St. Louis 3

NBA Finals: Boston 4, Los Angeles 3

NBA 1966–67

Eastern Division	Won	Lost	Pct.
Philadelphia	68	13	.840
Boston	60	21	.741
Cincinnati	39	42	.481
New York	36	45	.444
Baltimore	20	61	.247

Division Semifinals: Boston 3, New York 1; Philadelphia 3, Cincinnati 1
Division Finals: Philadelphia 4, Boston 1

Western Division	Won	Lost	Pct.
San Francisco	44	37	.543
St. Louis	39	42	.481
Los Angeles	36	45	.444
Chicago	33	48	.407
Detroit	30	51	.370

1966–67 (continued)

Division Semifinals: St. Louis 3, Chicago 0; San Francisco 3, Los Angeles 0

Division Finals: San Francisco 4, St. Louis 2

NBA Finals: Philadelphia 4, San Francisco 2

NBA 1967–68

Eastern Division	Won	Lost	Pct.
Philadelphia	62	20	.756
Boston	54	28	.659
New York	43	39	.524
Detroit	40	42	.488
Cincinnati	39	43	.476
Baltimore	36	46	.439

Division Semifinals: Boston 4, Detroit 2; Philadelphia 4, New York 2

Division Finals: Boston 4, Philadelphia 3

Western Division	Won	Lost	Pct.
St. Louis	56	26	.683
Los Angeles	52	30	.634
San Francisco	43	39	.524
Chicago	29	53	.354
Seattle	23	59	.280
San Diego	15	67	.183

Division Semifinals: San Francisco 4, St. Louis 2; Los Angeles 4, Chicago 1

Division Finals: Los Angeles 4, San Francisco 0

NBA Finals: Boston 4, Los Angeles 2

NBA 1968–69

Eastern Division	Won	Lost	.Pct.
Baltimore	57	25	.695
Philadelphia	55	27	.671
New York	54	28	.659
Boston	48	34	.585
Cincinnati	41	41	.500
Detroit	32	50	.390
Milwaukee	27	55	.329

Division Semifinals: Boston 4, Philadelphia 1; New York 4, Baltimore 0

Division Finals: Boston 4, New York 2

Western Division	Won	Lost	Pct.
Los Angeles	55	27	.671
Atlanta	48	34	.585
San Francisco	41	41	.500
San Diego	37	45	.451
Chicago	33	49	.402
Seattle	30	52	.366
Phoenix	16	66	.195

Division Semifinals: Atlanta 4, San Diego 2; Los Angeles 4, San Francisco 2

Division Finals: Los Angeles 4, Atlanta 1

NBA Finals: Boston 4, Los Angeles 3

NBA 1969–70

Eastern Division	Won	Lost	Pct.
New York	60	22	.732
Milwaukee	56	26	.683
Baltimore	50	32	.610
Philadelphia	42	40	.512
Cincinnati	36	46	.439
Boston	34	48	.415
Detroit	31	51	.378

Division Semifinals: Milwaukee 4, Philadelphia 1; New York 4, Baltimore 3

Division Finals: New York 4, Milwaukee 1

Western Division	Won	Lost	Pct.
Atlanta	48	34	.585
Los Angeles	46	36	.561
Chicago	39	43	.476
Phoenix	39	43	.476
Seattle	36	46	.439
San Francisco	30	52	.366
San Diego	27	55	.329

Division Semifinals: Atlanta 4, Chicago 1; Los Angeles 4, Phoenix 3

Division Finals: Los Angeles 4, Atlanta 0

NBA Finals: New York 4, Los Angeles 3

eorge Gervin

NBA 1970–71

Eastern Conference

Atlantic Division	Won	Lost	Pct.
New York	52	30	.634
Philadelphia	47	35	.573
Boston	44	38	.537
Buffalo	22	60	.268

Central Division	Won	Lost	Pct.
Baltimore	42	40	.512
Atlanta	36	46	.439
Cincinnati	33	49	.402
Cleveland	15	67	.183

Conference Semifinals: New York 4, Atlanta 1; Baltimore 4, Philadelphia 3

Conference Finals: Baltimore 4, New York 3

Western Conference

Midwest Division	Won	Lost	Pct.
Milwaukee	66	16	.805
Chicago	51	31	.622
Phoenix	48	34	.585
Detroit	45	37	.549

Pacific Division	Won	Lost	Pct.
Los Angeles	48	34	.585
San Francisco	41	41	.500
San Diego	40	42	.488
Seattle	38	44	.463
Portland	29	53	.354

Conference Semifinals: Los Angeles 4, Chicago 3; Milwaukee 4, San Francisco 1
Conference Finals: Milwaukee 4, Los Angeles 1

NBA Finals: Milwaukee 4, Baltimore 0

NBA 1971–72

Eastern Conference

Atlantic Division	Won	Lost	Pct.
Boston	56	26	.683
New York	48	34	.585
Philadelphia	30	53	.366
Buffalo	22	60	.268

Central Division	Won	Lost	Pct.
Baltimore	38	44	.463
Atlanta	36	46	.439
Cincinnati	30	52	.366
Cleveland	23	59	.280

Conference Semifinals: Boston 4, Atlanta 2; New York 4, Baltimore 2
Conference Finals: New York 4, Boston 1

Western Conference

Midwest Division	Won	Lost	Pct.
Milwaukee	63	19	.768
Chicago	57	25	.695
Phoenix	49	33	.598
Detroit	26	56	.317

1971–72 (continued)

Pacific Division	Won	Lost	Pct.
Los Angeles	69	13	.841
Golden State	51	31	.622
Seattle	47	35	.573
Houston	34	48	.415
Portland	18	64	.220

Conference Semifinals: Los Angeles 4, Chicago 0; Milwaukee 4, Golden State 1

Conference Finals: Los Angeles 4, Milwaukee 2

NBA Finals: Los Angeles 4, New York 1

NBA 1972–73

Eastern Conference

Atlantic Division	Won	Lost	Pct.
Boston	68	14	.829
New York	57	25	.695
Buffalo	21	61	.256
Philadelphia	9	73	.110

Central Division	Won	Lost	Pct.
Baltimore	52	30	.634
Atlanta	46	36	.561
Houston	33	49	.402
Cleveland	32	50	.390

Conference Semifinals: Boston 4, Atlanta 2; New York 4, Baltimore 1

Conference Finals: New York 4, Boston 3

Western Conference
Midwest Division	Won	Lost	Pct.
Milwaukee	60	22	.732
Chicago	51	31	.622
Detroit	40	42	.488
Kansas City–Omaha	36	46	.439

Pacific Division	Won	Lost	Pct.
Los Angeles	60	22	.732
Golden State	47	35	.573
Phoenix	38	44	.463
Seattle	26	56	.317
Portland	21	61	.256

Conference Semifinals: Los Angeles 4, Chicago 3; Golden State 4, Milwaukee 2
Conference Finals: Los Angeles 4, Golden State 1

NBA Finals: New York 4, Los Angeles 1

NBA 1973–74

Eastern Conference
Atlantic Division	Won	Lost	Pct.
Boston	56	26	.683
New York	49	33	.598
Buffalo	42	40	.512
Philadelphia	25	57	.305

Central Division	Won	Lost	Pct.
Capital	47	35	.573
Atlanta	35	47	.427
Houston	32	50	.390
Cleveland	29	53	.354

1973–74 (continued)

Conference Semifinals: Boston 4, Buffalo 2; New York 4, Capital 3

Conference Finals: Boston 4, New York 1

Western Conference

Midwest Division	Won	Lost	Pct.
Milwaukee	59	23	.720
Chicago	54	28	.659
Detroit	52	30	.634
Kansas City–Omaha	33	49	.402

Pacific Division	Won	Lost	Pct.
Los Angeles	47	35	.573
Golden State	44	38	.537
Seattle	36	46	.439
Phoenix	30	52	.366
Portland	27	55	.329

Conference Semifinals: Chicago 4, Detroit 3; Milwaukee 4, Los Angeles 1

Conference Finals: Milwaukee 4, Chicago 0

NBA Finals: Boston 4, Milwaukee 3

NBA 1974–75

Eastern Conference

Atlantic Division	Won	Lost	Pct.
Boston	60	22	.732
Buffalo	49	33	.598
New York	40	42	.488
Philadelphia	34	48	.415

Central Division	Won	Lost	Pct.
Washington	60	22	.732
Houston	41	41	.500
Cleveland	40	42	.488
Atlanta	31	51	.378
New Orleans	23	59	.280

Conference First Round: Houston 2, New York 1
Conference Semifinals: Boston 4, Houston 1;
Washington 4, Buffalo 3
Conference Finals: Washington 4, Boston 2

Western Conference

Midwest Division	Won	Lost	Pct.
Chicago	47	35	.573
Kansas City–Omaha	44	38	.537
Detroit	40	42	.488
Milwaukee	38	44	.463

Pacific Division	Won	Lost	Pct.
Golden State	48	34	.585
Seattle	43	39	.524
Portland	38	44	.463
Phoenix	32	50	.390
Los Angeles	30	52	.366

Conference First Round: Seattle 2, Detroit 1
Conference Semifinals: Chicago 4, Kansas
City–Omaha 2; Golden State 4, Seattle 2
Conference Finals: Golden State 4, Chicago 3

NBA Finals: Golden State 4, Washington 0

Walter Davis

NBA 1975–76

Eastern Conference

Atlantic Division	Won	Lost	Pct.
Boston	54	28	.659
Buffalo	46	36	.561
Philadelphia	46	36	.561
New York	38	44	.463

Central Division	Won	Lost	Pct.
Cleveland	49	33	.598
Washington	48	34	.585
Houston	40	42	.488
New Orleans	38	44	.463
Atlanta	29	53	.354

Conference First Round: Buffalo 2, Philadelphia 1
Conference Semifinals: Boston 4, Buffalo 2; Cleveland 4, Washington 3
Conference Finals: Boston 4, Cleveland 2

Western Conference

Midwest Division	Won	Lost	Pct.
Milwaukee	38	44	.463
Detroit	36	46	.439
Kansas City	31	51	.378
Chicago	24	58	.293

Pacific Division	Won	Lost	Pct.
Golden State	59	23	.720
Seattle	43	39	.524
Phoenix	42	40	.512
Los Angeles	40	42	.488
Portland	37	45	.451

1975–76 (continued)
Conference First Round: Detroit 2, Milwaukee 1
  Conference Semifinals: Golden State 4, Detroit 2;
Phoenix 4, Seattle 2
  Conference Finals: Phoenix 4, Golden State 3

  NBA Finals: Boston 4, Phoenix 2

NBA 1976–77

Eastern Conference

Atlantic Division	Won	Lost	Pct.
Philadelphia	50	32	.610
Boston	44	38	.537
N.Y. Knicks	40	42	.488
Buffalo	30	52	.366
N.Y. Nets	22	60	.268

Central Division	Won	Lost	Pct.
Houston	49	33	.598
Washington	48	34	.585
San Antonio	44	38	.537
Cleveland	43	39	.524
New Orleans	35	47	.427
Atlanta	31	51	.378

  Conference First Round: Boston 2, San Antonio 0;
Washington 2, Cleveland 1
  Conference Semifinals: Philadelphia 4, Boston 3;
Houston 4, Washington 2
  Conference Finals: Philadelphia 4, Houston 2

Western Conference

Midwest Division	Won	Lost	Pct.
Denver	50	32	.610
Detroit	44	38	.537
Chicago	44	38	.537
Kansas City	40	42	.488
Indiana	36	46	.439
Milwaukee	30	52	.366

Pacific Division	Won	Lost	Pct.
Los Angeles	53	29	.646
Portland	49	33	.598
Golden State	46	36	.561
Seattle	40	42	.488
Phoenix	34	48	.415

Conference First Round: Portland 2, Chicago 1; Golden State 2, Detroit 1

Conference Semifinals: Portland 4, Denver 2; Los Angeles 4, Golden State 3

Conference Finals: Portland 4, Los Angeles 0

NBA Finals: Portland 4, Philadelphia 2

NBA 1977–78

Eastern Conference

Atlantic Division	Won	Lost	Pct.
Philadelphia	55	27	.671
New York	43	39	.524
Boston	32	50	.390
Buffalo	27	55	.329
New Jersey	24	58	.293

1977–78 (continued)

Central Division	Won	Lost	Pct.
San Antonio	52	30	.634
Washington	44	38	.537
Cleveland	43	39	.524
Atlanta	41	41	.500
New Orleans	39	43	.476
Houston	28	54	.341

Conference First Round: Washington 2, Atlanta 0; New York 2, Cleveland 0

Conference Semifinals: Philadelphia 4, New York 0; Washington 4, San Antonio 2

Conference Finals: Washington 4, Philadelphia 2

Western Conference

Midwest Division	Won	Lost	Pct.
Denver	48	34	.585
Milwaukee	44	38	.537
Chicago	40	42	.488
Detroit	38	44	.463
Indiana	31	51	.378
Kansas City	31	51	.378

Pacific Division	Won	Lost	Pct.
Portland	58	24	.707
Phoenix	49	33	.598
Seattle	47	35	.573
Los Angeles	45	37	.549
Golden State	43	39	.524

Conference First Round: Seattle 2, Los Angeles 1; Milwaukee 2, Phoenix 0

Conference Semifinals: Denver 4, Milwaukee 3; Seattle 4, Portland 2

Conference Finals: Seattle 4, Denver 2

NBA Finals: Washington 4, Seattle 3

NBA 1978–79

Eastern Conference

Atlantic Division	Won	Lost	Pct.
Washington	54	28	.659
Philadelphia	47	35	.573
New Jersey	37	45	.451
New York	31	51	.378
Boston	29	53	.354

Central Division	Won	Lost	Pct.
San Antonio	48	34	.585
Houston	47	35	.573
Atlanta	46	36	.561
Cleveland	30	52	.366
Detroit	30	52	.366
New Orleans	26	56	.317

Conference First Round: Atlanta 2, Houston 0; Philadelphia 2, New Jersey 0

Conference Semifinals: Washington 4, Atlanta 3; San Antonio 4, Philadelphia 3

Conference Finals: Washington 4, San Antonio 3

1978–79 (continued)
Western Conference

Midwest Division	Won	Lost	Pct.
Kansas City	48	34	.585
Denver	47	35	.573
Indiana	38	44	.463
Milwaukee	38	44	.463
Chicago	31	51	.378

Pacific Division	Won	Lost	Pct.
Seattle	52	30	.634
Phoenix	50	32	.610
Los Angeles	47	35	.573
Portland	45	37	.549
San Diego	43	39	.524
Golden State	38	44	.463

Conference First Round: Los Angeles 2, Denver 1; Phoenix 2, Portland 1

Conference Semifinals: Seattle 4, Los Angeles 1; Phoenix 4, Kansas City 1

Conference Finals: Seattle 4, Phoenix 3

NBA Finals: Seattle 4, Washington 1

NBA 1979–80

Eastern Conference

Atlantic Division	Won	Lost	Pct.
Boston	61	21	.744
Philadelphia	59	23	.720
Washington	39	43	.476
New York	39	43	.476
New Jersey	34	48	.415

Central Division	Won	Lost	Pct.
Atlanta	50	32	.610
Houston	41	41	.500
San Antonio	41	41	.500
Indiana	37	45	.451
Cleveland	37	45	.451
Detroit	16	66	.195

Conference First Round: Houston 2, San Antonio 1; Philadelphia 2, Washington 0

Conference Semifinals: Philadelphia 4, Atlanta 1; Boston 4, Houston 0

Conference Finals: Philadelphia 4, Boston 1

Western Conference

Midwest Division	Won	Lost	Pct.
Milwaukee	49	33	.598
Kansas City	47	35	.573
Denver	30	52	.366
Chicago	30	52	.366
Utah	24	58	.293

Pacific Division	Won	Lost	Pct.
Los Angeles	60	22	.732
Seattle	56	26	.683
Phoenix	55	27	.671
Portland	38	44	.463
San Diego	35	47	.427
Golden State	24	58	.293

Calvin Murphy

1979–80 (continued)

Conference First Round: Phoenix 2, Kansas City 1; Seattle 2, Portland 1

Conference Semifinals: Los Angeles 4, Phoenix 1; Seattle 4, Milwaukee 3

Conference Finals: Los Angeles 4, Seattle 1

NBA Finals: Los Angeles 4, Philadelphia 2

NBA 1980–81

Eastern Conference

Atlantic Division	Won	Lost	Pct.
Boston	62	20	.756
Philadelphia	62	20	.756
New York	50	32	.610
Washington	39	43	.476
New Jersey	24	58	.293

Central Division	Won	Lost	Pct.
Milwaukee	60	22	.732
Chicago	45	37	.549
Indiana	44	38	.537
Atlanta	31	51	.378
Cleveland	28	54	.341
Detroit	21	61	.256

Conference First Round: Chicago 2, New York 0; Philadelphia 2, Indiana 0

Conference Semifinals: Boston 4, Chicago 0; Philadelphia 4, Milwaukee 3

Conference Finals: Boston 4, Philadelphia 3

1980–81 (continued)
Western Conference

Midwest Division	Won	Lost	Pct.
San Antonio	52	30	.634
Kansas City	40	42	.488
Houston	40	42	.488
Denver	37	45	.451
Utah	28	54	.341
Dallas	15	67	.183

Pacific Division	Won	Lost	Pct.
Phoenix	57	25	.695
Los Angeles	54	28	.659
Portland	45	37	.549
Golden State	39	43	.476
San Diego	36	46	.439
Seattle	34	48	.415

Conference First Round: Houston 2, Los Angeles 1; Kansas City 2, Portland 1

Conference Semifinals: Houston 4, San Antonio 3; Kansas City 4, Phoenix 3

Conference Finals: Houston 4, Kansas City 1

NBA Finals: Boston 4, Houston 2

NBA 1981–82

Eastern Conference

Atlantic Division	Won	Lost	Pct.
Boston	63	19	.768
Philadelphia	58	24	.707
New Jersey	44	38	.537
Washington	43	39	.524
New York	33	49	.402

Central Division	Won	Lost	Pct.
Milwaukee	55	27	.671
Atlanta	42	40	.512
Detroit	39	43	.476
Indiana	35	47	.427
Chicago	34	48	.415
Cleveland	15	67	.183

Conference First Round: Philadelphia 2, Atlanta 0; Washington 2, New Jersey 0

Conference Semifinals: Boston 4, Washington 1; Philadelphia 4, Milwaukee 2

Conference Finals: Philadelphia 4, Boston 3

Western Conference

Midwest Division	Won	Lost	Pct.
San Antonio	48	34	.585
Denver	46	36	.561
Houston	46	36	.561
Kansas City	30	52	.366
Dallas	28	54	.341
Utah	25	57	.305

Pacific Division	Won	Lost	Pct.
Los Angeles	57	25	.695
Seattle	52	30	.634
Phoenix	46	36	.561
Golden State	45	37	.549
Portland	42	40	.512
San Diego	17	65	.207

1981–82 (continued)

Conference First Round: Phoenix 2, Denver 1; Seattle 2, Houston 1

Conference Semifinals: Los Angeles 4, Phoenix 0; San Antonio 4, Seattle 1

Conference Finals: Los Angeles 4, San Antonio 0

NBA Finals: Los Angeles 4, Philadelphia 2

NBA 1982–83

Eastern Conference

Atlantic Division	Won	Lost	Pct.
Philadelphia	65	17	.793
Boston	56	26	.683
New Jersey	49	33	.598
New York	44	38	.537
Washington	42	40	.512

Central Division	Won	Lost	Pct.
Milwaukee	51	31	.622
Atlanta	43	39	.524
Detroit	37	45	.451
Chicago	28	54	.341
Cleveland	23	59	.280
Indiana	20	62	.244

Conference First Round: Boston 2, Atlanta 1; New York 2, New Jersey 0

Conference Semifinals: Milwaukee 4, Boston 0; Philadelphia 4, New York 0

Conference Finals: Philadelphia 4, Milwaukee 1

Western Conference

Midwest Division	Won	Lost	Pct.
San Antonio	53	29	.646
Denver	45	37	.549
Kansas City	45	37	.549
Dallas	38	44	.463
Utah	30	52	.366
Houston	14	68	.171

Pacific Division	Won	Lost	Pct.
Los Angeles	58	24	.707
Phoenix	53	29	.646
Seattle	48	34	.585
Portland	46	36	.561
Golden State	30	52	.366
San Diego	25	57	.305

Conference First Round: Denver 2, Phoenix 1; Portland 2, Seattle 0

Conference Semifinals: San Antonio 4, Denver 1; Los Angeles 4, Portland 1

Conference Finals: Los Angeles 4, San Antonio 2

NBA Finals: Philadelphia 4, Los Angeles 0

NBA 1983–84

Eastern Conference

Atlantic Division	Won	Lost	Pct.
Boston	62	20	.756
Philadelphia	52	30	.634
New York	47	35	.573
New Jersey	45	37	.549
Washington	35	47	.427

1983–84 (continued)

Central Division	Won	Lost	Pct.
Milwaukee	50	32	.610
Detroit	49	33	.598
Atlanta	40	42	.488
Cleveland	28	54	.341
Chicago	27	55	.329
Atlanta	26	56	.317

Conference First Round: Milwaukee 3, Atlanta 2; Boston 3, Washington 1; New York 3, Detroit 2; New Jersey 3, Philadelphia 2

Conference Semifinals: Boston 4, New York 3; Milwaukee 4, New Jersey 2

Conference Finals: Boston 4, Milwaukee 1

Western Conference

Midwest Division	Won	Lost	Pct.
Utah	45	37	.549
Dallas	43	39	.524
Denver	38	44	.463
Kansas City	38	44	.463
San Antonio	37	45	.451
Houston	29	53	.354

Pacific Division	Won	Lost	Pct.
Los Angeles	54	28	.659
Portland	48	34	.585
Seattle	42	40	.512
Phoenix	41	41	.500
Golden State	37	45	.451
San Diego	30	52	.366

Mark Aguirre

1983–84 (continued)

Conference First Round: Dallas 3, Seattle 2; Utah 3, Denver 2; Los Angeles 3, Kansas City 0; Phoenix 3, Portland 2

Conference Semifinals: Los Angeles 4, Dallas 1; Phoenix 4, Utah 2

Conference Finals: Los Angeles 4, Phoenix 2

NBA Finals: Boston 4, Los Angeles 3

NBA 1984–85

Eastern Conference

Atlantic Division	Won	Lost	Pct.
Boston	63	19	.768
Philadelphia	58	24	.707
New Jersey	42	40	.512
Washington	40	42	.488
New York	24	58	.293

Central Division	Won	Lost	Pct.
Milwaukee	59	23	.720
Detroit	46	36	.561
Chicago	38	44	.463
Cleveland	36	46	.439
Atlanta	34	48	.415
Indiana	22	60	.268

Conference First Round: Boston 3, Cleveland 1; Milwaukee 3, Chicago 1; Detroit 3, New Jersey 0; Philadelphia 3, Washington 1

Conference Semifinals: Boston 4, Detroit 2; Philadelphia 4, Milwaukee 0

Conference Finals: Boston 4, Philadelphia 1

Western Conference
Midwest Division

Midwest Division	Won	Lost	Pct.
Denver	52	30	.634
Houston	48	34	.585
Dallas	44	38	.537
San Antonio	41	41	.500
Utah	41	41	.500
Kansas City	31	51	.378

Pacific Division	Won	Lost	Pct.
L.A. Lakers	62	20	.756
Portland	42	40	.512
Phoenix	36	46	.439
L.A. Clippers	31	51	.378
Seattle	31	51	.378
Golden State	22	60	.268

Conference First Round: Portland 3, Dallas 1; Denver 3, San Antonio 2; Utah 3, Houston 2; L.A. Lakers 3, Phoenix 0

Conference Semifinals: Denver 4, Utah 1; L.A. Lakers 4, Portland 1

Conference Finals: L.A. Lakers 4, Denver 1

NBA Finals: L.A. Lakers 4, Boston 2

NBA 1985–86

Eastern Conference

Atlantic Division	Won	Lost	Pct.
Boston	67	15	.817
Philadelphia	54	28	.659
Washington	39	43	.476
New Jersey	39	43	.476
New York	23	59	.280

1985-86 (continued)

Central Division	Won	Lost	Pct.
Milwaukee	57	25	.695
Atlanta	50	32	.610
Detroit	46	36	.561
Chicago	30	52	.366
Cleveland	29	53	.354
Indiana	26	56	.317

Conference First Round: Atlanta 3, Detroit 1; Boston 3, Chicago 0; Milwaukee 3, New Jersey 0; Philadelphia 3, Washington 2

Conference Semifinals: Boston 4, Atlanta 1; Milwaukee 4, Philadelphia 3

Conference Finals: Boston 4, Milwaukee 0

Western Conference

Midwest Division	Won	Lost	Pct.
Houston	51	31	.622
Denver	47	35	.573
Dallas	44	38	.537
Utah	42	40	.512
Sacramento	37	45	.451
San Antonio	35	47	.427

Pacific Division	Won	Lost	Pct.
L.A. Lakers	62	20	.756
Portland	40	42	.488
L.A. Clippers	32	50	.390
Phoenix	32	50	.390
Seattle	31	51	.378
Golden State	30	52	.366

Conference First Round: Dallas 3, Utah 1; Denver 3, Portland 1; Houston 3, Sacramento 0; L.A. Lakers 3, San Antonio 0

Conference Semifinals: L.A. Lakers 4, Dallas 2; Houston 4, Denver 2

Conference Finals: Houston 4, L.A. Lakers 1

NBA Finals: Boston 4, Houston 2

NBA 1986–87

Eastern Conference

Atlantic Division	Won	Lost	Pct.
Boston	59	23	.720
Philadelphia	45	37	.549
Washington	42	40	.512
New Jersey	24	58	.293
New York	24	58	.293

Central Division	Won	Lost	Pct.
Atlanta	57	25	.695
Detroit	52	30	.634
Milwaukee	50	32	.610
Indiana	41	41	.500
Chicago	40	42	.488
Cleveland	31	51	.378

Conference First Round: Atlanta 3, Indiana 1; Boston 3, Chicago 0; Detroit 3, Washington 0; Milwaukee 3, Philadelphia 2

Conference Semifinals: Detroit 4, Atlanta 1; Boston 4, Milwaukee 3

Conference Finals: Boston 4, Detroit 3

1986-87 (continued)
Western Conference

Midwest Division	Won	Lost	Pct.
Dallas	55	27	.671
Utah	44	38	.537
Houston	42	40	.512
Denver	37	45	.451
Sacramento	29	53	.354
San Antonio	28	54	.341

Pacific Division	Won	Lost	Pct.
L.A. Lakers	65	17	.793
Portland	49	33	.598
Golden State	42	40	.512
Seattle	39	43	.476
Phoenix	36	46	.439
L.A. Clippers	12	70	.146

Conference First Round: Seattle 3, Dallas 1; L.A. Lakers 3, Denver 0; Golden State 3, Utah 2; Houston 3, Portland 1

Conference Semifinals: L.A. Lakers 4, Golden State 1; Seattle 4, Houston 2

Conference Finals: L.A. Lakers 4, Seattle 0

NBA Finals: L.A. Lakers 4, Boston 2

NBA 1987-88

Eastern Conference

Atlantic Division	Won	Lost	Pct.
Boston	57	25	.695
Washington	38	44	.463
New York	38	44	.463
Philadelphia	36	46	.439
New Jersey	19	63	.232

Central Division	Won	Lost	Pct.
Detroit	54	28	.659
Atlanta	50	32	.610
Chicago	50	32	.610
Cleveland	42	40	.512
Milwaukee	42	40	.512
Indiana	38	44	.463

Conference First Round: Atlanta 3, Milwaukee 2; Boston 3, New York 1; Chicago 3, Cleveland 2; Detroit 3, Washington 2

Conference Semifinals: Boston 4, Atlanta 3; Detroit 4, Chicago 1

Conference Finals: Detroit 4, Boston 2

Western Conference

Midwest Division	Won	Lost	Pct.
Denver	54	28	.659
Dallas	53	29	.646
Utah	47	35	.573
Houston	46	36	.561
San Antonio	31	51	.378
Sacramento	24	58	.293

Pacific Division	Won	Lost	Pct.
L.A. Lakers	62	20	.756
Portland	53	29	.646
Seattle	44	38	.537
Phoenix	28	54	.341
Golden State	20	62	.244
L.A. Clippers	17	65	.207

1987–88 (continued)

Conference First Round: Dallas 3, Houston 1; Denver 3, Seattle 2; L.A. Lakers 3, San Antonio 0; Utah 3, Portland 1

Conference Semifinals: Dallas 4, Denver 2; L.A. Lakers 4, Utah 3

Conference Finals: L.A. Lakers 4, Dallas 3

NBA Finals: L.A. Lakers 4, Detroit 3

NBA 1988–89

Eastern Conference

Atlantic Division	Won	Lost	Pct.
New York	52	30	.634
Philadelphia	46	36	.561
Boston	42	40	.512
Washington	40	42	.488
New Jersey	26	56	.317
Charlotte	20	62	.244

Central Division	Won	Lost	Pct.
Detroit	63	19	.768
Cleveland	57	25	.695
Atlanta	52	30	.634
Milwaukee	49	33	.598
Chicago	47	35	.573
Indiana	28	54	.341

Conference First Round: Milwaukee 3, Atlanta 2; Detroit 3, Boston 0; Chicago 3, Cleveland 2; New York 3, Philadelphia 0

Conference Semifinals: Chicago 4, New York 2; Detroit 4, Milwaukee 0

Conference Finals: Detroit 4, Chicago 2

Western Conference

Midwest Division	Won	Lost	Pct.
Utah	51	31	.622
Houston	45	37	.549
Denver	44	38	.537
Dallas	38	44	.463
San Antonio	21	61	.256
Miami	15	67	.183

Pacific Division	Won	Lost	Pct.
L.A. Lakers	57	25	.695
Phoenix	55	27	.671
Seattle	47	35	.573
Golden State	43	39	.524
Portland	39	43	.476
Sacramento	27	55	.329
L.A. Clippers	21	61	.256

Conference First Round: Phoenix 3, Denver 0; Golden State 3, Utah 0; Seattle 3, Houston 1; L.A. Lakers 3, Portland 0

Conference Semifinals: Phoenix 4, Golden State 1; L.A. Lakers 4, Seattle 0

Conference Finals: L.A. Lakers 4, Phoenix 0

NBA Finals: Detroit 4, L.A. Lakers 0

NBA 1989–90

Eastern Conference

Atlantic Division	Won	Lost	Pct.
Philadelphia	53	29	.646
Boston	52	30	.634
New York	45	37	.549
Washington	31	51	.378
Miami	18	64	.220
New Jersey	17	65	.207

Central Division	Won	Lost	Pct.
Detroit	59	23	.720
Chicago	55	27	.671
Milwaukee	44	38	.537
Cleveland	42	40	.512
Indiana	42	40	.512
Atlanta	41	41	.500
Orlando	18	64	.220

Conference First Round: New York 3, Boston 2; Chicago 3, Milwaukee 1; Philadelphia 3, Cleveland 2; Detroit 3, Indiana 0

Conference Semifinals: Chicago 4, Philadelphia 1; Detroit 4, New York 1

Conference Finals: Detroit 4, Chicago 3

Western Conference

Midwest Division	Won	Lost	Pct.
San Antonio	56	26	.683
Utah	55	27	.671
Dallas	47	35	.573
Denver	43	39	.524
Houston	41	41	.500
Minnesota	22	60	.268
Charlotte	19	63	.232

Pacific Division	Won	Lost	Pct.
L.A. Lakers	63	19	.768
Portland	59	23	.720
Phoenix	54	28	.659
Seattle	41	41	.500
Golden State	37	45	.451
L.A. Clippers	30	52	.366
Sacramento	23	59	.280

Conference First Round: Portland 3, Dallas 0; San Antonio 3, Denver 0; L.A. Lakers 3, Houston 1; Phoenix 3, Utah 2

Conference Semifinals: Phoenix 4, L.A. Lakers 1; Portland 4, San Antonio 3

Conference Finals: Portland 4, Phoenix 2

NBA Finals: Detroit 4, Portland 1

NBA 1990–91

Eastern Conference

Atlantic Division	Won	Lost	Pct.
Boston	56	26	.683
Philadelphia	44	38	.537
New York	39	43	.476
Washington	30	52	.366
New Jersey	26	56	.317
Miami	24	58	.293

1990–91 (continued)

Central Division	Won	Lost	Pct.
Chicago	61	21	.744
Detroit	50	32	.610
Milwaukee	48	34	.585
Atlanta	43	39	.524
Indiana	41	41	.500
Cleveland	33	49	.402
Charlotte	26	56	.317

Conference First Round: Detroit 3, Atlanta 2; Boston 3, Indiana 2; Chicago 3, New York 0; Philadelphia 3, Milwaukee 0

Conference Semifinals: Detroit 4, Boston 2; Chicago 4, Philadelphia 1

Conference Finals: Chicago 4, Detroit 0

Western Conference

Midwest Division	Won	Lost	Pct.
San Antonio	55	27	.671
Utah	54	28	.659
Houston	52	30	.634
Orlando	31	51	.378
Minnesota	29	53	.354
Dallas	28	54	.341
Denver	20	62	.244

Pacific Division	Won	Lost	Pct.
Portland	63	19	.768
L.A. Lakers	58	24	.707
Phoenix	55	27	.671
Golden State	44	38	.537
Seattle	41	41	.500
L.A. Clippers	31	51	.378
Sacramento	25	57	.305

Conference First Round: Golden State 3, San Antonio 1; L.A. Lakers 3, Houston 0; Utah 3, Phoenix 1; Portland 3, Seattle 2

Conference Semifinals: L.A. Lakers 4, Golden State 1; Portland 4, Utah 1

Conference Finals: L.A. Lakers 4, Portland 2

NBA Finals: Chicago 4, L.A. Lakers 1

NBA 1991–92

Eastern Conference

Atlantic Division	Won	Lost	Pct.
Boston	51	31	.622
New York	51	31	.622
New Jersey	40	42	.488
Miami	38	44	.463
Philadelphia	35	47	.427
Washington	25	57	.305
Orlando	21	61	.256

Central Division	Won	Lost	Pct.
Chicago	67	15	.817
Cleveland	57	25	.695
Detroit	48	34	.585
Indiana	40	42	.488
Atlanta	38	44	.463
Charlotte	31	51	.378
Milwaukee	31	51	.378

Conference First Round: Boston 3, Indiana 0; Chicago 3, Miami 0; Cleveland 3, New Jersey 1; New York 3, Detroit 2

Conference Semifinals: Cleveland 4, Boston 3; Chicago 4, New York 3

Conference Finals: Chicago 4, Cleveland 2

1991–92 (continued)
Western Conference

Midwest Division	Won	Lost	Pct.
Utah	55	27	.671
San Antonio	47	35	.573
Houston	42	40	.512
Denver	24	58	.293
Dallas	22	60	.268
Minnesota	15	67	.183

Pacific Division	Won	Lost	Pct.
Portland	57	25	.695
Golden State	55	27	.671
Phoenix	53	29	.646
Seattle	47	35	.573
L.A. Clippers	45	37	.549
L.A. Lakers	43	39	.524
Sacramento	29	53	.354

Conference First Round: Seattle 3, Golden State 1; Utah 3, L.A. Clippers 2; Portland 3, L.A. Lakers 1; Phoenix 3, San Antonio 0

Conference Semifinals: Portland 4, Phoenix 1; Utah 4, Seattle 1

Conference Finals: Portland 4, Utah 2

NBA Finals: Chicago 4, Portland 2

NBA 1992–93

Eastern Conference

Atlantic Division	Won	Lost	Pct.
New York	60	22	.732
Boston	48	34	.585
New Jersey	43	39	.524
Orlando	41	41	.500
Miami	36	46	.439
Philadelphia	26	56	.317
Washington	22	60	.268

Central Division	Won	Lost	Pct.
Chicago	57	25	.695
Cleveland	54	28	.659
Charlotte	44	38	.537
Atlanta	43	39	.524
Indiana	41	41	.500
Detroit	40	42	.488
Milwaukee	28	54	.341

Conference First Round: Chicago 3, Atlanta 0; Charlotte 3, Boston 1; Cleveland 3, New Jersey 2; New York 3, Indiana 1

Conference Semifinals: New York 4, Charlotte 1; Chicago 4, Cleveland 0

Conference Finals: Chicago 4, New York 2

Western Conference

Midwest Division	Won	Lost	Pct.
Houston	55	27	.671
San Antonio	49	33	.598
Utah	47	35	.573
Denver	36	46	.439
Minnesota	19	63	.232
Dallas	11	71	.134

1992–93 (continued)

Pacific Division	Won	Lost	Pct.
Phoenix	62	20	.756
Seattle	55	27	.671
Portland	51	31	.622
L.A. Clippers	41	41	.500
L.A. Lakers	39	43	.476
Golden State	34	48	.415
Sacramento	25	57	.305

Conference First Round: Houston 3, L.A. Clippers 2; Phoenix 3, L.A. Lakers 2; San Antonio 3, Portland 1; Seattle 3, Utah 2

Conference Semifinals: Seattle 4, Houston 3; Phoenix 4, San Antonio 2

Conference Finals: Phoenix 4, Seattle 3

NBA Finals: Chicago 4, Phoenix 2

NBA 1993–94

Eastern Conference

Atlantic Division	Won	Lost	Pct.
New York	57	25	.695
Orlando	50	32	.610
New Jersey	45	37	.549
Miami	42	40	.512
Boston	32	50	.390
Philadelphia	25	57	.305
Washington	24	58	.293

Central Division	Won	Lost	Pct.
Atlanta	57	25	.695
Chicago	55	27	.671
Cleveland	47	35	.573
Indiana	47	35	.573
Charlotte	41	41	.500
Detroit	20	62	.244
Milwaukee	20	62	.244

Conference First Round: Atlanta 3, Miami 2; Chicago 3, Cleveland 0; Indiana 3, Orlando 0; New York 3, New Jersey 1

Conference Semifinals: Indiana 4, Atlanta 2; New York 4, Chicago 3

Conference Finals: New York 4, Indiana 3

Western Conference

Midwest Division	Won	Lost	Pct.
Houston	58	24	.707
San Antonio	55	27	.671
Utah	53	29	.646
Denver	42	40	.512
Minnesota	20	62	.244
Dallas	13	69	.159

Pacific Division	Won	Lost	Pct.
Seattle	63	19	.768
Phoenix	56	26	.683
Golden State	50	32	.610
Portland	47	35	.573
L.A. Lakers	33	49	.402
Sacramento	28	54	.341
L.A. Clippers	27	55	.329

1993–94 (continued)

Conference First Round: Denver 3, Seattle 2; Phoenix 3, Golden State 0; Houston 3, Portland 1; Utah 3, San Antonio 1

Conference Semifinals: Houston 4, Phoenix 3; Utah 4, Denver 3

Conference Finals: Houston 4, Utah 1

NBA Finals: Houston 4, New York 3

NBA 1994–95

Eastern Conference

Atlantic Division	Won	Lost	Pct.
Orlando	57	25	.695
New York	55	27	.671
Boston	35	47	.427
Miami	32	50	.390
New Jersey	30	52	.366
Philadelphia	24	58	.293
Washington	21	61	.256

Central Division	Won	Lost	Pct.
Indiana	52	30	.634
Charlotte	50	32	.610
Chicago	47	39	.573
Cleveland	43	40	.524
Atlanta	42	40	.512
Milwaukee	34	48	.415
Detroit	28	54	.341

Conference First Round: Chicago 3, Charlotte 1; Indiana 3, Atlanta 0; New York 3, Cleveland 1; Orlando 3, Boston 1

Conference Semifinals: Indiana 4, New York 3; Orlando 4, Chicago 2

Conference Finals: Orlando 4, Indiana 3

Western Conference

Midwest Division	Won	Lost	Pct.
San Antonio	62	20	.756
Utah	60	22	.732
Houston	47	35	.573
Denver	41	41	.500
Dallas	36	46	.439
Minnesota	21	61	.256

Pacific Division	Won	Lost	Pct.
Phoenix	59	23	.720
Seattle	57	25	.695
L.A. Lakers	48	34	.585
Portland	44	38	.537
Sacramento	39	43	.476
Golden State	26	56	.317
L.A. Clippers	17	65	.207

Conference First Round: Houston 3, Utah 2; L.A. Lakers 3, Seattle 1; Phoenix 3, Portland 0; San Antonio 3, Denver 0

Conference Semifinals: Houston 4, Phoenix 3; San Antonio 4, L.A. Lakers 2

Conference Finals: Houston 4, San Antonio 2

NBA Finals: Houston 4, Orlando 0

NBA 1995-96

Eastern Conference

Atlantic Division	Won	Lost	Pct.
Orlando	60	22	.732
New York	47	35	.573
Miami	42	40	.512
Washington	39	43	.476
Boston	33	49	.402
New Jersey	30	52	.366
Philadelphia	18	64	.220

Central Division	Won	Lost	Pct.
Chicago	72	10	.878
Indiana	52	30	.634
Cleveland	47	35	.573
Atlanta	46	36	.561
Detroit	46	36	.561
Charlotte	41	41	.500
Milwaukee	25	57	.305
Toronto	21	61	.256

Conference First Round: Chicago 3, Miami 0; Orlando 3, Detroit 0; Atlanta 3, Indiana 2; New York 3, Cleveland 0

Conference Semifinals: Chicago 4, New York 1; Orlando 4, Atlanta 1

Conference Finals: Chicago 4, Orlando 0

Western Conference

Midwest Division	Won	Lost	Pct.
San Antonio	59	23	.720
Utah	55	27	.671
Houston	48	34	.585
Denver	35	47	.427
Dallas	26	56	.317
Minnesota	26	56	.317
Vancouver	15	67	.183

Pacific Division	Won	Lost	Pct.
Seattle	64	18	.780
L.A. Lakers	53	29	.646
Portland	44	38	.537
Phoenix	41	41	.500
Sacramento	39	43	.476
Golden State	36	46	.439
L.A. Clippers	29	53	.354

Conference First Round: Seattle 3, Sacramento 1; San Antonio 3, Phoenix 1; Utah 3, Portland 2; Houston 3, L.A. Lakers 1

Conference Semifinals: Seattle 4, Houston 0; Utah 4, San Antonio 2

Conference Finals: Seattle 4, Utah 3

NBA Finals: Chicago 4, Seattle 2

AMERICA'S SPORTS BIBLE FOR PREVIEWS AND PREDICTIONS

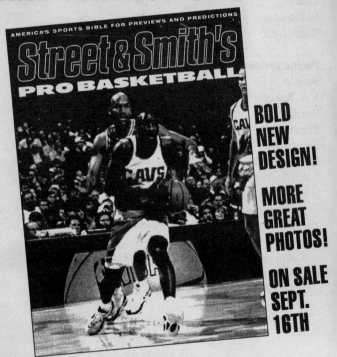